Annual Editions: Social Problems, 42/e

**Kurt Finsterbusch**

http://create.mheducation.com

ISBN-10: 1260488365    ISBN-13: 9781260488364

# Contents

# Detailed Table of Contents

## Unit 4: Institutional Problems

**The American Family: An Endangered and Disappearing Species**, Lynn Wardle, *CNS News*, 2015
Wardle presents many more facts than Krogstad about the American family today. The key point is traditional families (husband and wife with children) and family life are significantly declining in America. This process has adverse impacts including lower grades, less accomplishments, psychological problems, behavioral problems, suicide, and higher poverty rates.

**The Case for Single-Price Health Care**, Paul S. Hewitt and Phillip Longman, *Washington Monthly*, 2018
Washington makes the case for single price health care which would reduce health care costs. Obama Care expanded coverage but health care costs increased greatly hurting the public. The article argues that this problem is mostly the result of monopolistic hospitals engaging in price discrimination as they exploit their increasing market power over private purchasers of health care.

**Why Is Health Care So Expensive?** *Consumer Reports,* 2014
Health care in the United States costs about twice as much as it does in the rest of the developed world and is not as good as the European systems. There is a lot that health insurance does not cover in America and drugs and doctor fees are very high.

**The War on Public Schools**, Erika Christakis, *The Atlantic*, 2017
Christakis cites Bush, Obama, and Trump blasting public schools for poor performance. However, few people care more about individual students than public-school teachers. 21st-century public schools, with their record numbers of graduates and expanded missions, are nothing close to the cesspools portrayed by political hyperbole. But we've underestimated their strengths. I am concerned with how the current discussion has ignored public schools' victories, while also detracting from their civic role which is to prepare people to work together to advance society.

**Protecting Religious Liberty**, Bernard G. Prusak, *Commonweal*, 2018
The role of religion in America today is complex. The religious ideas of one religious group should not be legally prescribed to force other Americans to do or not do what they may want. The law should apply to everyone equally. Religious minorities should be protected not prosecuted. Scripture denies gay rights, but gay marriage is legal. Prusak presents many applicable thoughts of the past to guide our thinking about the proper standing of religion today.

## Unit 5: Crime, Violence, and Law Enforcement

**Sex Slavery/Trafficking**, *Soroptimist*, 2012
Sex slavery and trafficking are horrible crimes that are under the radar. Soroptimist describes this problem including its surprising and brutal aspects. It is a $32 billion industry and involves 2.5 million people. Women and girls are typically trafficked into the commercial sex industry, i.e. prostitution or other forms of sexual exploitation. Not all slaves are trafficked, but all trafficking victims are victims of slavery. This slavery removes the victim from all that is familiar to her, rendering her completely isolated and alone, often unable to speak the language of her captors or fellow victims. Women and girls are typically trafficked into the commercial sex industry, i.e. prostitution or other forms of sexual exploitation. Organized crime is largely responsible for the spread of international human trafficking.

**Getting Tough on Devastating Corporate Crime**, Ralph Nader, *Huffington Post*, 2013
Do you think that the U.S. is tough on Crime? Many people are in prison, police arrest many young men in poor neighborhoods, and many complain that sentences are too tough. However, Nader points out that the legal system is way too lenient on corporate crime which is responsible for much greater financial costs than "street" crime and almost no one goes to jail for these crimes.

**Rough Justice**, Mychal Denzel Smith, *The New Republic*, 2018
Smith's thesis is that America is over policed. He covers a lot of history to establish why the public currently has a high regard for the police. He also points out that 31 percent of people killed by police in 2012 were black. However, most of the book is dedicated to describing the consequences of over-policing.

**Public Safety, Public Justice**, Daniel Rose, *Harlem Times,* 2015
Rose argues that we must change our criminal justice philosophy and our punitive laws. Imprisonment rates are too high and unfair to Blacks who are imprisoned six times as much as whites. Rose advocates rehabilitation and many other reforms.

**This Man Was Sentenced to Die in Prison for Shoplifting a $159 Jacket: This Happens More Than You Think**, Ed Pilkington, *AlterNet*, 2013
Timothy Jackson was caught shoplifting a jacket and sentenced to life in prison without the possibility of parole. He has already served 16 years. He is used by the author to prove that the criminal justice system in many parts of the United States is too punitive. There are 3,281 people incarcerated for life in America for non-violent crimes. One was sentenced to die in prison for siphoning gas from a truck. The point of the article is that some laws and some judicial judgments are crazy but "the law is the law" so petty criminals die in prison. Change is needed.

**The Price of Justice**, Peter Edelman, *The Nation*, 2017
Edelman presents evidence that state and local governments are plundering the poor. His first story is about a woman who rolled through a stop in 2014. The judge hit her with a $135 fine and ordered her to pay it in full immediately which she could not do. It is a long story, but the upshot is that the system took hundreds of dollars from her and was about to jail her but she got a lawyer and got off. Many other stories and evidence show how cruel our legal system is to the poor.

**Statement for the Record: Worldwide Threat Assessment of the US Intelligence Community**, James R. Clapper, *Office of the Director of National Intelligence,* 2015
Clapper presents the official assessment of worldwide terrorist threats. This report covers cyber-attacks, potential use of weapons of mass destruction, and other terrorist attacks. We must remain on the alert but this report does not suggest that the American mainland has a lot to be afraid of.

**Low-Tech Terrorism**, Bruce Hoffman, *The National Interest*, 2014
This article is a rather extensive assessment of all (despite the title) current terrorist threats to America. Fortunately, terrorists have not yet acquired and successfully set off a weapon of mass destruction, though they have tried. The article extensively reviews Al Qaeda's and other terrorist groups' considerable efforts to acquire such weapons and their failure. As a result, most terrorism involves guns and bombs.

## Unit 6: Problems of Population, Environment, Resources, and the Future

**How Will We Feed the New Global Middle Class?** Charles C. Mann, *The Atlantic*, 2018
Mann introduces his article with the statement "In 2050 the world population will be 10 billion. Can everyone eat without destroying the Earth?" Mann uses Voigt to present the pessimist answer to this question and Borlaug to present the positive answer. The green revolution saved the day in the 1970s and 1980s, but world food production has been declining ever since so the question is Germaine today. Technology plays a decisive role in this issue and is thoroughly discussed by Mann. However, some very productive technologies have negative effects on the environment, so the issue is somewhat in determinant.

# Preface

The reason we study social problems is so that we can do something about them. Corrective action, however, is not taken until the situation is seen as a problem and the fire of concern is kindled in a number of citizens. A democratic country gives those citizens means for legally trying to change things, and this freedom and opportunity is a great pride for our country. In fact, most college students have already given time or money to some cause in which they believe. This is necessary because each generation will face struggles for rights and justice. Daily forces operate to corrupt, distort, bias, exploit, and defraud as individuals and groups seek their own advantage at the expense of others and the public interest. Those dedicated to a good society, therefore, constantly struggle against these forces. Furthermore, the struggle is often complex and confusing. Not always are the defenders of the status quo wrong and the champions of change right. *Important values will be championed by both sides.*

Today there is much debate about the best way to improve education. Opposing spokespersons think that they are serving the good of the children and of the United States. In a similar manner, conscientious students in the same college class and reading the same material will hotly disagree. Therefore, solving problems is usually not a peaceful process. First, it requires information and an understanding of the problem, and we can expect disagreements on both the facts and the interpretations. Second, it requires discussion, compromise, and a plan with majority support, or at least the support of the powerful groups. Third, it requires action. In a democratic society, this process should involve tolerance and even goodwill toward one's opponents as long as they act honestly, fairly, and democratically. Class discussions should involve respect for each other's opinions.

In some ways, the study of social problems is easy and in some ways it is hard. The easy aspect is that most people know quite a lot about the problems that this book addresses; the hard part is that solving those problems is very difficult. If the solutions were easy, the problems would have been solved by now, and we would not be studying these particular issues. It may be easy to plan solutions, but it is hard to implement them. In general, however, Americans are optimistic and believe in progress; we learn from our mistakes and keep trying until conditions are acceptable. For instance, the members of Common Cause, including myself, have worked for campaign finance reform since 1970. Our efforts failed until Watergate created a huge public demand for it, and both campaign finance reform and public-right-to-know laws were passed. The reform, however, led to the formation of PACs (Political Action Committees) to get around the law and buy influence legally.

In 2002 a new campaign finance reform law, the McCain–Feingold Act, was passed. Nevertheless, the role of big money in campaign finances is today larger than it has been for many decades. This will eventually precipitate yet another major reform effort. It could be that at the end of the twenty-first century, Americans will still be struggling with many of the same problems as today. But it is reasonable to believe that things will be somewhat better at that point because throughout this century people will mobilize again and again to improve our society; some will even do this at considerable cost to themselves.

The articles presented here were selected for three reasons: (1) their attention to important issues, (2) the value of the information and ideas they present, and/or (3) their ability to move the reader to concern and possibly even action toward correcting social problems. This edition of *Annual Editions: Social Problems* begins by broadly describing the United States and recent changes in forces that affect our lifestyles. It then examines some big issues in the political and economic systems that have societywide impacts, as well as issues of inequality and injustice that challenge basic American values. The next section considers how well the various institutions of society work. Most institutions are being heavily criticized—these articles help to explain why. The following section studies the traditional problem of crime and law enforcement. Fortunately, there is some good news here. Finally, the last section focuses on the future and problems of population, environment, technology, globalization, community, and long-term change.

## Editor

Kurt Finsterbusch received a bachelor's degree in history from Princeton University in 1957 and a bachelor of divinity degree from Grace Theological Seminary in 1960. His PhD in sociology, from Columbia University, was conferred in 1969. Dr. Finsterbusch is the author of several books, including *Understanding Social Impacts* (Sage Publications,1980), *Social Research for Policy Decisions* (Wadsworth Publishing, 1980, with Annabelle Bender

Motz), and Organizational Change as a Development Strategy (Lynne Rienner Publishers, 1987, with Jerald Hage). He is currently teaching at the University of Maryland, College Park, and, in addition to serving as editor for Annual Editions: Social Problems, he is also editor of Annual Editions: Sociology and Taking Sides: Clashing Views on Social issues.

## Dedication
Dedicated to the many heroes and heroines who are trying to fix the various social problems addressed here.

## Academic Advisory Board
Members of the Academic Advisory Board are instrumental in the final selection of articles for each edition of ANNUAL EDITIONS.

Their review of articles for content, level, and appropriateness provides critical direction to the editors and staff. We think that you will find their careful consideration well reflected in this volume.

**Pamela Altman**
*Georgia Southern University*

**Thomas E. Arcaro**
*Elon University*

**Sylven Beck**
*The George Washington University*

**Heather Boone**
*Atlantic Cape Community College*

**Mamie Bridgeforth**
*Essex County College*

**M. Jennifer Brougham**
*Arizona State University*

**Shakira Cain-Bell**
*Jackson State University*

**Judy Chiasson**
*California State University*

**Elizabeth F. Cohen**
*Syracuse University*

**Lynn Connolly**
*Chestnut Hill College*

**Maria Cuevas**
*Yakima Valley Community College*

**Roger G. Dunham**
*University of Miami*

**Kathy Edwards**
*KCTCS—Ashland Community & Technical College*

**Nancy Federman**
*San Diego State University*

**David Hunt**
*Augusta State University*

**Mark Killian**
*University of Cincinnati*

**Rosalind Kopfstein**
*Western Connecticut State University*

**Timothy LaFountaine**
*Quinsigamond Community College*

**Diane Lindley**
*University of Mississippi*

**John P. Lynxwiler**
*University of Central Florida, Orlando*

**James F. MacNair**
*Atlantic Cape Community College*

**Karith Meyers**
*Moorpark College*

**Christopher P. Morley**
*SUNY Upstate Medical University*

**Kathryn S. Mueller**
*Baylor University*

**Robert G. Newby**
*Central Michigan University*

**Wendy Parker**
*Albany College of Pharmacy*

**Larry Rosenberg**
*Millersville University*

**Karl Smith**
*University of Maryland Eastern Shore*

**Leretta Smith**
*North Dakota State University*

**Casey Welch**
*Flagler College*

# Unit 1

# UNIT

Prepared by: Kurt Finsterbusch, *University of Maryland, College Park*

# Introduction: Clashing Values and Problematic Transformations of Social Life

This unit offers an introduction to the study of American social problems. It looks at American culture that provides the value system by which we decide what are the significant social problems. Immediately we recognize that people have different values. Some of these value differences are related to different positions in the social structure and different experiences. Racial, religious, gender, income, occupational, and age differences lead to different experiences, and therefore, different perspectives. For example, all races in America will share a common culture but also have different subcultures. Same with each generation. Some of these differences will be explored in this unit.

We propose a perspective that should be helpful as we observe value differences. We suggest that most people share roughly the same set of values. They differ however, on how these values should be ranked. For example, almost all Americans are both materialists and environmentalists. Even the business person who pollutes the environment while producing products for sale and profits wants to live in a clean and healthy environment. Even an environmentalist drives a car to work and uses air conditioning in warm weather. Both have the same values but rank them differently and therefore act differently. In this unit, we try to get a general picture of American culture and then select specific areas for closer examination. Some of the areas examined are civic virtue, Facebook impacts, and generational differences.

## Article

Prepared by: Kurt Finsterbusch, *University of Maryland, College Park*

# The American Narrative: Is There One & What Is It?

WILLIAM H. CHAFE

## Learning Outcomes

*After reading this article, you will be able to:*

- Trace the role of the culture of serving the public good and the role of the culture of individual freedom in American history.

- Analyze how these two value systems are opposing each other today.

- Discuss the importance of balance between these sets of values and the danger of destroying that balance today.

Who are we? Where have we been? Where are we going? Can we even agree on who "we" includes? At no time in our history have these questions been more relevant. The American political system seems dysfunctional, if not permanently fractured. A generational gap in technological expertise and familiarity with the social network divides the country to an even greater extent than the culture wars of the 1960s and 1970s. Soon, more "Americans" will speak Spanish as their first language than English. For some, access to health care is a universal right, for others, a privilege that must be earned. Rarely—and certainly not since the Civil War—have we been so divided on which direction we should be heading as a country. How can there be an American narrative when it is not clear what it means to talk about an American people or nation? Two overriding paradigms have long competed in defining who we are. The first imagines America as a community that places the good of the whole first; the second envisions the country as a gathering of individuals who prize individual freedom and value more than anything else each person's ability to determine his own fate.

When the Puritans arrived in the Massachusetts Bay Colony in 1630, their leader, John Winthrop, told his shipmates aboard the *Arabella* that their mission was to create a "city upon a hill," a blessed society that would embody values so noble that the entire world would admire and emulate the new colony. Entitled "A Modell of Christian Charity," Winthrop's sermon described what it would take to create that beloved community: "We must love one another. We must bear one another's burdens . . . make others' conditions our own. We must rejoice together, mourn together, labor, and suffer together, always having before our eyes a community [where we are all] members of the same body."

Consistent with Winthrop's vision, Massachusetts was governed in its early decades by a sense of communal well-being. While the colony tolerated differences of status and power, the ruling norm was that the common good took precedence. Thus, "just prices" were prescribed for goods for sale, and punishment was imposed on businesses that sought excess profits. Parents who mistreated their children were shamed; people who committed adultery were exposed and humiliated.

Soon enough, a surge of individualism challenged the reigning norms. Entrepreneurs viewed communal rules as shackles to be broken so that they could pursue individual aspirations—and profits. The ideal of a "just price" was discarded. While religion remained a powerful presence, secularism ruled everyday business life, and Christianity was restricted to a once-a-week ritual. Class distinctions proliferated, economic inequality increased, and the values of *laissez-faire individualism* displaced the once-enshrined "common wealth." Aid to the poor became an act of individual charity rather than a communal responsibility.

Not surprisingly, the tensions between those who put the good of the community first and those who value individual freedom foremost have reverberated throughout our history. Thomas Jefferson sought to resolve the conflict in the Declaration of Independence by embracing the idea of "equal opportunity" for all. Note that he championed not equality of results, but equality of opportunity. Every citizen might have an "inalienable" right to "life, liberty, and the pursuit of happiness," but what happened to each person's "equal opportunity" depended on the performance of that particular individual. Success was not guaranteed.

Throughout American history, the tensions between the value of the common good and the right to unbridled individual freedom have resurfaced. The federal government sought to build roads and canals across state lines to serve the general good. The nation fought a Civil War because slavery contradicted the belief in the right of equal citizenship. In the aftermath of the war, the Constitution guaranteed all males the right to vote, and its Fourteenth Amendment promised each citizen "equal protection" under the law.

But by the end of the nineteenth century, rampant economic growth had created myriad enterprises that threatened the common good. In *The Jungle*, Upton Sinclair highlighted the danger of workers falling into vats of boiling liquid at meatpacking plants. The influx of millions of immigrants brought new dangers of infectious disease. As sweatshops, germ-filled tenements, and unsafe factories blighted American cities, more and more Americans insisted on legislation that fostered the general welfare. Led by women reformers such as Jane Addams and Florence Kelley, social activists succeeded in getting laws passed that ended child labor, protected workers from injury from dangerous factory machines, and created standards for safe meat and food. The Progressive Era still left most people free to pursue their own destiny, but under President Theodore Roosevelt, the government became the ultimate arbiter of minimal standards for industry, railroads, and consumer safety.

The tensions between the two narratives continued to grow as the nation entered the Great Depression. Nearly a million mortgages were foreclosed, the stock market crashed, 25 percent of all American workers were chronically unemployed, and banks failed. When Franklin Roosevelt was elected president, he promised to use "bold, persistent experimentation" to find answers to people's suffering. The legislation of the first 100 days of his presidency encompassed unprecedented federal intervention in the regulation of industry, agriculture, and the provision of welfare payments to the unemployed. The good of the whole reemerged as a dominant concern. By 1935, however, the American Liberty League, a political group formed by conservative Democrats to oppose New Deal legislation, was

indicting **fdr** as a socialist and demanding a return to laissez-faire individualism. But the New Deal rolled on. In 1935, Congress enacted Social Security, the single greatest collective investment America had ever made, for *all* people over 65, and the Wagner Labor Relations Act gave unions the right to organize. Roosevelt ran his 1936 reelection campaign on a platform emphasizing that "one third of [our] nation is ill-housed, ill-clothed, and ill-fed."

This focus on the good of the whole culminated during World War II, a time when everyone was reminded of being part of a larger battle to preserve the values that "equal opportunity" represented: the dignity of every citizen, as well as the right to freedom of religion, freedom from want, and freedom of political expression. For the first time since Reconstruction, the government acted to prohibit discrimination against African-Americans, issuing an executive order to allow blacks as well as whites to be hired in the war industries. Similarly, it supported policies of equal pay to women workers while leading a massive effort to recruit more women into the labor force to meet wartime demands. From wage and price controls to the universal draft, government action on behalf of the good of the whole reached a new height.

After the war ended, the tension between the competing value systems returned, but, significantly, even most Republicans accepted as a given the fundamental reforms achieved under the New Deal. Anyone who suggested repeal of Social Security, President Dwight Eisenhower wrote to his brother Milton midway through his term in office, was "out of his mind." Eisenhower even created a new Cabinet department to oversee health and welfare.

The stage was set for the revolutions of the 1960s: that is, the civil rights movement, the women's movement, the student movement, and the War on Poverty. Blacks had no intention of accepting the status quo of prewar Jim Crow segregation when they returned from serving in World War II. Building on the community institutions they had created during the era of Jim Crow, they mobilized to confront racism. When a black woman was raped by six white policemen in Montgomery, Alabama, in the late 1940s, the Women's Political Council, organized by local black women, and the Brotherhood of Sleeping Car Porters, an all-black union, took on the police and forced a trial. That same network of black activists sought improvements in the treatment of blacks at downtown department stores and on public transport. Thus, when one of their members, Rosa Parks, was arrested in 1955 for refusing to give up her seat on a city bus to a white person, both groups took action. By initiating a phone tree and printing 4,000 leaflets, they organized a mass rally overnight. Held at a local

Baptist church to consider a bus boycott, the rally featured an address by Martin Luther King, Jr., who later became the embodiment of the movement (though it should be noted that the movement created King and not vice versa). After that night, Montgomery's black community refused to ride the city buses for 381 consecutive days, until the buses were desegregated.

A few years later, four first-year students at the all-black North Carolina Agricultural and Technical College in Greensboro, North Carolina, carried the movement a step further. Although they had come of age after the Supreme Court outlawed school segregation, little had changed. Now that their generation was reaching maturity, they asked what they could do. The young men had gone to an all-black high school where their teachers had asked them to address voter registration envelopes to community residents and encouraged them to think of themselves as first-class citizens. They had participated in an **naacp** youth group in which weekly discussions had centered on events such as the Montgomery Bus Boycott. They attended a Baptist church where the pastor preached the social gospel and asked for "justice now." Embittered by how little the status of black Americans had improved, they sought new ways of carrying forward what they had learned.

Their solution was simple: highlight the absurdity of segregation by going to a downtown department store and acting like regular customers. At the Woolworth's in Greensboro, they bought notebooks at one counter, purchased toothpaste at another, then sat down at the lunch counter and ordered a cup of coffee. "We don't serve colored people here," they were told. "But you served us over there," they responded, showing their receipts. Opening their school books, they sat for three hours until the store closed. The next day, they returned to the lunch counter with 23 of their classmates. The day after there were 66, the next day 100. On the fifth day, 1000 black students and adults crowded the streets of downtown Greensboro.

The direct-action civil rights movement had begun. Within two months, sit-ins occurred in 54 cities in nine states. By April 1960, the Student Nonviolent Co-ordinating Committee (sncc) had been founded. Soon, *The New York Times* was devoting a special section each day to civil rights demonstrations in the South. On August 28, 1963, a quarter-million people came together for the March on Washington. There, Martin Luther King, Jr., gave his "I Have a Dream" speech, a contemporary version of what John Winthrop had said 238 years earlier that celebrated the same idea of a "beloved community" where "neither Jew nor Gentile, black man, or white man" could be separated from each other.

At long last, the government responded. The Civil Rights Act of 1964 ended Jim Crow. The Voting Rights Act of 1965 restored the franchise to black Americans. The War on Poverty gave hope to millions who had been left out of the American dream. Medicare offered health care to all senior citizens, and Medicaid offered it to those who could not otherwise afford to go to the doctor. Federal Aid to Education created new and better schools. The Model Cities Program offered a way for blighted neighborhoods to be revitalized.

The narrative of progress toward the common good reached a new crescendo. With the civil rights movement as an inspiration, women started their own movement for social equality. Access to previously closed careers opened up under pressure. By 1990, half of all medical, law, and business students were women. Young girls grew up with the same aspirations as young boys. Latinos, gay Americans, and other minorities soon joined the march demanding greater equality. It seemed as though a permanent turning point had occurred.

But the counternarrative eventually rediscovered its voice. Millions of white Americans who might have supported the right of blacks to vote or eat at a lunch counter were appalled by affirmative action and demands for Black Power. When the war in Vietnam caused well-off students to take to the streets in protest against their country's military actions, thousands of ordinary workers were angered by the rebellion of the young against authority. Traditional families were outraged when feminists questioned monogamy and dared to challenge male authority.

By 1968, the nation was divided once more, and the events of that election year crystallized the issues. Incumbent Lyndon Johnson withdrew from the presidential race at the end of March. Martin Luther King, Jr., was assassinated in April, with riots spreading like wildfire across the country in response. Student protestors took over Columbia University in May, making a mockery of the idea of civil discourse and respect for authority. Robert F. Kennedy was assassinated in June, just as he seemed ready to move decisively toward the Democratic presidential nomination. And when the Democratic party met for its convention in Chicago, thousands of protestors were pummeled by police as they demonstrated against conventional politics.

At the same time, Richard Nixon was nominated by the Republican party on a platform of "law and order" and respect for authority. Adopting a "Southern strategy," he appealed for white Southern votes by opposing forced desegregation of schools. Lambasting students who protested the war, he pleaded for a return to respect for traditional institutions. Nixon claimed to speak on behalf of "the silent majority" who remained proud to be American citizens, who celebrated the flag rather than mocked it, and who affirmed the rights of individuals to do as they wished.

Richard Nixon's election in Fall 1968 launched the resurgence of a conservative consensus in American politics. Though on issues such as the environment Nixon pursued many policies consistent with the "good of the whole" framework, on most issues he moved in the opposite direction. He opposed busing as a tool to create greater school desegregation, started to dismantle War on Poverty programs, based his 1972 reelection campaign on attacking the "collectivism" of the Democratic party, and insisted on defending the values of "traditional" Americans against attacks by the young, minorities, and women.

As social issues provided a rallying point for those set against further social change, the conservative narrative gained new proponents. Those opposed to gay rights mobilized to curtail further efforts to make sexuality a civil rights issue. Evangelical Christians joined groups such as Jerry Falwell's Moral Majority or Pat Robertson's "Praise the Lord" clubs to lobby against advances for minority rights. Direct mail campaigns and the use of cable television helped the Right galvanize new audiences of potential supporters.

Presidential politics also continued on a conservative path. Even though Richard Nixon was compelled to resign in shame over his illegal activities in the Watergate scandal, each of his successors—even Democrats—advanced the conservative agenda he initiated. Gerald Ford vetoed more legislation in two years than most presidents veto in eight. Jimmy Carter, though a liberal on gender equality and black civil rights, proved conservative on most economic issues. Ronald Reagan personified the conservative revival. He not only celebrated patriotism, but also revived the viewpoint that the best America was one without government intervention in the economy, and one that venerated the ideal of individualism.

Even Democrat Bill Clinton, excoriated by the Right as a demonic embodiment of counterculture values, was in practice more a Dwight Eisenhower Republican than a Lyndon Johnson Democrat. Dedicated to cultivating the political mainstream, he achieved legislative victories primarily on traditionally Republican issues: deficit reduction; the North American Free Trade Agreement; an increased police presence on the streets; welfare reform that took people off the public dole after two years; and the use of V-chips to allow parents to control their children's television viewing habits. Only his failed health care proposal acted in tune with the ideology of fdr and lbj.

George W. Bush simply extended the conservative tradition. With massive tax cuts, he created lower rates for the wealthy than had been seen in more than a half-century. His consistent support of deregulation freed up countless companies and investment capital firms to pursue profits without restriction. He made nationalism a cherished part of his political legacy, including the pursuit of a doctrine that emphasized unilateral initiatives defined as in the best interests of the United States, and downplayed multilateral cooperation that would subject America to constraint by the wishes of its partners and allies.

From 1968 to 2008, the American political and ideological trajectory hewed to a conservative narrative that celebrates individualism over collective action and criticizes government activity on behalf of the common good.

In recent years, the tension between the two narratives has escalated to an alarming degree. Barack Obama's 2008 election appeared to revitalize a focus on the common good. More people voted, embracing the idea of change, and elected a black American who seemed to embody those values. The fact that Obama became the first president in 100 years to successfully pass national health care reform—albeit without the provision of a public alternative to private insurance companies—appeared to validate that presumption.

But with the midterm elections of 2010, the rejection of Democratic politics—especially state intervention on behalf of the common good—resulted in the most dramatic electoral turnaround since 1946, when President Harry Truman's Democrats lost 81 seats in the House of Representatives. "Tea Party" Republicans not only stood for conservative positions on most social issues, but most dramatically, they insisted that all taxes should be cut, that federal expenditures for Medicare, Social Security, and other social programs must be slashed, and that it is preferable for the government to default on its financial responsibilities than to raise the national debt ceiling.

A backward glance through United States history would reveal no clearer example of the tension between the two competing American narratives, existing side by side, seemingly irreconcilable. The moment is historic, particularly at a time when climate change, stalled immigration reform, and a depressed global economy cry out for action. Thus, the conflict between the good of the whole and the ascendancy of individualist freedom has reached new heights. The choice that voters make in the 2012 presidential election will define our country's political future. Which narrative will we pursue? Are health care and quality education universal rights or privileges reserved for only those with the means to pay? Do we wish to bear "one another's burdens . . . make others' conditions our own . . . mourn together [and] labor and suffer together?" Or do we wish to make each individual responsible for his or her own fate? These questions are not new. But now, more than ever, they challenge us to find an answer: Who are we? In which direction do we wish to go?

Despite the trend over the past three-and-a-half centuries toward legislation that creates a safety net to protect the larger community, millions of Americans appear committed to dismantling government, slashing federal spending, and walking away from previous commitments to the good of the whole. A number of candidates running for the Republican presidential nomination in 2012 wish to curtail federal responsibility for Social Security for senior citizens. Every Republican candidate seeks to repeal Obama's national health insurance program. Cutting taxes has become a holy mantra. While it is true that in the coming decades demographic change will dramatically increase the number of Latino voters, who historically have favored legislation on behalf of the common good, it is not inconceivable that a reversal of social welfare legislation will happen first.

The tension between these two narratives is as old as the country itself. More often than not, it has been a healthy tension, with one set of values checking and balancing the other. But the polarization of today is unparalleled. The decisions the electorate makes in 2012 are of historic importance in determining which direction the country will take.

# Critical Thinking

1. How does the value system focused on the public good benefit American society and how might it hurt American society?
2. How does the value system focused on individual freedom benefit American society and how might it hurt American society?

3. How can balance between these two value systems be maintained?

# Internet References

**New American Studies Web**
www.georgetown.edu/crossroads/asw
**Social Science Information Gateway**
http://www.sosig.esrc.bris.ac.uk
**Sociosite**
http://www.topsite.com/goto/sociosite.net
**Socioweb**
http://www.topsite.com/goto/socioweb.com
**Sociology—Study Sociology Online**
http://edu.learnsoc.org
**Sociology Web Resources**
http://www.mhhe.com/socscience/sociology/resources/index.htm

**WILLIAM H. CHAFE,** a Fellow of the American Academy since 2001, is the Alice Mary Baldwin Professor of History at Duke University. His publications include *Private Lives/Public Consequences: Personality and Politics in Modern America* (2005) and *The Rise and Fall of the American Century: The United States from 1890 to 2008* (2008). His current project is titled *Behind the Veil: African American Life During the Age of Segregation.*

*Article* Prepared by: Kurt Finsterbusch, *University of Maryland, College Park*

# American Culture: Traditions and Customs of the United States

Kim Ann Zimmermann

## Learning Outcomes

*After reading this article, you will be able to:*

- Understand why the United States is one of the most culturally diverse countries in the world.

- Understand what it means that the United States is a melting pot.

- Be able to describe American culture in terms of language, religion, style, food, art, and holidays.

American culture encompasses the customs and traditions of the United States. "Culture encompasses religion, food, what we wear, how we wear it, our language, marriage, music, what we believe is right or wrong, how we sit at the table, how we greet visitors, how we behave with loved ones, and a million other things," said Cristina De Rossi, an anthropologist at Barnet and Southgate College in London.

The United States is the third largest country in the world with a population of more than 325 million, according to the U.S. Census Bureau. A child is born every 8 seconds, and a person dies every 12 seconds.

In addition to Native Americans who were already living on the continent, the population of the United States was built on immigration from other countries. Despite recent moves to close the U.S. borders to new immigrants and refugees, a new immigrant moves to the United States every 33 seconds, according to the Census Bureau.

Because of this, the United States is one of the most culturally diverse countries in the world. Nearly every region of the world has influenced American culture, most notably the English who colonized the country beginning in the early 1600s. U.S. culture has also been shaped by the cultures of Native Americans, Latin Americans, Africans and Asians.

The United States is sometimes described as a "melting pot" in which different cultures have contributed their own distinct "flavors" to American culture. Just as cultures from around the world have influenced American culture, today American culture influences the world. The term Western culture often refers broadly to the cultures of the United States and Europe.

The way people "melt" in the United States differs. "Different groups of immigrants integrate in different ways," De Rossi told Live Science. "For example, in the United States, Catholic Spanish-speaking communities might keep their language and other cultural family traditions, but are integrated in the urban community and have embraced the American way of life in many other ways."

The Northeast, South, Midwest, Southeast and Western regions of the United States all have distinct traditions and customs. Here is a brief overview of the culture of the United States.

## Language

There is no official language of the United States, according to the U.S. government. While almost every language in the world is spoken in the United States, the most frequently spoken non-English languages are Spanish, Chinese, French and German. Ninety percent of the U.S. population speaks and understands at least some English, and most official business is conducted in English. Some states have official or preferred languages. For example, English and Hawaiian are the official languages in Hawaii.

The Census Bureau estimates that more than 300 languages are spoken in the United States. The bureau divides those languages into four categories: Spanish; other Indo-European languages, which includes German, Yiddish, Swedish, French, Italian, Russian, Polish, Hindi, Punjabi, Greek and several others; Asian and Pacific Island languages, including Chinese, Korean, Japanese, Thai, Tamil and more; and "all other languages," which is a category for languages that didn't fit into the first three categories, such as Hungarian, Arabic, Hebrew, languages of Africa and languages of native people of North, Central and South America.

# Religion

Nearly every known religion is practiced in the United States, which was founded on the basis of religious freedom. About 71 percent of Americans identify themselves as Christians, according to information gathered by the Pew Research Center, a nonpartisan research group, in 2017. The research also found that about 23 percent had no religious affiliation at all and around 6 percent of the population is made up non-Christian religions.

The number of people who identify with no religion seems to be decreasing. According to the Pew Research Center, this category is expected to drop from 16 percent in 2015 to 13 percent in 2060.

# American Style

Clothing styles vary by social status, region, occupation and climate. Jeans, sneakers, baseball caps, cowboy hats and boots are some items of clothing that are closely associated with Americans. Ralph Lauren, Calvin Klein, Michael Kors and Victoria Secret are some well-known American brands.

American fashion is widely influenced by celebrities and the media, and fashion sales equal around $200 billion per year, according to a paper published by Harvard University in 2007. More and more Americans are buying fashion, electronics and more online. According to the Census Bureau, U.S. retail e-commerce sales for the first quarter of 2017 totaled around $98.1 billion.

# American Food

American cuisine was influenced by Europeans and Native Americans in its early history. Today, there are a number of foods that are commonly identified as American, such as hamburgers, hot dogs, potato chips, macaroni and cheese, and meat loaf. "As American as apple pie" has come to mean something that is authentically American.

There are also styles of cooking and types of foods that are specific to a region. Southern-style cooking is often called "American comfort food" and includes dishes such as fried chicken, collard greens, black-eyed peas and corn bread.

Tex-Mex, popular in Texas and the Southwest, is a blend of Spanish and Mexican cooking styles and includes items such as chili and burritos, and relies heavily on shredded cheese and beans.

Jerky, dried meats that are served as snacks, is also a food that was created in the United States, according to NPR.

# The Arts

The United States is widely known around the world as a leader in mass media production, including television and movies. According to the U.S. Department of Commerce, the United States comprises one-third of the worldwide media and entertainment industry.

The television broadcasting industry took hold in the United States in the early 1950s, and American television programs are now shown around the world. The United States also has a vibrant movie industry, centered in Hollywood, California, and American movies are popular worldwide. The U.S. film industry earned $31 billion in revenues in 2013, and is expected to reach $771 billion by 2019, according to the U.S. Department of Commerce.

The United States' arts culture extends beyond movies and television shows, though. New York is home to Broadway, and Americans have a rich theatrical history. American folk art is an artistic style and is identified with quilts and other hand-crafted items. American music is very diverse with many, many styles, including rhythm and blues, jazz, gospel, country and western, bluegrass, rock 'n' roll and hip hop.

# Sports

The United States is a sports-minded country, with millions of fans who follow football, baseball, basketball and hockey, among other sports. Baseball, which was developed in colonial America and became an organized sport in the mid-1800s, is known as America's favorite pastime, although its popularity has been eclipsed by football for the past three decades, according to the Harris Poll.

# American Holidays

Many holidays are celebrated only in the United States. Americans celebrate their independence from Britain on July 4. Memorial Day, celebrated on the last Monday in May, honors those who have died in military service. Labor Day, observed on the first Monday in September, celebrates the country's workforce. Thanksgiving, another distinctive American holiday, falls on the fourth Thursday in November and dates back to colonial times to celebrate the harvest. Presidents' Day, marking the birthdays of George Washington and Abraham Lincoln, is a federal holiday that occurs on the third Monday in February. The contributions of veterans are honored on Veterans' Day, observed on Nov. 11. The contributions of civil rights leader Martin Luther King Jr. are remembered on the third Monday in January.

## Critical Thinking

1. What is unique about American culture?
2. Why do people change their culture when they migrate?
3. What is considered right and what is considered wrong in American culture?

## Internet References

**New American Studies Web**
www.georgetown.edu/crossroads/asw

**Social Science Information Gateway**
http://sosig.esrc.bris.ac.uk

**Sociology Web Resources**
http://www.mhhe.com/socscience/sociology/resources/index.htm

**Sociology—Study Sociology Online**
http://edu.learnsoc.org

**Sociosite**
http://www.topsite.com/goto/sociosite.net

Zimmermann, Kim Ann. "American Culture: Traditions and Customs of the United States," Live Science, July 13, 2017. Copyright ©2015 by EnVeritas Group. Used with permission.

*Article*                                Prepared by: Kurt Finsterbusch, *University of Maryland, College Park*

# Is the American Idea Doomed?

Not yet—but it has precious few supporters on either the left or the right.

YONI APPELBAUM

## Learning Outcomes

*After reading this article, you will be able to:*

- Understand the history of the democratic ideals of government of all the people, by all the people, and for all the people.

- Understand the current threats to these ideals.

- Understand the necessity of opposing groups working together.

On May 5, 1857, eight men sat down to dinner at Boston's Parker House hotel. They had gathered to plan a magazine, but by the time they stood up five hours later, they had laid the intellectual groundwork for a second American revolution.

These men were among the leading literary lights of their day, but they had more in mind that night than literary pursuits. The magazine they envisioned would, its prospectus later promised, "honestly endeavor to be the exponent of what its conductors believe to be the American idea."

That prospectus bore the unmistakable stamp of *The Atlantic*'s founding editor, James Russell Lowell, but "the American idea" had been popularized by Theodore Parker, the radical preacher and abolitionist. The American idea, Parker declared in an 1850 speech, comprised three elements: that all people are created equal, that all possess unalienable rights, and that all should have the opportunity to develop and enjoy those rights. Securing them required "a government of all the people, by all the people, for all the people," Parker said.

Ralph Waldo Emerson, another *Atlantic* founder, put the matter more concisely. There was, he observed, a single phrase, offered by the little republicans of the schoolyard, that summed the whole thing up: "I'm as good as you be."

As a vision, it was bold and improbable—but the magazine these men launched that November, 160 years ago, helped spur the nation to redefine itself around the pursuit of the American idea. And as the United States grew and prospered, other peoples around the globe were attracted to its success, and the idea that produced it.

Now, though, the idea they articulated is in doubt. America no longer serves as a model for the world as it once did; its influence is receding. At home, critics on the left reject the notion that the U.S. has a special role to play; on the right, nationalists push to define American identity around culture, not principles. Is the American idea obsolete?

From the first, the idea provoked skepticism. It was radical to claim that a nation as new as America could have its own idea to give the world, it was destabilizing to discard rank and station and allow people to define their own destinies, and it bordered on absurd to believe that a nation so sprawling and heterogeneous could be governed as a democratic republic. By 1857, the experiment's failure seemed imminent.

Across Europe, the 19th century had dawned as a democratic age, but darkened as it progressed. The revolutions of 1848 failed. Prussia busily cemented its dominance over the German states. In 1852, France's Second Republic gave way to its Second Empire. Spain's Progressive Biennium ended in 1856 as it began, with a coup d'état. Democracy was in full retreat. Even where it endured, the right to vote or hold office was generally restricted to a small, propertied elite.

On the surface, things appeared different in Boston, where *The Atlantic*'s eight founders—Emerson, Lowell, Moses Dresser Phillips, Henry Wadsworth Longfellow, John Lothrop Motley, James Elliot Cabot, Francis H. Underwood, and Oliver

Wendell Holmes Sr.—dined in May 1857. Almost all adult males in Massachusetts, black and white alike, could vote, and almost all did. Almost all were literate. And they stood equal before the law. The previous Friday, the state had ratified a new constitutional amendment stripping out the last significant property qualifications for running for state Senate.

But even in Boston, democracy was embattled. The state's government was in the grip of the nativist Know-Nothings, who resented recent waves of immigrants. That same Friday, voters had ratified an amendment imposing a literacy test for voting, a mostly symbolic effort at exclusion. But slavery, the diners believed, posed an even greater threat to democracy. Most of them had been radicalized three years before by the Anthony Burns case, when federal troops marched into their commonwealth to return Burns, an escaped slave then living and working in Boston, to bondage in Virginia—inspiring protests and lethal violence on his behalf. To the west, Kansas was bloodied by fighting between pro- and antislavery elements; to the south, politicians had begun defending slavery not as a necessary evil but as a positive ideal.

The fight against slavery had become a struggle for the American idea; the two could not coexist. In 1860, Abraham Lincoln's election led the South to conclude that it had lost the argument. The seceding states left Congress with a Republican majority, able to translate the principles of equality, rights, and opportunity into practical action: homesteads for all who sought them; land-grant colleges to spread the fruits of education; tariffs to protect fledgling industries; and a transcontinental railroad to promote commerce and communication. Here was the American idea made manifest.

But the Civil War tested whether a nation built around that idea could "long endure," as Lincoln told his audience at Gettysburg in 1863. His address aimed to rally support for the war by framing it as a struggle for equality, rights, and opportunity. He echoed Parker's speech defining the American idea in order to make clear to his listeners that it fell to them to determine whether "government of the people, by the people, for the people, shall not perish from the earth."

When the Union prevailed, it enshrined this vision in the Constitution with a series of amendments banning slavery, extending equal protection of the law, and safeguarding the right to vote for Americans of all races. In the ensuing decades, the rapid growth of the United States attracted further waves of immigrants and transformed the country into a global power. Some countries and peoples attempted to replicate American success by embracing American principles. Others recoiled and embraced alternatives—monarchy, empire, communism, and fascism among them.

The United States and its allies triumphed in two world wars and in a third that was undeclared—the first, Woodrow Wilson said, waged so that the world might "be made safe for democracy"; the second, Franklin D. Roosevelt explained, "to meet the threat to our democratic faith"; and the third, Ronald Reagan declared, to settle "the question of freedom for all mankind." Each victory brought with it a fresh surge of democratization around the world. And each surge ebbed, in part because the pursuit of equality, rights, and opportunity guarantees ongoing contention while the alternatives offer the illusion of stability.

The American story isn't simply an arc of history bending toward justice; it's far messier. Americans have never agreed on when to prioritize the needs of individuals and when their collective project should come first. If this tension wasn't itself unifying, it nonetheless helped stake out the terrain over which productive national debate could be waged.

So where does the American idea stand today? To some extent, it is a victim of its own success: Its spread to other nations has left America less distinctive than it once was. But the country has also failed to live up to its own ideals. In 1857, the United States was remarkable for its high levels of democratic participation and social equality. Recent reports rank the U.S. 28th out of 35 developed countries in the percentage of adults who vote in national elections, and 32nd in income equality. Its rates of intergenerational economic mobility are among the lowest in the developed world.

On opportunity, too, the United States now falls short. In its rate of new-business formation and in the percentage of jobs new businesses account for, it ranks in the lower half of nations tracked by the Organization for Economic Cooperation and Development. Today, Americans describe China as Europeans once described the United States—as an uncouth land of opportunity and rising economic might.

It is no surprise that younger Americans have lost faith in a system that no longer seems to deliver on its promise—and yet, the degree of their disillusionment is stunning. Nearly three-quarters of Americans born before the Second World War assign the highest value—10 out of 10—to living in a democracy; less than a third of those born since 1980 do the same. A quarter of the latter group say it's unimportant to choose leaders in free elections; just shy of a third think civil rights are needed to protect people's liberties. Americans are not alone; much of western Europe is similarly disillusioned.

Around the globe, those who dislike American ideas about democracy now outnumber those who favor them. Vladimir Putin's Russia offers a bellicose, authoritarian alternative. China whispers seductively to rulers of developing nations that they, too, can keep a tight grip on power while enjoying the spoils of economic growth.

All of this has left many Americans feeling disoriented, their faith that their nation has something distinctive to offer the world shaken. On the left, many have gravitated toward a strange sort of universalism, focusing on America's flaws while admiring other nations' virtues. They decry nationalism and covet open borders, imagining a world in which ideas can prevail without nations to champion them.

Even as the left is made queasy by the notion that an idea can be both good and distinctively American, many on the right now doubt that America is a land defined by a distinctive idea at all. President Donald Trump's rhetoric is curiously devoid of references to a common civic creed. He promotes instead a more generic nationalism—one defined, like any nation's, by culture and borders and narrow interests and enemies.

Both of these visions are corrosive, although not equally. America is an ethnically, geographically, and economically varied land. What helped reunite the states a century and a half ago was a nationalism grounded in a shared set of ideals, ideals that served as a source of national pride and future promise. But nationalism, the greatest force for social cohesion the world has yet discovered, can be wielded to varied ends. Trump embraces an arid nationalism defined by blood and soil, by culture and tradition. It accounts for his moral blindness after the protests in Charlottesville, Virginia—his inability to condemn the "very fine people" who rallied with the Ku Klux Klan and neo-Nazis against "changing culture." That sort of cultural nationalism can easily shade into something uglier, and glues together only a fraction of Americans.

With democracy in retreat abroad, its contradictions and shortcomings exposed at home, and its appeal declining with each successive generation, it's 1857 all over again. But if the challenges are the same, the solution may also be familiar. Vitriol and divisiveness are commonly blamed for the problems of contemporary politics. But Americans aren't fighting too hard; they're engaged in the wrong fights. The universalism of the left and cultural nationalism of the right are battering America's sense of common national purpose. Under attack on both flanks, and weakened by its failure to deliver exceptional results, the nation's shared identity is crumbling.

Americans have been most successful when fighting over how to draw closer to the promise of their democracy; how to fulfill their threefold commitment to equality, rights, and opportunity; and how to distribute the resulting prosperity. They have been held together by the conviction that the United States had a unique mission, even as they debated how to pursue it.

The greatest danger facing American democracy is complacence. The democratic experiment is fragile, and its continued survival improbable. Salvaging it will require enlarging opportunity, restoring rights, and pursuing equality, and thereby renewing faith in the system that delivers them. This, really, is the American idea: that prosperity and justice do not exist in tension, but flow from each other. Achieving that ideal will require fighting as if the fate of democracy itself rests upon the struggle—because it does.

## Critical Thinking

1. Why is slavery antithetical to democracy?
2. Was the civil war a fight for democracy?
3. What was required for democracy to survive in America?

## Internet References

**New American Studies Web**
www.georgetown.edu/crossroads/asw
**Social Science Information Gateway**
http://sosig.esrc.bris.ac.uk
**Sociology Web Resources**
http://www.mhhe.com/socscience/sociology/resources/index.htm
**Sociology—Study Sociology Online**
http://edu.learnsoc.org
**Sociosite**
http://www.topsite.com/goto/sociosite.net

*Article*          Prepared by: Kurt Finsterbusch, *University of Maryland, College Park*

# Culture as a Cause of Poverty Has Been Wilfully Misinterpreted

The new poverty – a culture of the poor – has little power to relieve its own suffering, as welfare sanctions and cuts demonstrate

JEREMY SEABROOK

## Learning Outcomes

*After reading this article, you will be able to:*

- Explain the culture of poverty thesis.

- Present the arguments against the culture of poverty thesis.

- Be able to explain poverty or at least present the major theories that try to explain the causes of poverty.

When the term "culture of poverty" was first used by the anthropologist Oscar Lewis in 1959, it was seized upon as "evidence" that poverty is not caused primarily by an absence of material resources. This was never Lewis's intention. In a 1966 essay for Scientific American, he wrote: "A culture of poverty is not just a matter of deprivation or disorganisation – a term signifying the absence of something. It is a culture in the traditional anthropological sense in that it provides human beings with a design for living, a ready-made set of solutions for human problems, and so serves a significant adaptive function."

This was wilfully misinterpreted by those who believed poverty could not be abated by throwing money at it (that sole remedy for all other social ills); it was absorbed into an ancient moral critique of the poor; identified in modern industrial society with chaotic, disorganised lives, absence of parental ambition for children, aversion to hard labour and a tendency to addiction.

Lewis's work influenced a report by Daniel Moynihan during the Lyndon B Johnson presidency's "war on poverty" in 1965, which spoke of a "tangle of pathology" in relation to black families, and highlighted a "deviant maternalism" as a consequence of the fugitive male – a claim feminists later vehemently rebutted. In any case, riots in Los Angeles, Detroit and other US cities in the late 60s eclipsed theories of culture, which yielded to more pragmatic social programmes of investment and renewal of urban areas.

But the idea of culture as a cause of poverty has been tenacious; because it not only is readily assimilated to earlier ideas of "the undeserving", but also lends a shimmer of scientific authority to ancient prejudice. It certainly animates the reformist zealots of Britain's coalition government. This culture poses an anthropological problem, similar to that faced by imperialism when it confronted the "savage" societies of its overseas possessions. It requires colonisation of unorthodox or aberrant beliefs, and conformity with "correct", universal values, which always coincide with those of the rich and powerful.

The culture of poverty today presents itself as "a culture of welfare dependency" – a useful distraction from material deprivation. The word "culture" is also widely misused by politicians and journalists: we hear of a culture of bullying, a culture of neglect, a culture of fear, a culture of secrecy – so many cultures to be changed by fiat of the Talcott Parsons of suburbia, the Durkheims of the inner city!

Rather than a "culture of poverty" (which implies passivity of poor people), we should perhaps think of "the culture of the poor". This culture does exist. It has not remained static, but is dynamic, and follows changes in industrial society.

In the early industrial era, poverty was a forced frugality, a want of the necessities for survival – a lack of nutrition, shelter, fuel. Resources at the disposal of industrial workers were inadequate for a dignified sufficiency; people used desperate expedients – pawning clothes and redeeming them on payday, scavenging in the rural hinterland for dietary supplements, dependency on loans, frequent removals to avoid bailiffs.

This culture was superseded in an age of affluence, when to be poor came to mean living off the remains of wealth, the throwaway surplus of the rich. If contemporary poverty is less divisive than its predecessor, this is because rich and poor are now united in a common endeavour – a desire for more, which coincides with the imperatives of capitalism. The earlier culture of the poor offered a different solution: it was, to some degree, self-conscious, since the labour of the people was indispensable to industrial society, and this gave them considerable power.

With the removal of much industry from the rich world, the poor were remade in the image of wealth. This is different from the incipient consciousness of the impoverished workers of Victorian Britain, who had a collective character. It responded to, and recognised, a common human destiny. It was, of course, dominated by male labour, since the labour of men was, in most industries, the only thing that stood between women and children and total destitution. This has been overlooked by those who have exulted in both the diminution of men's power (high time though it may have been), and – perhaps involuntarily – the loss of any sense of a shared predicament; since the culture of contemporary poverty is characterised by a ruthless, unsentimental individualism.

The new poverty, the triumphant poverty of modernity, unlike its predecessor, is not in opposition to capitalism. Quite the contrary; it pays homage to it, fealty almost. It represents the extinction of social hope – the saving grace of an earlier, though even more grinding, capitalist poverty. Present-day poverty has little power to relieve its own suffering, as demonstrated by the misery created by "benefit sanctions", a reduction in allowances and cuts to welfare. It illuminates the wider dependency of humanity upon the market; market-dependency, a condition that does not name itself.

Since capitalism has extinguished significant alternatives – belief systems, values or ideologies that could conceivably replace it – the new poverty has nothing to offer in its own stead; only the sharp, opportunistic wisdom of getting by, surviving;

living, as they say, one day at a time. The poor are victims of capitalism's realm of freedom, which favours those chosen by fortune or chance – the holder of the lucky number or the winning ticket, the windfall, the possessor of the startling talent or stupendous prowess, the bonanza in the lottery of a capitalism identified as life itself.

This "culture of the poor" scarcely contains the seed of an alternative, or even of opposition: occasional outbreaks of violence, looting and destruction, occur, but are put down with considerable severity, as the riots of August 2011 showed. This is modernised poverty, which must console itself with the overflow from the waste pipes of wealth. The only promise of emancipation for the poor comes from within the very structures that oppress them. No wonder the culture of poverty is a theory for our time: it lends an aura of academic authority to the idea that poverty is transmitted culturally, and economics has little or nothing to do with it.

## Critical Thinking

1. Identify cultural norms that make it difficult for teenagers to get ahead.
2. Identify the structural conditions that make it difficult for teenagers to get ahead.
3. How can norms and conditions be changed to give poor teenagers a better chance to get ahead?

## Internet References

**New American Studies Web**
https://blogs.commons.georgetown.edu/vkp/
**Social Science Information Gateway**
http://www.ariadne.ac.uk/issue2/sosig
**Sociology—Study Sociology Online**
http://edu.learnsoc.org/
**Sociology Web Resources**
http://www.mhhe.com/socscience/sociology/resources/index.htm
**Sociosite**
http://www.topsite.com/goto/sociosite.net
**Socioweb**
http://www.topsite.com/goto/socioweb.com

*Article* Prepared by: Kurt Finsterbusch, *University of Maryland, College Park*

# Is Facebook Making Us Lonely?

Social media—from Facebook to Twitter—have made us more densely networked than ever. Yet for all this connectivity, new research suggests that we have never been lonelier (or more narcissistic)—and that this loneliness is making us mentally and physically ill. A report on what the epidemic of loneliness is doing to our souls and our society.

STEPHEN MARCHE

## Learning Outcomes

*After reading this article, you will be able to:*

- Know the trends in loneliness over the past several decades.
- Understand the role of Facebook in present-day loneliness.
- Understand the effects of loneliness on the mental and physical health of individuals and on society.

Yvette Vickers, a former *Playboy* playmate and B-movie star, best known for her role in *Attack of the 50 Foot Woman*, would have been 83 last August, but nobody knows exactly how old she was when she died. According to the Los Angeles coroner's report, she lay dead for the better part of a year before a neighbor and fellow actress, a woman named Susan Savage, noticed cobwebs and yellowing letters in her mailbox, reached through a broken window to unlock the door, and pushed her way through the piles of junk mail and mounds of clothing that barricaded the house. Upstairs, she found Vickers's body, mummified, near a heater that was still running. Her computer was on too, its glow permeating the empty space.

The *Los Angeles Times* posted a story headlined "Mummified Body of Former Playboy Playmate Yvette Vickers Found in Her Benedict Canyon Home," which quickly went viral. Within two weeks, by Technorati's count, Vickers's lonesome death was already the subject of 16,057 Facebook posts and 881 tweets. She had long been a horror-movie icon, a symbol of Hollywood's capacity to exploit our most basic fears in the silliest ways; now she was an icon of a new and different kind of

horror: our growing fear of loneliness. Certainly, she received much more attention in death than she did in the final years of her life. With no children, no religious group, and no immediate social circle of any kind, she had begun, as an elderly woman, to look elsewhere for companionship. Savage later told *Los Angeles* magazine that she had searched Vickers's phone bills for clues about the life that led to such an end. In the months before her grotesque death, Vickers had made calls not to friends or family but to distant fans who had found her through fan conventions and Internet sites.

Vickers's web of connections had grown broader but shallower, as has happened for many of us. We are living in an isolation that would have been unimaginable to our ancestors, and yet we have never been more accessible. Over the past three decades, technology has delivered to us a world in which we need not be out of contact for a fraction of a moment. In 2010, at a cost of $300 million, 800 miles of fiber-optic cable was laid between the Chicago Mercantile Exchange and the New York Stock Exchange to shave three milliseconds off trading times. Yet within this world of instant and absolute communication, unbounded by limits of time or space, we suffer from unprecedented alienation. We have never been more detached from one another, or lonelier. In a world consumed by ever more novel modes of socializing, we have less and less actual society. We live in an accelerating contradiction: the more connected we become, the lonelier we are. We were promised a global village; instead we inhabit the drab cul-de-sacs and endless freeways of a vast suburb of information.

At the forefront of all this unexpectedly lonely interactivity is Facebook, with 845 million users and $3.7 billion in revenue last year. The company hopes to raise $5 billion in an initial public offering later this spring, which will make it by far the largest Internet IPO in history. Some recent estimates put the company's potential value at $100 billion, which would make it larger than the global coffee industry—one addiction preparing to surpass the other. Facebook's scale and reach are hard to comprehend: last summer, Facebook became, by some counts, the first website to receive one trillion page views in a month. In the last three months of 2011, users generated an average of 2.7 billion "likes" and comments every day. On whatever scale you care to judge Facebook—as a company, as a culture, and as a country—it is vast beyond imagination.

Despite its immense popularity, or more likely because of it, Facebook has, from the beginning, been under something of a cloud of suspicion. The depiction of Mark Zuckerberg, in *The Social Network,* as a bastard with symptoms of Asperger's syndrome, was nonsense. But it felt true. It felt true to Facebook, if not to Zuckerberg. The film's most indelible scene, the one that may well have earned it an Oscar, was the final, silent shot of an anomic Zuckerberg sending out a friend request to his ex-girlfriend, then waiting and clicking and waiting and clicking—a moment of superconnected loneliness preserved in amber. We have all been in that scene: transfixed by the glare of a screen, hungering for response.

When you sign up for Google+ and set up your Friends circle, the program specifies that you should include only "your real friends, the ones you feel comfortable sharing private details with." That one little phrase, *Your real friends*— so quaint, so charmingly mothering—perfectly encapsulates the anxieties that social media have produced: the fears that Facebook is interfering with our real friendships, distancing us from each other, making us lonelier; and that social networking might be spreading the very isolation it seemed designed to conquer.

Facebook arrived in the middle of a dramatic increase in the quantity and intensity of human loneliness, a rise that initially made the site's promise of greater connection seem deeply attractive. Americans are more solitary than ever before. In 1950, less than 10 percent of American households contained only one person. By 2010, nearly 27 percent of households had just one person. Solitary living does not guarantee a life of unhappiness, of course. In his recent book about the trend toward living alone, Eric Klinenberg, a sociologist at NYU, writes: "Reams of published research show that it's the quality, not the quantity of social interaction, that best predicts loneliness." True. But before we begin the fantasies of happily eccentric singledom, of divorcées dropping by their knitting circles after work for glasses of Drew Barrymore pinot grigio, or recent college graduates with perfectly articulated, Steampunk-themed, 300-square-foot apartments organizing

croquet matches with their book clubs, we should recognize that it is not just isolation that is rising sharply. It's loneliness, too. And loneliness makes us miserable.

We know intuitively that loneliness and being alone are not the same thing. Solitude can be lovely. Crowded parties can be agony. We also know, thanks to a growing body of research on the topic, that loneliness is not a matter of external conditions; it is a psychological state. A 2005 analysis of data from a longitudinal study of Dutch twins showed that the tendency toward loneliness has roughly the same genetic component as other psychological problems such as neuroticism or anxiety.

Still, loneliness is slippery, a difficult state to define or diagnose. The best tool yet developed for measuring the condition is the UCLA Loneliness Scale, a series of 20 questions that all begin with this formulation: "How often do you feel . . . ?" As in: "How often do you feel that you are 'in tune' with the people around you?" And. "How often do you feel that you lack companionship?" Measuring the condition in these terms, various studies have shown loneliness rising drastically over a very short period of recent history. A 2010 AARP survey found that 35 percent of adults older than 45 were chronically lonely, as opposed to 20 percent of a similar group only a decade earlier. According to a major study by a leading scholar of the subject, roughly 20 percent of Americans—about 60 million people— are unhappy with their lives because of loneliness. Across the Western world, physicians and nurses have begun to speak openly of an epidemic of loneliness.

The new studies on loneliness are beginning to yield some surprising preliminary findings about its mechanisms. Almost every factor that one might assume affects loneliness does so only some of the time, and only under certain circumstances. People who are married are less lonely than single people, one journal article suggests, but only if their spouses are confidants. If one's spouse is not a confidant, marriage may not decrease loneliness. A belief in God might help, or it might not, as a 1990 German study comparing levels of religious feeling and levels of loneliness discovered. Active believers who saw God as abstract and helpful rather than as a wrathful, immediate presence were less lonely. "The mere belief in God," the researchers concluded, "was relatively independent of loneliness."

But it is clear that social interaction matters. Loneliness and being alone are not the same thing, but both are on the rise. We meet fewer people. We gather less. And when we gather, our bonds are less meaningful and less easy. The decrease in confidants—that is, in quality social connections—has been dramatic over the past 25 years. In one survey, the mean size of networks of personal confidants decreased from 2.94 people in 1985 to 2.08 in 2004. Similarly, in 1985, only 10 percent of

Americans said they had no one with whom to discuss important matters, and 15 percent said they had only one such good friend. By 2004, 25 percent had nobody to talk to and 20 percent had only one confidant.

In the face of this social disintegration, we have essentially hired an army of replacement confidants, an entire class of professional carers. As Ronald Dworkin pointed out in a 2010 paper for the Hoover Institution, in the late 40s, the United States was home to 2,500 clinical psychologists, 30,000 social workers, and fewer than 500 marriage and family therapists. As of 2010, the country had 77,000 clinical psychologists, 192,000 clinical social workers, 400,000 nonclinical social workers, 50,000 marriage and family therapists, 105,000 mental-health counselors, 220,000 substance-abuse counselors, 17,000 nurse psychotherapists, and 30,000 life coaches. The majority of patients in therapy do not warrant a psychiatric diagnosis. This raft of psychic servants is helping us through what used to be called regular problems. We have outsourced the work of everyday caring.

We need professional careers more and more, because the threat of societal breakdown, once principally a matter of nostalgic lament, has morphed into an issue of public health. Being lonely is extremely bad for your health. If you're lonely, you're more likely to be put in a geriatric home at an earlier age than a similar person who isn't lonely. You're less likely to exercise. You're more likely to be obese. You're less likely to survive a serious operation and more likely to have hormonal imbalances. You are at greater risk of inflammation. Your memory may be worse. You are more likely to be depressed, to sleep badly, and to suffer dementia and general cognitive decline. Loneliness may not have killed Yvette Vickers, but it has been linked to a greater probability of having the kind of heart condition that did kill her.

And yet, despite its deleterious effect on health, loneliness is one of the first things ordinary Americans spend their money achieving. With money, you flee the cramped city to a house in the suburbs or, if you can afford it, a McMansion in the exurbs, inevitably spending more time in your car. Loneliness is at the American core, a by-product of a long-standing national appetite for independence: The Pilgrims who left Europe willingly abandoned the bonds and strictures of a society that could not accept their right to be different. They did not seek out loneliness, but they accepted it as the price of their autonomy. The cowboys who set off to explore a seemingly endless frontier likewise traded away personal ties in favor of pride and self-respect. The ultimate American icon is the astronaut: Who is more heroic, or more alone? The price of self-determination and self-reliance has often been loneliness. But Americans have always been willing to pay that price.

Today, the one common feature in American secular culture is its celebration of the self that breaks away from the constrictions of the family and the state, and, in its greatest expressions, from all limits entirely. The great American poem is Whitman's "Song of Myself." The great American essay is Emerson's "Self-Reliance." The great American novel is Melville's *Moby-Dick,* the tale of a man on a quest so lonely that it is incomprehensible to those around him. American culture, high and low, is about self-expression and personal authenticity. Franklin Delano Roosevelt called individualism "the great watchword of American life."

Self-invention is only half of the American story, however. The drive for isolation has always been in tension with the impulse to cluster in communities that cling and suffocate. The Pilgrims, while fomenting spiritual rebellion, also enforced ferocious cohesion. The Salem witch trials, in hindsight, read like attempts to impose solidarity—as do the McCarthy hearings. The history of the United States is like the famous parable of the porcupines in the cold, from Schopenhauer's *Studies in Pessimism*—the ones who huddle together for warmth and shuffle away in pain, always separating and congregating.

We are now in the middle of a long period of shuffling away. In his 2000 book *Bowling Alone,* Robert D. Putnam attributed the dramatic postwar decline of social capital—the strength and value of interpersonal networks—to numerous interconnected trends in American life: suburban sprawl, television's dominance over culture, the self-absorption of the Baby Boomers, and the disintegration of the traditional family. The trends he observed continued through the prosperity of the aughts, and have only become more pronounced with time: the rate of union membership declined in 2011, again; screen time rose; the Masons and the Elks continued their slide into irrelevance. We are lonely because we want to be lonely. We have made ourselves lonely.

The question of the future is this: Is Facebook part of the separating or part of the congregating; is it a huddling-together for warmth or a shuffling-away in pain?

Well before facebook, digital technology was enabling our tendency for isolation, to an unprecedented degree. Back in the 1990s, scholars started calling the contradiction between an increased opportunity to connect and a lack of human contact the "Internet paradox." A prominent 1998 article on the phenomenon by a team of researchers at Carnegie Mellon showed that increased Internet usage was already coinciding with increased loneliness. Critics of the study pointed out that the two groups that participated in the study—high-school journalism students who were heading to university and socially active members of community-development boards—were statistically likely to become lonelier over time. Which brings us to a more fundamental question: Does the Internet make people lonely, or are lonely people more attracted to the Internet?

The question has intensified in the Facebook era. A recent study out of Australia (where close to half the population is active on Facebook), titled "Who Uses Facebook?," found a complex and sometimes confounding relationship between loneliness and social networking. Facebook users had slightly lower levels of "social loneliness"—the sense of not feeling bonded with friends—but "significantly higher levels of family loneliness"—the sense of not feeling bonded with family. It may be that Facebook encourages more contact with people outside of our household, at the expense of our family relationships—or it may be that people who have unhappy family relationships in the first place seek companionship through other means, including Facebook. The researchers also found that lonely people are inclined to spend more time on Facebook: "One of the most noteworthy findings," they wrote, "was the tendency for neurotic and lonely individuals to spend greater amounts of time on Facebook per day than nonlonely individuals." And they found that neurotics are more likely to prefer to use the wall, while extroverts tend to use chat features in addition to the wall.

Moira Burke, until recently a graduate student at the Human-Computer Institute at Carnegie Mellon, used to run a longitudinal study of 1,200 Facebook users. That study, which is ongoing, is one of the first to step outside the realm of self-selected college students and examine the effects of Facebook on a broader population, over time. She concludes that the effect of Facebook depends on what you bring to it. Just as your mother said: you get out only what you put in. If you use Facebook to communicate directly with other individuals—by using the "like" button, commenting on friends' posts, and so on—it can increase your social capital. Personalized messages, or what Burke calls "composed communication," are more satisfying than "one-click communication"—the lazy click of a like. "People who received composed communication became less lonely, while people who received one-click communication experienced no change in loneliness," Burke tells me. So, you should inform your friend in writing how charming her son looks with Harry Potter cake smeared all over his face, and how interesting her sepia-toned photograph of that tree-framed bit of skyline is, and how cool it is that she's at whatever concert she happens to be at. That's what we all want to hear. Even better than sending a private Facebook message is the semi-public conversation, the kind of back-and-forth in which you half ignore the other people who may be listening in. "People whose friends write to them semi-publicly on Facebook experience decreases in loneliness," Burke says.

On the other hand, nonpersonalized use of Facebook—scanning your friends' status updates and updating the world on your own activities via your wall, or what Burke calls "passive consumption" and "broadcasting"—correlates to feelings of disconnectedness. It's a lonely business, wandering the labyrinths of our friends' and pseudo-friends' projected identities, trying to figure out what part of ourselves we ought to project, who will listen, and what they will hear. According to Burke, passive consumption of Facebook also correlates to a marginal increase in depression. "If two women each talk to their friends the same amount of time, but one of them spends more time reading about friends on Facebook as well, the one reading tends to grow slightly more depressed," Burke says. Her conclusion suggests that my sometimes unhappy reactions to Facebook may be more universal than I had realized. When I scroll through page after page of my friends' descriptions of how accidentally eloquent their kids are, and how their husbands are endearingly bumbling, and how they're all about to eat a home-cooked meal prepared with fresh local organic produce bought at the farmers' market and then go for a jog and maybe check in at the office because they're so busy getting ready to hop on a plane for a week of luxury dogsledding in Lapland, I do grow slightly more miserable. A lot of other people doing the same thing feel a little bit worse, too.

Still, Burke's research does not support the assertion that Facebook creates loneliness. The people who experience loneliness on Facebook are lonely away from Facebook, too, she points out; on Facebook, as everywhere else, correlation is not causation. The popular kids are popular, and the lonely skulkers skulk alone. Perhaps, it says something about me that I think Facebook is primarily a platform for lonely skulking. I mention to Burke the widely reported study, conducted by a Stanford graduate student, that showed how believing that others have strong social networks can lead to feelings of depression. What does Facebook communicate, if not the impression of social bounty? Everybody else looks so happy on Facebook, with so many friends, that our own social networks feel emptier than ever in comparison. Doesn't that *make* people feel lonely? "If people are reading about lives that are much better than theirs, two things can happen," Burke tells me. "They can feel worse about themselves, or they can feel motivated."

Burke will start working at Facebook as a data scientist this year.

John Cacioppo, the director of the Center for Cognitive and Social Neuroscience at the University of Chicago, is the world's leading expert on loneliness. In his landmark book, *Loneliness,* released in 2008, he revealed just how profoundly the epidemic of loneliness is affecting the basic functions of human physiology. He found higher levels of epinephrine, the stress hormone, in the morning urine of lonely people. Loneliness burrows deep: "When we drew blood from our older adults and analyzed their white cells," he writes, "we found that loneliness somehow penetrated the deepest recesses of the cell to alter the way genes were being expressed." Loneliness affects not only the brain, then, but the basic process of DNA transcription. When you are lonely, your whole body is lonely.

To Cacioppo, Internet communication allows only ersatz intimacy. "Forming connections with pets or online friends or even God is a noble attempt by an obligatorily gregarious creature to satisfy a compelling need," he writes. "But surrogates can never make up completely for the absence of the real thing." The "real thing" being actual people, in the flesh. When I speak to Cacioppo, he is refreshingly clear on what he sees as Facebook's effect on society. Yes, he allows, some research has suggested that the greater the number of Facebook friends a person has, the less lonely she is. But he argues that the impression this creates can be misleading. "For the most part," he says, "people are bringing their old friends, and feelings of loneliness or connectedness, to Facebook." The idea that a website could deliver a more friendly, interconnected world is bogus. The depth of one's social network outside Facebook is what determines the depth of one's social network within Facebook, not the other way around. Using social media doesn't create new social networks; it just transfers established networks from one platform to another. For the most part, Facebook doesn't destroy friendships—but it doesn't create them, either.

In one experiment, Cacioppo looked for a connection between the loneliness of subjects and the relative frequency of their interactions via Facebook, chat rooms, online games, dating sites, and face-to-face contact. The results were unequivocal. "The greater the proportion of face-to-face interactions, the less lonely you are," he says. "The greater the proportion of online interactions, the lonelier you are." Surely, I suggest to Cacioppo, this means that Facebook and the like inevitably make people lonelier. He disagrees. Facebook is merely a tool, he says, and like any tool, its effectiveness will depend on its user. "If you use Facebook to increase face-to-face contact," he says, "it increases social capital." So if social media let you organize a game of football among your friends, that's healthy. If you turn to social media instead of playing football, however, that's unhealthy.

"Facebook can be terrific, if we use it properly," Cacioppo continues. "It's like a car. You can drive it to pick up your friends. Or you can drive alone." But hasn't the car increased loneliness? If cars created the suburbs, surely they also created isolation. "That's because of how we use cars," Cacioppo replies. "How we use these technologies can lead to more integration, rather than more isolation."

The problem, then, is that we invite loneliness, even though it makes us miserable. The history of our use of technology is a history of isolation desired and achieved. When the Great Atlantic and Pacific Tea Company opened its A&P stores, giving Americans self-service access to groceries, customers stopped having relationships with their grocers. When the telephone arrived, people stopped knocking on their neighbors' doors. Social media bring this process to a much wider set of relationships. Researchers at the HP Social Computing Lab who studied the nature of people's connections on Twitter came to a depressing, if not surprising, conclusion: "Most of the links declared within Twitter were meaningless from an interaction point of view." I have to wonder: What other point of view is meaningful?

Loneliness is certainly not something that Facebook or Twitter or any of the lesser forms of social media is doing to us. We are doing it to ourselves. Casting technology as some vague, impersonal spirit of history forcing our actions is a weak excuse. We make decisions about how we use our machines, not the other way around. Every time I shop at my local grocery store, I am faced with a choice. I can buy my groceries from a human being or from a machine. I always, without exception, choose the machine. It's faster and more efficient, I tell myself, but the truth is that I prefer not having to wait with the other customers who are lined up alongside the conveyor belt: the hipster mom who disapproves of my high-carbon-footprint pineapple; the lady who tenses to the point of tears while she waits to see if the gods of the credit-card machine will accept or decline; the old man whose clumsy feebleness requires a patience that I don't possess. Much better to bypass the whole circus and just ring up the groceries myself.

Our omnipresent new technologies lure us toward increasingly superficial connections at exactly the same moment that they make avoiding the mess of human interaction easy. The beauty of Facebook, the source of its power, is that it enables us to be social while sparing us the embarrassing reality of society—the accidental revelations we make at parties, the awkward pauses, the farting and the spilled drinks, and the general gaucherie of face-to-face contact. Instead, we have the lovely smoothness of a seemingly social machine. Everything's so simple: status updates, pictures, your wall.

But the price of this smooth sociability is a constant compulsion to assert one's own happiness, one's own fulfillment. Not only must we contend with the social bounty of others; we must foster the appearance of our own social bounty. Being happy all the time, pretending to be happy, actually attempting to be happy—it's exhausting. Last year a team of researchers led by Iris Mauss at the University of Denver published a study looking into "the paradoxical effects of valuing happiness." Most goals in life show a direct correlation between valuation and achievement. Studies have found, for example, that students who value good grades tend to have higher grades than those who don't value them. Happiness is an exception. The study came to a disturbing conclusion:

Valuing happiness is not necessarily linked to greater happiness. In fact, under certain conditions, the opposite is true. Under conditions of low (but not high) life stress, the more people valued happiness, the lower were their hedonic balance, psychological well-being, and life satisfaction, and the higher their depression symptoms.

The more you try to be happy, the less happy you are. Sophocles made roughly the same point.

Facebook, of course, puts the pursuit of happiness front and center in our digital life. Its capacity to redefine our very concepts of identity and personal fulfillment is much more worrisome than the data mining and privacy practices that have aroused anxieties about the company. Two of the most compelling critics of Facebook—neither of them a Luddite—concentrate on exactly this point. Jaron Lanier, the author of *You Are Not a Gadget,* was one of the inventors of virtual-reality technology. His view of where social media are taking us reads like dystopian science fiction: "I fear that we are beginning to design ourselves to suit digital models of us, and I worry about a leaching of empathy and humanity in that process." Lanier argues that Facebook imprisons us in the business of self-presenting, and this, to his mind, is the site's crucial and fatally unacceptable downside.

Sherry Turkle, a professor of computer culture at MIT who in 1995 published the digital-positive analysis *Life on the Screen,* is much more skeptical about the effects of online society in her 2011 book, *Alone Together:* "These days, insecure in our relationships and anxious about intimacy, we look to technology for ways to be in relationships and protect ourselves from them at the same time." The problem with digital intimacy is that it is ultimately incomplete: "The ties we form through the Internet are not, in the end, the ties that bind. But they are the ties that preoccupy," she writes. "We don't want to intrude on each other, so instead we constantly intrude on each other, but not in 'real time.'"

Lanier and Turkle are right, at least in their diagnoses. Self-presentation on Facebook is continuous, intensely mediated, and possessed of a phony nonchalance that eliminates even the potential for spontaneity. (Look how casually I threw up these three photos from the party at which I took 300 photos!) Curating the exhibition of the self has become a 24/7 occupation. Perhaps not surprisingly, then, the Australian study "Who Uses Facebook?" found a significant correlation between Facebook use and narcissism: "Facebook users have higher levels of total narcissism, exhibitionism, and leadership than Facebook non-users," the study's authors wrote. "In fact, it could be argued that Facebook specifically gratifies the narcissistic individual's need to engage in self-promoting and superficial behavior."

Rising narcissism isn't so much a trend as the trend behind all other trends. In preparation for the 2013 edition of its diagnostic manual, the psychiatric profession is currently struggling to update its definition of narcissistic personality disorder. Still, generally speaking, practitioners agree that narcissism manifests in patterns of fantastic grandiosity, craving for attention, and lack of empathy. In a 2008 survey, 35,000 American respondents were asked if they had ever had certain symptoms of narcissistic personality disorder. Among people older than 65, 3 percent reported symptoms. Among people in their 20s, the proportion was nearly 10 percent. Across all age groups, one in 16 Americans has experienced some symptoms of NPD. And loneliness and narcissism are intimately connected: a longitudinal study of Swedish women demonstrated a strong link between levels of narcissism in youth and levels of loneliness in old age. The connection is fundamental. Narcissism is the flip side of loneliness, and either condition is a fighting retreat from the messy reality of other people.

A considerable part of Facebook's appeal stems from its miraculous fusion of distance with intimacy, or the illusion of distance with the illusion of intimacy. Our online communities become engines of self-image, and self-image becomes the engine of community. The real danger with Facebook is not that it allows us to isolate ourselves, but that by mixing our appetite for isolation with our vanity, it threatens to alter the very nature of solitude. The new isolation is not of the kind that Americans once idealized, the lonesomeness of the proudly nonconformist, independent-minded, solitary stoic, or that of the astronaut who blasts into new worlds. Facebook's isolation is a grind. What's truly staggering about Facebook usage is not its volume—750 million photographs uploaded over a single weekend—but the constancy of the performance it demands. More than half its users—and one of every 13 people on Earth is a Facebook user—log on every day. Among 18 to 34-year-olds, nearly half check Facebook minutes after waking up, and 28 percent do so before getting out of bed. The relentlessness is what is so new, so potentially transformative. Facebook never takes a break. We never take a break. Human beings have always created elaborate acts of self-presentation. But not all the time, not every morning, before we even pour a cup of coffee. Yvette Vickers's computer was on when she died.

Nostalgia for the good old days of disconnection would not just be pointless, it would be hypocritical and ungrateful. But the very magic of the new machines, the efficiency and elegance with which they serve us, obscures what isn't being served: everything that matters. What Facebook has revealed about human nature—and this is not a minor revelation—is that a connection is not the same thing as a bond, and that instant and total connection is no salvation, no ticket to a happier, better world or a more liberated version of humanity. Solitude used to be good for self-reflection and self-reinvention. But now we are left thinking about who we are all the time, without ever really thinking about who we are. Facebook denies us a pleasure whose profundity we had underestimated: the chance to forget about ourselves for a while, the chance to disconnect.

## Critical Thinking

1. What are the advantages of social media for mental health?
2. What are the tradeoffs for time using social media?
3. What in your opinion are the best ways to use social media?

## Internet References

**Global X Social Media Index ETF**
　　http://www.globalxfunds.com/SOCL
**Social Science Information Gateway**
　　http://sosig.esrc.bris.ac.uk
**Sociology Web Resources**
　　http://www.mhhe.com/socscience/sociology/resources/index.htm
**Sociology—Study Sociology Online**
　　http://edu.learnsoc.org
**Sociosite**
　　http://www.topsite.com/goto/sociosite.net
**Socioweb**
　　http://www.topsite.com/goto/socioweb.com
**The American Studies Web**
　　http://lamp.georgetown.edu/asw

# Unit 2

# UNIT

Prepared by: Kurt Finsterbusch, *University of Maryland, College Park*

# Problems of the Political Economy

Since the political system and the economy interpenetrate each other to a high degree, it is now common to study them together under the label political economy. The political economy is the most basic aspect of society, and it should be studied first. The way it functions affects how problems in other areas can or cannot be addressed. Here, we encounter issues of power, control, and influence. It is in this arena that society acts corporately to address the problems that are of public concern. It is important, therefore, to ascertain the degree to which the economic elite control the political system. The answer determines how democratic America is. Next, we want to know how effective the American political economy is. Can government agencies be effective? Can government regulations be effective? Can the economy be effective? Can the economy make everyone, and not just the owners and top administrators, prosper and be happy?

The first section of this unit covers the political system. The most basic issue is the extent that the economic elite and major corporations control the government. If their control is tight, then democracy is a sham. The following section includes topics such as the degree that the governing institutions can provide for the common good and the question of whether American organizations and institutions have gotten so big that they have become unaccountable. The next section deals with the type of capitalism that is dominate today, the devolution of the relations between capitalism and labor, and the general conditions of the working class. The final section covers urbanism and immigration policy.

*Article*    Prepared by: Kurt Finsterbusch, *University of Maryland, College Park*

# A Problem Only Politics Can Solve

MATT MAZEWSKI

## Learning Outcomes

*After reading this article, you will be able to:*

- Understand Piketty's masterful explanation of increasing inequality under current capitalism.

- Be aware of many criticisms of Piketty's work without falsifying it.

- Understand that Piketty's disturbing thesis is not likely to change the political economy.

In a 2008 interview with Jim Lehrer shortly after becoming a Nobel laureate, economist Paul Krugman sheepishly revealed that he first became interested in economics because of his childhood love of science fiction. And no, it was not, as some might say, because economics is science fiction, but rather because studying it seemed to the young Krugman to be the closest he could come to practicing psychohistory-an imaginary social science developed by the mathematician Hari Seldon in Isaac Asimov's science-fiction series Foundation.

Psychohistory in Foundation is essentially an advanced form of what today goes by the name of "big-data analytics." Armed with ultra-sophisticated mathematical models, Seldon is able to predict the exact timing of a societal collapse and develop a plan to limit the fallout. The prediction must remain secret, however; otherwise it will trigger a chain of events that will make the calamity even worse.

The soothsaying abilities of presentday economists remain far more limited than those of the godlike Seldon (see Recession, The Great), but self fulfilling and self-defeating prophecies involving the economy are quite real. If forecasts of looming inflation convince the Federal Reserve to preemptively raise interest rates, they may in fact ensure that inflation never materializes. The act of making a prediction about the trajectory of the economy can itself shape the future.

Heather Boushey of the Washington Center for Economic Growth, J. Bradford DeLong of the University of California, Berkeley, and Marshall Steinbaum of the Roosevelt Institute contemplate this very paradox in their introduction to After Piketty: The Agenda for Economics and Inequality, an edited volume containing twenty-one "arguments, critiques, extensions, and explorations" written in response to French economist Thomas Piketty's 2013 work on the history and future of inequality in the West, Capital in the Twenty-First Century. To understand what they find puzzling, it helps to first understand what it is that Piketty sets out to show.

Krugman explains in "Why We're in a New Gilded Age" (Chapter 3) that Piketty's thesis is "all about r versus g-the rate of return on capital versus the rate of economic growth," where "capital" refers not only to financial capital but to productive assets of any kind, such as industrial plants or equipment. Capital argues that for most of history the rate of return on capital (r) has been greater than the rate of growth (g), and that this pattern is so consistent that it is virtually a fundamental law of capitalism. In addition, whenever the difference between r and g becomes greater the result is that a larger share of the national income accrues to the owners of capital. Piketty maintains that g is currently declining because of reduced population growth and slowing technological progress, but that r is declining more slowly and that the gap between the two rates is therefore growing. This portends a future of worsening inequality, in which inheritance rather than work becomes the main path to amassing wealth.

Piketty claims that the major exceptions to the historical norm of r &gt; g were the result of cataclysmic events like the Second World War, when wartime taxation and widespread destruction of factories and machines reduced capital's income share across the industrialized world. The editors write that Piketty's Capital "portrays the forces favoring the formation of a dominant plutocracy as being so strong that they can be countered only by world wars and global revolutions-and even then, the correction is only temporary."

In an essay titled "The Piketty Phenomenon" (Chapter 1), Capital's English-language translator, Arthur Goldhammer, ponders how "a work by an academic economist comprising nearly 700 pages dense with statistical tables and graphs" could become the fastest-selling book in the history of Harvard University Press, and its author "the 'rock star' of a profession more commonly regarded as a 'dismal science.'" He attributes the book's stunning success and the "readiness of so many to wade into the unfamiliar waters of economic history" at least in part to widespread public anger at the injustices of the post-recession recovery, when "the portfolios of the wealthy recovered quickly, whereas people who lost their homes lost them for good."

It is here that the editors spot a "contradiction" in the book's "dual nature as work of scholarship and global intellectual phenomenon." On the one hand, Capital contends that increasing inequality is the result of fundamental laws of capitalism. But in speaking before standing-room-only crowds at universities and high-level forums like the UN and IMF about possible policy remedies, "Piketty himself as a celebrity public intellectual is not behaving like a passive chronicler of unavoidable destiny. He is acting as if he believes that the forces he describes in his book can be resisted-that we collectively make our own destiny."

The essays in After Piketty are impressively diverse, not only in their subject matter but also in the way they relate to Piketty's original text. Several launch straightforward critiques of his work-both of what he has done and what he has failed to do- while others present complementary ideas that aim to enrich his arguments. Daina Ramey Berry (Chapter 6, "The Ubiquitous Nature of Slave Capital") laments that Piketty did not say more about the institution of slavery, a form of "literal human capital," and its role in wealth accumulation up through the nineteenth century. Laura Tyson and Michael Spence (Chapter 8, "Exploring the Effects of Technology and Wealth Inequality") show how technological change has also been an important driver of income inequality, and how advances in automation could weaken the link between income and work to such an extent that policies like a universal basic income become necessary.

The contributors also span a wide spectrum of ideological orientations. Some, such as Eric Nielsen, operate from squarely within the mainstream neoclassical tradition in economics. In "Human Capital and Wealth before and after Capital in the Twenty-First Century" (Chapter 7), Nielsen criticizes Piketty's neglect of "human capital" (of the non-literal kind) and somewhat unconvincingly suggests that education, rather than Piketty's own "contentious and divisive policy program" of global wealth taxation, is the surest path to reducing inequality. Piketty's proposed wealth tax is not without its problems,

including the inherent difficulty in coordinating international agreements and monitoring tax havens, but education alone will not reverse our slide toward oligarchy.

Others offer more heterodox perspectives that draw on feminist theory or Marxist analysis. Heather Boushey's "Feminist Interpretation of Patrimonial Capitalism" (Chapter 15) comments on the virtual absence of gender from Piketty's narrative and considers how social norms surrounding marriage, childrearing, and inheritance can affect the intergenerational propagation of inequality. She highlights evidence that women, while "just as likely as men to inherit wealth from their parents," are less likely to inherit a family business, and that parents are twice as likely to ask Google, "Is my son gifted?" as they are to ask, "Is my daughter gifted?"

Suresh Naidu (Chapter 5, "A Political Economy Take on W/Y") posits a tension in Capital between a "Domesticated Piketty" who works with standard economic models that are "institution-and politics free" and a "Wild Piketty" who sees capital as "the alchemy of today's income transmuted into secure claims on future income." Wealth, in this latter view, is not simply money saved from past income but a collection of rights to future income that are shaped by politics and power. If, for instance, intellectual property protections are strengthened, the holders of patents or copyrights will find that what they own-namely, the right to a stream of revenue-has been rendered more valuable.

The sheer variety of approaches in this volume would pose a challenge for any attempt at editorial curation. Boushey, DeLong, and Steinbaum have chosen to arrange the chapters in four sections, with a fifth and final section devoted to a response from Piketty himself. The first section ("Reception") contains the essay by Goldhammer and previously published reviews of Capital by Robert Solow and Krugman. All of these are supremely useful as introductions to the book and its academic and cultural significance. The ordering of the chapters in the subsequent triptych ("Conceptions of Capital," "Dimensions of Inequality," and "The Political Economy of Capital and Capitalism") seems fairly random.

An alternative would have been to group chapters according to their level of technical detail. Most of After Piketty is accessible to the general reader, but anyone who has done more practical things than take graduate-level courses in economic theory will almost certainly find parts of the book to be a slog. For example, "Macro Models of Wealth Inequality" (Chapter 14), with its discussions of "logarithmic preferences" and "nonhomothetic bequest motives," will be of interest only to specialists.

The math-phobic may be more interested in the chapters that offer broader philosophical or epistemological perspectives on Piketty's project. David Singh Grewal, in the "The Legal

Constitution of Capitalism" (Chapter 19), critiques the way in which Piketty treats r &gt; g as a law of nature akin to gravity. Instead, he tries to "historicize the laws of capitalism understood as laws" by tracing the development of modern theories of property and contract and showing how these often "work to entrench the privileged place of capital."

Although the competition is fierce, the most fascinating chapter is the final one, Elisabeth Jacobs' "Everywhere and Nowhere: Politics in Capital in the Twenty-First Century" (Chapter 21). Jacobs circles back to the paradox highlighted at the outset by asking, "How can we have both fundamental laws of economics and historically contingent, institutionally bound processes that shape the relationship between the distribution of economic gains and the pace of economic growth?" She finds fault with Piketty's discussions of proposals like international wealth taxation for their depiction of policy intervention as something that comes from outside the economic system rather than from actors and institutions that live within it. Capital, she says, fails to attend to the "mechanisms through which inequality might erode the promise of democratic governance." The diminution of the voice of working people as wealthy donors and high-paid corporate lobbyists come to drive the agenda and write the legislation is but one example of "feedback loops" between economic and political inequality. Jacobs maintains that "promising economic policy ideas such as Piketty's utopian vision of a global wealth tax are likely to remain a fantasy" unless coupled with a sustained effort to "build countervailing political power."

Paul Krugman realized early on that he could never be Hari Seldon, but it sometimes seems as if he and many other economists have not entirely given up on the dream. The premise of psychohistory lives on in the technocratic conceit that economic policy can be formulated and implemented by an elite group of experts with minimal input from the masses. In Chapter 3, Krugman writes that it's "easy to be cynical" about the prospect of meaningful action against the problem of inequality. "But surely Piketty's masterly diagnosis of where we are and where we're heading makes such a thing considerably more likely," he continues, for Piketty "has transformed our economic discourse; we'll never talk about wealth and inequality the same way we used to."

Yet transforming the "economic discourse" will not by itself transform the world. It is not enough to have white papers or bullet points on a campaign website if you cannot amass the political power needed to implement your agenda and defend it once implemented. To do that, you have to organize people around a concrete vision of how your policies will improve their lives. Inequality will persist as long as we assume that the technocrats will eventually fix it for us. "We collectively make our own destiny," say the editors of After Piketty, "even if the circumstances under which we make it are not those of our choosing." A more egalitarian future is possible, but only if we build it for ourselves.

## Critical Thinking

1. What needs to be done to increase income equality?

2. What are the chances that enough political power can be assembled to make the necessary changes?

3. The Piketty argument and its criticism is scholarly and complex. Give a simple version of it?

## Internet References

**New American Studies Web**
   www.georgetown.edu/crossroads/asw
**Social Science Information Gateway**
   http://sosig.esrc.bris.ac.uk
**Sociology Web Resources**
   http://www.mhhe.com/socscience/sociology/resources/index.htm
**Sociology—Study Sociology Online**
   http://edu.learnsoc.org
**Sociosite**
   http://www.topsite.com/goto/sociosite.net

*Article*  Prepared by: Kurt Finsterbusch, *University of Maryland, College Park*

# The New Era of Monopoly Is Here

Today's markets are characterised by the persistence of high monopoly profits

JOSEPH STIGLITZ

## Learning Outcomes

*After reading this article, you will be able to:*

- Describe the two schools of thought about the distribution of income and how the economy functions.

- Understand both the benefits of competitive markets and their tendency to evolve into monopolies.

- Understand how companies erect and maintain barriers to entry and how the government assists this process.

For 200 years, there have been two schools of thought about what determines the distribution of income and how the economy functions. One, emanating from Adam Smith and 19th-century liberal economists, focuses on competitive markets. The other, cognisant of how Smith's brand of liberalism leads to rapid concentration of wealth and income, takes as its starting point unfettered markets' tendency toward monopoly. It is important to understand both, because our views about government policies and existing inequalities are shaped by which of the two schools of thought one believes provides a better description of reality.

For the 19th-century liberals and their latter-day acolytes, because markets are competitive, individuals' returns are related to their social contributions their "marginal product", in the language of economists. Capitalists are rewarded for saving rather than consuming for their *abstinence*, in the words of Nassau Senior, one of my predecessors in the Drummond Professorship of Political Economy at Oxford. Differences in income were then related to their ownership of "assets" human and financial capital. Scholars of inequality thus focused on the determinants of the distribution of assets, including how they are passed on across generations.

The second school of thought takes as its starting point "power", including the ability to exercise monopoly control or, in labour markets, to assert authority over workers. Scholars in this area have focused on what gives rise to power, how it is maintained and strengthened, and other features that may prevent markets from being competitive. Work on exploitation arising from asymmetries of information is an important example.

In the west in the post-second world war era, the liberal school of thought has dominated. Yet, as inequality has widened and concerns about it have grown, the competitive school, viewing individual returns in terms of marginal product, has become increasingly unable to explain how the economy works. So, today, the second school of thought is ascendant.

After all, the large bonuses paid to banks' CEOs as they led their firms to ruin and the economy to the brink of collapse are hard to reconcile with the belief that individuals' pay has *anything* to do with their social contributions. Of course, historically, the oppression of large groups slaves, women, and minorities of various types are obvious instances where inequalities are the result of power relationships, not marginal returns.

In today's economy, many sectors telecoms, cable TV, digital branches from social media to internet search, health insurance, pharmaceuticals, agro-business, and many more cannot be understood through the lens of competition. In these sectors, what competition exists is oligopolistic, not the "pure" competition depicted in textbooks. A few sectors can be defined as "price taking"; firms are so small that they have no effect on market price. Agriculture is the clearest example, but government intervention in the sector is massive, and prices are not set primarily by market forces.

Barack Obama's council of economic advisers (CEA), led by Jason Furman, has attempted to tally the extent of the increase in market concentration and some of its implications. In most industries, according to the CEA, standard metrics show large and in some cases, dramatic increases in market concentration. The top 10 banks' share of the deposit market, for example, increased from about 20% to 50% in just 30 years, from 1980 to 2010.

Some of the increase in market power is the result of changes in technology and economic structure: consider network economies and the growth of locally provided service-sector industries. Some is because firms  Microsoft and drug companies are good examples  have learned better how to erect and maintain entry barriers, often assisted by conservative political forces that justify lax anti-trust enforcement and the failure to limit market power on the grounds that markets are "naturally" competitive. And some of it reflects the naked abuse and leveraging of market power through the political process: Large banks, for example, lobbied the US Congress to amend or repeal legislation separating commercial banking from other areas of finance.

The consequences are evident in the data, with inequality rising at every level, not only across individuals, but also across firms. The CEA report noted that the "90th percentile firm sees returns on investments in capital that are more than five times the median. This ratio was closer to two just a quarter of a century ago."

Joseph Schumpeter, one of the great economists of the 20th century, argued that one shouldn't be worried by monopoly power: monopolies would only be temporary. There would be fierce competition *for* the market and this would replace competition in the market and ensure that prices remained competitive. My own theoretical work long ago showed the flaws in Schumpeter's analysis, and now empirical results provide strong confirmation. Today's markets are characterised by the persistence of high monopoly profits.

The implications of this are profound. Many of the assumptions about market economies are based on acceptance of the competitive model, with marginal returns commensurate with social contributions. This view has led to hesitancy about official intervention: If markets are fundamentally efficient and fair, there is little that even the best of governments could do to improve matters. But if markets are based on exploitation, the rationale for laissez-faire disappears. Indeed, in that case, the battle against entrenched power is not only a battle for democracy; it is also a battle for efficiency and shared prosperity.

## Critical Thinking

1. What evidence is there that competitive markets are not working in some areas?

2. How does power figure into the way the economy works and how income is distributed?

3. How do oligopolies function in the American economy?

## Internet References

**New American Studies Web**
   www.georgetown.edu/crossroads/asw
**Social Science Information Gateway**
   http://sosig.esrc.bris.ac.uk
**Sociology Web Resources**
   http://www.mhhe.com/socscience/sociology/resources/index.htm
**Sociology—Study Sociology Online**
   http://edu.learnsoc.org
**Sociosite**
   http://www.topsite.com/goto/sociosite.net

**JOSEPH STIGLITZ** is a Nobel-prize winning economist, professor at Columbia University, former senior chief economist of the World Bank, and chair of the council of economic advisers under Bill Clinton.

*Article*  Prepared by: Kurt Finsterbusch, *University of Maryland, College Park*

# Corporate Collusion Is Rampant and We All Pay the Steep Price

The big banks even referred to themselves as "cartels," but government will do nothing to stop them.

ROBERT REICH

## Learning Outcomes

*After reading this article, you will be able to:*

- Understand that our antitrust law and agencies have failed to control the banks, medications, health insurance, TV and communications, airlines, and food.

- Many antitrust failures are discussed by Reich. Discuss the specifics in one or two cases.

- Present some antitrust cases which Reich did not mention.

L ast week's settlement between the Justice Department and five giant banks reveals the appalling weakness of modern antitrust.

The banks had engaged in the biggest price-fixing conspiracy in modern history. Their self-described "cartel" used an exclusive electronic chat room and coded language to manipulate the $5.3 trillion-a-day currency exchange market. It was a "brazen display of collusion" that went on for years, said Attorney General Loretta Lynch.

**But there will be no trial, no executive will go to jail, the banks can continue to gamble in the same currency markets, and the fines – although large – are a fraction of the banks' potential gains and will be treated by the banks as costs of doing business.**

**America used to have antitrust laws that permanently stopped corporations from monopolizing markets, and often broke up the biggest culprits.**

**No longer. Now, giant corporations are taking over the economy – and they're busily weakening antitrust enforcement.**

**The result has been higher prices for the many, and higher profits for the few. It's a hidden upward redistribution from the majority of Americans to corporate executives and wealthy shareholders.**

**Wall Street's five largest banks now account for 44 percent of America's banking assets – up from about 25 percent before the crash of 2008 and 10 percent in 1990. That means higher fees and interest rates on loans, as well as a greater risk of another "too-big-to-fail" bailout.**

**But politicians don't dare bust them up because Wall Street pays part of their campaign expenses.**

Similar upward distributions are occurring elsewhere in the economy.

**Americans spend far more on medications per person than do citizens in any other developed country, even though the typical American takes fewer prescription drugs.** A big reason is the power of pharmaceutical companies to keep their patents going way beyond the twenty years they're supposed to run.

**Drug companies pay the makers of generic drugs to delay cheaper versions. Such "pay-for-delay" agreements are illegal in other advanced economies, but antitrust enforcement hasn't laid a finger on them in America. They cost you and me an estimated $3.5 billion a year.**

**Or consider health insurance. Decades ago health insurers wangled from Congress an exemption to the antitrust laws that allowed them to fix prices, allocate markets, and collude over the terms of coverage, on the assumption they'd be regulated by state insurance commissioners.**

**But America's giant insurers outgrew state regulation. Consolidating into a few large national firms and operating**

across many different states, they've gained considerable economic and political power.

Why does the United States have the highest **broadband prices** among advanced nations and the slowest speeds?

Because more than 80 percent of Americans have no choice but to rely on their local cable company for high capacity wired data connections to the Internet – usually **Comcast, AT&T, Verizon, or Time-Warner**. And these corporations are among the most politically potent in America (although, thankfully, not powerful enough to grease the merger of Comcast with Time-Warner).

Have you wondered why your airline ticket prices have remained so high even though the cost of jet fuel has plummeted 40 percent?

Because U.S. airlines have consolidated into a handful of **giant carriers** that divide up routes and collude on fares. In 2005 the U.S. had nine major airlines. Now we have just four. And all are politically well-connected.

Why does **food cost so much**? Because the four largest food companies control 82 percent of beef packing, 85 percent of soybean processing, 63 percent of pork packing, and 53 percent of chicken processing.

Monsanto alone owns the key genetic traits to more than 90 percent of the soybeans planted by farmers in the United States, and 80 percent of the corn.

Big Agribusiness wants to keep it this way.

Google's search engine is so dominant "google" has become a verb. Three years ago the staff of the Federal Trade Commission recommended suing Google for "conduct [that] has resulted – and will result – in real harm to consumers and to innovation."

The commissioners decided against the lawsuit, perhaps because Google is also the biggest lobbyist in Washington.

The list goes on, industry after industry, across the economy.

**Antitrust has been ambushed by the giant companies it was designed to contain.**

**Congress has squeezed the budgets of the antitrust division of the Justice Department and the bureau of competition of the Federal Trade Commission. Politically-powerful** interests have squelched major investigations and lawsuits. Right-wing judges have stopped or shrunk the few cases that get through.

We're now in a new gilded age of wealth and power similar to the first gilded age when the nation's antitrust laws were enacted. But unlike then, today's biggest corporations have enough political clout to neuter antitrust.

**Conservatives rhapsodize about the "free market" and condemn government intrusion. Yet the market is rigged. And unless government unrigs it through bold antitrust action to restore competition, the upward distributions hidden inside the "free market" will become even larger.**

## Critical Thinking

1. Can the government get back control of powerful and unaccountable corporations?

2. Does campaign funding adequately explain the power of the corporations?

3. Rule by the superrich has existed before and then gets swept away. Will that happen again?

## Internet References

**New American Studies Web**
   www.georgetown.edu/crossroads/asw

**Social Science Information Gateway**
   http://sosig.esrc.bris.ac.uk

**Sociology Web Resources**
   http://www.mhhe.com/socscience/sociology/resources/index.htm

**Sociology—Study Sociology Online**
   http://edu.learnsoc.org

**Sociosite**
   http://www.topsite.com/goto/sociosite.net

**ROBERT B. REICH** has served in three national administrations, most recently as secretary of labor under President Bill Clinton. He also served on President Obama's transition advisory board. His latest book is "Aftershock: The Next Economy and America's Future."

*Article*    Prepared by: Kurt Finsterbusch, *University of Maryland, College Park*

# A Fitful Union: What the Founders Wrought?

JAMES T. KLOPPENBERG

## Learning Outcomes

*After reading this article, you will be able to:*

- Provide an explanation for the 2016 election outcome as the outcome of traditional political ideas and forces.

- Throughout our history, many Americans have an animosity toward federal authority and toward federal government.

- Understand the political developments today by understanding the forces enshrined in the constitutions of the states and the federal government.

To the state governments, by contrast, the "founders" gave all but unlimited authority to regulate citizens by invoking "police power," or "coercion," which Gerstle traces to the traditions of civic republicanism and English common law. [ . . . ]incompatible defenses of liberty, on the one hand, and reliance on coercion, on the other hand, "bound together from the earliest days of the republic," have coexisted uneasily ever since. If we understand it instead as setting in motion a dynamic framework of self-government—a "living" set of rules that can be altered not only by the dramatic step of amending the Constitution but also reshaped incrementally, by juries and city councils, by state legislatures and district courts, and by the endless struggles fought between the executive, legislative, and judicial branches of the federal government as well as between the national and state governments—we will see instead that our challenges are those always facing a democracy.

Hatred is as American as apple pie. Progressives who are struggling to understand the catastrophic result of the 2016 presidential election should return to American history. A candidate who proudly trumpeted his disdain for women, African

Americans, Mexicans, Muslims, gays, and the disabled, and who wore his lack of experience in public office as a badge of honor, struck many Americans as unfit as well as unqualified for the presidency. Yet that candidate tapped into some of the most venerable traditions in our nation's past, traditions that have survived the attacks of the past six decades. Now that many self-styled conservatives are openly embracing such traditions, progressives—including the majority of voters who preferred Hillary Clinton—must face facts. Our past is alive. As Ta-Nehisi Coates has put it, "racism is heritage."

In his ambitious study of governance in U.S. history, the distinguished American historian Gary Gerstle shows that Americans have distrusted each other ever since they forged a single nation from states that considered themselves as independent of each other as they were of Great Britain. That suspicion has manifested itself in an apparent contradiction that Gerstle probes in Liberty and Coercion: The Paradox of American Government from the Founding to the Present (Princeton University Press, $36, 472 pp.). Whereas the U.S. Constitution gave limited authority to the central government, state governments reserved much more robust and too-seldom appreciated "police powers," long exercised by English authorities, that justified not only economic regulation but regimes of "surveillance" constraining the freedoms ostensibly guaranteed by the Bill of Rights.

A venerable tradition of animosity toward federal authority has animated foes of a stronger national government. Antifederalists opposed ratifying the Constitution. Flinty frontiersmen ignored demands that they respect Indian treaties. Jacksonians denigrated the nationalism (and antislavery activism) of their foes. Self-proclaimed "redeemers" thwarted post-Civil War attempts to end White supremacy in the former Confederacy. More recently, that animosity blunted or rolled back New Deal and Great Society programs, and it lives on among Tea Party activists who denounce Barack Obama as a socialist dictator.

The conflict between those who tried to empower the central government and those who fought to contain it, Gerstle insists, has defined American political history. The federal government, enfeebled by the Tenth Amendment, failed to consolidate temporary expansions of its authority in potentially "transformative" moments such as the Civil War, the New Deal, and the 1960s. Instead, in an effort to sidestep the states' dogged opposition, the federal government was forced into "improvisational" maneuvers, inadequate to establish the legitimacy of progressive social and economic reforms, as it tried vainly either to use the courts, enlist the states, or cooperate with private partners to reach its goals.

Many observers have tried to explain why contemporary conservatives, pledged to oppose the federal government and all its works, nevertheless insist that state governments outlaw abortion and gay marriage, secure the right to pray in school and carry assault rifles in malls, and impose strict regulations on who can work (under what conditions) and who can vote. Gerstle finds the answer to that apparent contradiction in Americans' peculiar fear of centralized power and their confidence in the authority of the states. This is a deeply pessimistic account of U.S. history. Changes that have led to greater freedom and equality, in Gerstle's view, are ultimately futile improvisations that violate the Constitution. Resistance to those changes is grounded solidly in the police powers reserved for the states.

My two reservations concerning Gerstle's provocative argument should not be taken as dissent from the praise the book has earned. Given that so much of Gerstle's case turns on his conception of the eighteenth-century origins of the "liberal" federal government and the limits placed on it by the "founders," his brief and schematic interpretation of that period offers a misleadingly straightforward account of devilishly complicated developments. When he gets to the nineteenth and especially the twentieth century, this author of two outstanding books, one on industrial labor and another on race and nationalism, and co-editor of two well-known essay collections, is on much more solid ground. For readers who want to know what the scholarly community thinks about the past two centuries of U.S. political history, Liberty and Coercion is a reliable and comprehensive guide.

Gerstle's overall argument, though, depends on a distinction that I consider problematic. He attributes the safeguards against a powerful national government—safeguards built into the Constitution—to the prevailing eighteenth-century "liberal" mistrust of centralized authority and Americans' commitment to securing liberty. To the state governments, by contrast, the "founders" gave all but unlimited authority to regulate citizens

by invoking "police power," or "coercion," which Gerstle traces to the traditions of civic republicanism and English common law. Thus, incompatible defenses of liberty, on the one hand, and reliance on coercion, on the other, "bound together from the earliest days of the republic," have coexisted uneasily ever since.

As historians have been pointing out for three decades, however, the split between "liberal" and "republican" ideas on which Gerstle's interpretation depends is a figment of the scholarly imagination. Those who wrote the state constitutions and the U.S. Constitution were the same people. They were not liberals obsessed with rights at one moment, then republicans focused on civic duties at another. The original state constitutions emerged in a flurry of writing during the period from 1775 to 1780; many delegates to the Constitutional Convention in Philadelphia in 1787, and to the state ratifying conventions that adopted the Constitution, had framed those documents. As John Adams wrote in the Massachusetts Constitution that he drafted in 1780, "government is instituted for the common good, for the protection, safety, prosperity, and happiness of the people and not for the profit, honor, or private interest of any one man, family, or class of men." The plan being adopted by Massachusetts was "Locke, Sidney, and Rousseau and de Mably reduced to practice."

Neither Adams nor Thomas Jefferson nor James Madison distinguished between the "liberal" Locke and the "republican" Rousseau, or between individual liberty and government coercion. Notwithstanding their real disagreements, all the members of the founding generation believed that individual rights must be exercised within the boundaries of laws written by representatives of the people themselves. That shared commitment to popular sovereignty, not a schizoid or incoherent yearning for unbounded freedom and unlimited surveillance, made the state constitutions and the U.S. Constitution emblems of the world's first democratic revolution. The architects of these founding documents, with very few exceptions (Alexander Hamilton, who wanted bankers to govern and the president to serve for life, comes to mind), prized equality and decentralization because they judged concentrated political power a threat to self-government. They also feared concentrated economic power, which is among the reasons that they thought the rich should pay more in taxes than the poor.

These God-fearing men, whether Deists or conventional Protestant Christians, knew they were flawed creatures incapable of establishing, once and for all, the delicate equilibrium between freedom and obligation, which explains the provision for amendments. They aimed to secure for citizens a wide array of liberties bounded by laws that would develop, over time, as a result of deliberations in sites ranging from town meetings and state legislatures to the Congress, and from local jury rooms to the Supreme Court. Gerstle concedes that references to the principle undergirding the states' police power, "salus populi," the people's welfare, "did slip in" to the Preamble of the Constitution and Article 1, Section 8. I believe instead that those references to the obligations shouldered by state and national government alike to "promote the general welfare" were central to all these founding documents and the reason why, despite the Antifederalists' anxieties, the Constitution was ratified by the states.

Although the founders did value rights, they also valued justice. They differed, though, about how both rights and justice—both liberty and coercion—should be secured, and for whom. From the earliest squabbling about whether to form a single nation until today, race and ethnicity have been among the most important issues underlying those disagreements. Whether the question was the survival of indigenous peoples, the immigration of Germans to the colony of Pennsylvania (Benjamin Franklin disparaged them as "Palatine boors"), or the suitability for citizenship of women, Catholics, Jews, Muslims, Asians, Latinos, or, most persistently, African Americans, disputes concerning federal or state authority stemmed from the unwillingness of many White Protestant Americans to accept as their equals people unlike themselves. Beneath the masquerade of battles over local or state control, I believe, lay struggles over White male supremacy. Although Gerstle understands that persistent animosity as well as any American historian, he chooses not to emphasize the persistence of racism or sexism in this book. In the wake of this year's presidential election, the consequences of those traditions loom larger.

The heart of Liberty and Coercion is a series of eight superb chapters dealing with the battles fought to establish and expand the power of the national government against forces defending two different oligarchies, those entrenched in the states and those spawned in the ever-rising tide of capitalism. Gerstle shows the stutter-step establishment of national authority, as the United States spread across the continent, and eventually around the world, by means of land distribution, post offices, local militias, and ultimately the nation's military forces. Usually that expansion occurred through cloaked partnerships with entrepreneurs, ranging from nineteenth-century railroad, banking, and industrial tycoons to those who used generous government funding to create the military-industrial complex in the region now known as the Sunbelt. All these champions of "private enterprise" profited handsomely from federal largesse, even though their shrill attacks on "big government" veiled their feeding at the public trough.

Along the way, Gerstle catalogues various measures adopted by state governments to regulate economic activity, many of which he labels "progressive," and others regulating religious belief, alcohol consumption, and sexual behavior, which he dubs "regressive." Although those categories are less stable

historically than Liberty or Coercion suggests, a generation of legal historians has puzzled over the fact that states undertook much more robust forms of regulation than did the federal government. Gerstle contends that the explanation lies in the Constitution's original shackling of federal authority. Yet debates over the role of government, at every level, have been at the heart of U.S. politics and law from the beginning: Federalists and Jeffersonian Republicans in the 1790s, Whigs and the Jackson Party in the 1830s, and, since 1860, Republicans and Democrats have all battled nonstop over the purpose and the proper scope of government, within the states as well as between the states and the federal government. The outcomes have varied; the struggle continues.

Gerstle argues that the fault line between states and nation has shaped our political history, but that emphasis leads him to understate the extent to which there has been, and continues to be, tension between the tectonic plate of the Southern states and the rest of the nation. Parties enjoying greater strength in the North showed stronger support for the rights of indigenous peoples, internal improvements, antislavery agitation, compulsory education, unionization of labor, social-welfare programs, and, in more recent decades, struggles to secure equal rights for African Americans, women, the disabled, and LGBTQ people. Of course, opposition to all those causes was never limited to one region, as the election reminded us, and the hardy band of Southern progressives cannot be ignored. Yet again and again, the strongest opposition to what Gerstle (and most readers of Commonweal) would consider forward-thinking legislation concerning agriculture, industrial relations, civil liberties, and especially the rights of minorities has come not just from "the states" but from particular states: those of the former Confederacy and its latter-day cultural outposts further west.

Those who view the expansion of the central government as the most effective way to advance an egalitarian agenda have often emphasized the transformative role of war. Although Gerstle agrees that the scope and scale of federal power expanded by necessity during wartime, he terms that expansion a "mirage." Opponents dismantled most of the improvised initiatives once peace returned, except after WWII, when the Cold War justified military spending on an unprecedented scale for an apparently endless time. In 1944, Franklin Roosevelt laid out ambitious plans for a postwar social-welfare state as generous as any of those created in Northern Europe. That agenda came to nothing, though, when southern Democrats made clear that they would never support programs that would have extended benefits to all citizens, Black as well as White. Gerstle shows brilliantly how and why New Deal efforts to assist struggling farmers and industrial workers, efforts that substantially shrank the gap between the richest and poorest Americans, ended up benefiting primarily the most organized and (relatively) affluent sectors of agriculture and labor. A fine chapter on the 1960s shows that enforcing civil rights and anti-poverty legislation required "breaking the power of the states," but he minimizes the extent to which the states that had to be "broken" clustered in the former Confederacy.

That campaign for equality and inclusiveness sparked a "conservative revolt" that has dominated American politics since the 1970s. Confronted with a flurry of federal regulations, the states reasserted their authority to resist the power of the central government with the significant exceptions of military spending and initiatives to police citizens' drug use and sexual behavior. Conservatives began to insist, in the face of the longest period of sustained economic growth in U.S. history and a steady decline in inequality, that government regulations and the steeply progressive income tax put in place in the 1930s had stifled initiative and productivity. They embarked on a campaign to reverse the central decisions of the Warren Court by demanding a return to what they conjured up as the "original meaning" of the Constitution. Under the leadership of President Ronald Reagan, they challenged the power of organized labor, slashed taxes, and campaigned against increases in the minimum wage, ostensibly out of renewed reverence for a "free market" that, as Liberty and Coercion makes abundantly clear, was always thoroughly regulated, albeit frequently in the interest of those who howled about preserving the freedom of contract.

Gerstle illuminates the novelty of recent conservatism by spotlighting President Dwight Eisenhower's March 15, 1954, address on Americans' civic duty to pay their fair share of taxes in order to expand Social Security and unemployment insurance, improve the nation's housing stock, and provide health care for all. The political center of gravity has shifted dramatically, in part due to the Reagan revolution and in part due to Jimmy Carter's and Bill Clinton's embrace of deregulation. President Obama's Affordable Care Act, as Gerstle points out, was modeled on the health-care law enacted in Massachusetts under Governor Mitt Romney. This plan, relying on private insurance exchanges, was conceived as a Republican Party alternative to the single-payer system that Hillary Clinton proposed in 1993. By 2010, all taxes—and all public–private partnerships—were being condemned as threats to Americans' freedom. By 2016, that refrain was being repeated endlessly, particularly by a real-estate developer who boasted about his shrewd and (so far at least) successful evasion of federal income taxes.

Among the fascinating features of Liberty and Coercion is Gerstle's analysis of the rise of political parties and the relation between partisanship and corruption. The founders neglected to address the necessity of funding elections because, as Gerstle acknowledges, they deemed parties inimical to the civic virtue necessary for popular government. If the common good, not the interest of any particular group, was to be every statesman's aim, then parties were dangerous, as Washington warned in his Farewell Address. Yet because of the vast size of the nation and the decentralization of political authority, Gerstle argues, the nation immediately split into factions, and electioneering was thus bound to be an expensive proposition. The founders' naïve unwillingness to provide for public funding spelled disaster. Private money inevitably seeped through even the tiniest cracks in the dams that "elite reformers"—a phrase that appears five times in less than two pages—have tried again and again to erect to stop corruption from flooding the political process. The fault lay, Gerstle insists, with "the deficiencies of the Constitution" rather than "the moral deficiencies of individual men." Perhaps because those "moral deficiencies" are so hard to overlook right now, that judgment seems debatable.

What is to be done? This reviewer was surprised that Gerstle endorses the view, for decades associated with the most conservative legal scholars but now embraced by some on the left as well, that the limits placed on the federal government by the Constitution render most forms of economic regulation unconstitutional. Moreover, decisions rendered by the Warren Court, based on the principle of substantive due process, are said to impinge illegitimately on the states' authority. Efforts to limit the influence of money in politics are dismissed as hopeless. So if we want to bolster the imperiled labor movement, shrink the widening gap between rich and poor, and secure the rights of minorities, Gerstle concludes, we must amend the Constitution. Because the founders really did intend "to limit and fragment federal power," and because they really did fail to give "the federal government a power to act for the good and welfare of the commonwealth," we must undo what they did. I disagree, and I believe that both John Adams and James Madison, the much misunderstood darlings of many conservatives today, would disagree as well.

Although I doubt there are differences that make a difference between Gerstle's vision of social democracy and my own, my second disagreement with the analysis offered in Liberty and Coercion centers on how we should understand the Constitution. Ever since the Progressive era, generations of reformers and scholars, some influenced by philosophical pragmatism and others informed by the best historical research on the founding period, have insisted on the idea of a "living Constitution," a charter that the founders understood would have to change and develop along with the nation itself. Partisans of that view, including constitutional scholars such as Jack Rakove and Akhil Amar, dismiss the idea of originalism as incoherent. The Constitution was a compromise forged by individuals from starkly different regions—slave and free—who cherished different ideals of what the United States should become. The document ratified by the states embodied the compromises they had to make in order to satisfy their fellow delegates. Many of the ideas it contains, particularly those about women and non-Whites but also those about many other aspects of the world we inhabit–including but not limited to ideas about economic regulation, religious, and ethnic pluralism, and the diversity of choices people can legitimately make about how they want to live their lives—no longer conform to the shared understandings of most Americans.

If we enshrine the Constitution in a glass case said to contain its "original meaning," we embalm it. If we understand it instead as setting in motion a dynamic framework of self-government—a "living" set of rules that can be altered not only by the dramatic step of amending the Constitution but also reshaped incrementally, by juries and city councils, by state legislatures and district courts, and by the endless struggles fought between the executive, legislative, and judicial branches of the federal government as well as between the national and state governments—we will see instead that our challenges are those always facing a democracy. We must make persuasive arguments for what we believe, we must elect those who share our convictions, and we must abide by the decisions they make whether we like it or not.

Seldom in U.S. history has our nation faced a choice as stark as that of 2016. Particularly in light of the result, we must resist the idea that nothing short of amending the Constitution is adequate. Our future will be shaped, as our past has been, by our democratic process, imperfect and in need of reform as it always is. We must build with the tools we have. We must resist the temptation to see the perfect as the enemy of the good, as so many of those who voted for Barack Obama but failed to vote at all in 2016 evidently did. Gary Gerstle has given us a masterful overview of the dynamics that have shaped American politics, including the persistent struggle between the states and the federal government. Anyone who shares Gerstle's conviction that our democracy should be moving toward greater equality and inclusion, and who seeks a clearer understanding of what we are up against as we work toward those ideals, should read Liberty and Coercion.

## Critical Thinking

1. Do you agree with Kloppenberg that the history of the United States constantly involves the struggle between freedom and rights on the one hand and law and order and regulations on the other hand?

2. Have regulations gone too far in the United States?

3. Do you agree with Kloppenberg that "hatred is as American as apple pie"?

## Internet References

**Sociology—Study Sociology Online**
http://edu.learnsoc.org/

**Sociology Web Resources**
http://www.mhhe.com/socscience/sociology/resources/index.htm

**Sociosite**
http://www.topsite.com/goto/sociosite.net

**Socioweb**
http://www.topsite.com/goto/socioweb.com

---

**JAMES T. KLOPPENBERG**, Charles Warren Professor of American History at Harvard, is the author of Toward Democracy: The Struggle for Self-Rule in European and American Thought (Oxford) and Reading Obama: Dreams, Hope, and the American Political Tradition (Princeton).

*Article*                 Prepared by: Kurt Finsterbusch, *University of Maryland, College Park*

# Why the 14 Most Common Arguments against Immigration Are All Wrong

CATO INSTITUTE

## Learning Outcomes

*After reading this article, you will be able to:*

- Understand that many arguments against immigration seem logical but are contradicted by facts.

- Correct the big myth that immigrants are a major source of crime when they have lower crime rates than native born Americans.

- Contradict Trump's claim that many criminals and terrorists are among the immigrants.

These are 14 most common arguments against immigration—and they're all wrong…
    Arguments against immigration are common, but rarely unique — and, frankly, they research proves them all wrong. These 14 are the ones you are most likely to hear…

**1. "Immigrants will take American jobs, lower our wages, and especially hurt the poor."** Immigration has over-all increased the wages and income of Americans. Immigrants are typically attracted to growing regions and they increase the supply and demand sides of the economy once they are there, expanding employment opportunities. The smallest estimated immigration surplus, as it is called, is equal to about 0.24% of GDP — and that's just looking at the benefits to native-born Americans, excluding the benefits to immigrants.

**2. "Immigrants abuse the welfare state."** Immigrants are less likely to use means-tested welfare benefits than similar native-born Americans. Most legal immigrants do not have access to means-tested welfare for their first five years here with few exceptions that are mostly determined on the state level and funded with state taxes. Illegal immigrants don't have access at all — except for emergency Medicaid.

**3. "Immigrants increase the budget deficit and government debt."** Immigrants in the United States have about a net-zero impact on government budgets. Between 50% and 75% of illegal immigrants comply with federal tax law, and states that rely on consumption or property taxes tend to garner a surplus from taxes paid by unlawful immigrants while those that rely on income taxes do not. Immigrants also grow the economy considerably, increasing tax revenue.

**4. "Immigrants increase economic inequality."** If an immigrant quadruples his income by coming to the United States, but barely affects the wages of native-born Americans, he increases economic inequality as a result. However, the standard of living is much more important than the earnings distribution and everybody in this situation either wins or is unaffected.

**5. "Today's immigrants don't assimilate like immigrants from previous waves did."** Assimilation is never perfect and always takes time, but it's going very well. Immigrants are assimilating as well as or better than previous immigrant groups, and basic indicators of assimilation (such as speaking English or becoming a naturalized citizen) are stronger now than they were a century ago.

**6. "Immigrants are a major source of crime."** Immigrants are less likely to be incarcerated for violent and property crimes and cities with more immigrants and their descendants are more peaceful. Illegal immigrants are much less likely to be incarcerated than native-born Americans but more likely than legal immigrants.

**7. "Immigrants pose a unique risk today because of terrorism."** The annual chance of being murdered in a terrorist attacked committed by a foreigner from 1975 through the end of 2015 was about 1 in 3.6 million per year. Almost 99% of the people murdered by foreign-born terrorists on U.S. soil were murdered on 9/11 and the attackers entered on tourist visas and one student visa, not immigrant visas. From 2002 through 2016, only one radicalized terrorist entered the United States for every 29 million visa or status approvals.

**8. "It's easy to immigrate to America and we're the most open country in the world."** It is very difficult to immigrate to the United States. Ellis Island closed down a long time ago. There isn't a line for most immigrants in most cases and when there is, it can take decades or centuries. It's true that America allows greater numbers of immigrants than any other country. However, the annual flow of immigrants as a percent of our population is below most other OECD countries.

**9. "Amnesty or a failure to enforce our immigration laws will destroy the Rule of Law in the United States."** For a law to be consistent with the principle of the Rule of Law, it must be applied equally, have roughly ex ante predictable outcomes based on the circumstances, and be consistent with our Anglo-Saxon traditions of personal autonomy and liberty. Our current immigration laws violate all of those principles. The immigration laws are applied differently based on people's country of birth via arbitrary quotas and other regulations, the outcomes are certainly not predictable, and they are hardly consistent with America's traditional immigration policy and our conceptions of liberty.

**10. "National sovereignty."** Even in the most extreme open immigration policy imaginable, total open borders, national sovereignty is not diminished. The main effect of our immigration laws is to prevent willing foreign workers from selling their labor to voluntary American purchasers. Such economic controls do not aid in the maintenance of national sovereignty and relaxing or removing them would not infringe upon the government's national sovereignty any more than a policy of unilateral free trade would.

**11. "Immigrants won't vote for the Republican Party — look at what happened to California."** The evidence is clear that Hispanic and immigrant voters in California in the early to mid-1990s did turn the state blue but that was as a reaction to California's GOP declaring political war on them. Those who claim that immigration-induced change in demographics is solely responsible for the shift in California's politics have to explain the severe drop-off in support for the GOP at exactly the same time that the party was using anti-immigration propositions and arguments to win the 1994 election. They would further have to explain why Texas Hispanics are so much more Republican than those in California are. Nativism has never been the path toward national party success and frequently contributes to their downfall. In other words, whether immigrants vote for Republicans is mostly up to how Republicans treat them.

**12. "Immigrants bring with them their bad cultures, ideas, or other factors that will undermine and destroy our economic and political institutions. The resultant weakening in economic growth means that immigrants will destroy more wealth than they will create over the long run."** Americans are not more supportive of free markets than most other people, we are just lucky that we inherited excellent institutions from our ancestors. The larger a country's immigrant population was in 1990, the more economic freedom increased in the same country by 2011. Immigrant countries of origin did not affect the outcome. It is very hard to upend established political and economic institutions through immigration. Immigrants change to fit into the existing order rather than vice versa, and those who decide to come here mostly admire American institutions or have opinions on policies that are very similar to those of native-born Americans. As a result, adding more immigrants who already broadly share the opinions of most Americans will not affect policy. Additionally, more open immigration makes native voters oppose welfare or expanded government because they believe immigrants will disproportionately consume the benefits (regardless of the fact that poor immigrants actually under-consume welfare compared to poor Americans).

**13. "The brain drain of smart immigrants to the United State impoverished other countries."** The flow of skilled workers from low-productivity countries to high-productivity nations increases the incomes of people in the destination country, enriches the immigrants, and helps (or at least does not hurt) those left behind. Furthermore, remittances that immigrants send home are often large enough to offset any loss in home country income through emigration. In the long run, the potential to immigrate and the higher returns from education increases the incentive for workers in the developing world to acquire skills that they otherwise might not — increasing the quantity of human capital. Instead of being called a brain drain, this phenomenon should be accurately called a skill flow.

**14. "Immigrants will increase crowding, harm the environment, and [insert misanthropic statement here]."** Many anti-immigration organizations today were funded and founded to oppose immigration because it would increase the number of Americans who would then harm the environment. However, people are an economic and environmental blessing, not a curse. Concerns about overcrowding are focused on publicly provided goods or services—like schools, roads, and heavily zoned urban areas. Private businesses do not complain about crowding as they can boost their profits by expanding to meet demand or charging higher prices. If crowding was really an issue then privatizing government functions so they would then have an incentive to rapidly meet demand is a cheap and easy option.

# Critical Thinking

1. Can you defend immigration from those who criticize immigrants?
2. Can there be too much immigration? Can there be too little?
3. What is your opinion of the wall that Trump advocates?

# Internet References

**New American Studies Web**
www.georgetown.edu/crossroads/asw
**Social Science Information Gateway**
http://sosig.esrc.bris.ac.uk
**Sociology—Study Sociology Online**
http://edu.learnsoc.org
**Sociosite**
https://www.sociosite.net/
**Socioweb**
http://topsite.com/goto/socioweb.com

*Article*   Prepared by: Kurt Finsterbusch, *University of Maryland, College Park*

# The Common Good

Manuel Velasquez, et al.

## Learning Outcomes

*After reading this article, you will be able to:*

- Recognize the societal benefit of people working for the common good and discuss the extent that people will sacrifice some personal benefits in the process.

- Understand what is required to produce the common good.

- Discuss the difficulty of reconciling America's emphasis on individualism, freedom, and personal rights with the common good.

Commenting on the many economic and social problems that American society confronts, Newsweek columnist Robert J. Samuelson once wrote: "We face a choice between a society where people accept modest sacrifices for a common good or a more contentious society where group selfishly protect their own benefits." Newsweek is not the only voice calling for a recognition of and commitment to the "common good."

Appeals to the common good have also surfaced in discussions of business' social responsibilities, discussions of environmental pollution, discussions of our lack of investment in education, and discussions of the problems of crime and poverty. Everywhere, it seems, social commentators are claiming that our most fundamental social problems grow out of a widespread pursuit of individual interests.

What exactly is "the common good", and why has it come to have such a critical place in current discussions of problems in our society? The common good is a notion that originated over two thousand years ago in the writings of Plato, Aristotle, and Cicero. More recently, the contemporary ethicist, John Rawls, defined the common good as "certain general conditions that are . . . equally to everyone's advantage". The Catholic religious tradition, which has a long history of struggling to define and promote the common good, defines it as "the sum of those conditions of social life which allow social groups and their individual members relatively thorough and ready access to their own fulfillment." The common good, then, consists primarily of having the social systems, institutions, and environments on which we all depend work in a manner that benefits all people. Examples of particular common goods or parts of the common good include an accessible and affordable public health care system, and effective system of public safety and security, peace among the nations of the world, a just legal and political system, and unpolluted natural environment, and a flourishing economic system. Because such systems, institutions, and environments have such a powerful impact on the well-being of members of a society, it is no surprise that virtually every social problem in one way or another is linked to how well these systems and institutions are functioning.

As these examples suggest, the common good does not just happen. Establishing and maintaining the common good require the cooperative efforts of some, often of many, people. Just as keeping a park free of litter depends on each user picking up after himself, so also maintaining the social conditions from which we all benefit requires the cooperative efforts of citizens. But these efforts pay off, for the common good is a good to which all members of society have access, and from whose enjoyment no one can be easily excluded. All persons, for example, enjoy the benefits of clean air or an unpolluted environment, or any of our society's other common goods. In fact, something counts as a common good only to the extent that it is a good to which all have access.

It might seem that since all citizens benefit from the common good, we would all willingly respond to urgings that we each cooperate to establish and maintain the common good. But numerous observers have identified a number of obstacles that hinder us, as a society, from successfully doing so.

First, according to some philosophers, the very idea of a common good is inconsistent with a pluralistic society like ours. Different people have different ideas about what is worthwhile or what constitutes "the good life for human beings", differences that have increased during the last few decades as the voices of more and more previously silenced groups, such as women and minorities, have been heard. Given these differences, some people urge, it will be impossible for us to agree on what particular kind of social systems, institutions, and environments we will all pitch in to support.

And even if we agreed upon what we all valued, we would certainly disagree about the relative values things have for us. While all may agree, for example, that an affordable health system, a healthy educational system, and a clean environment are all parts of the common good, some will say that more should be invested in health than in education, while others will favor directing resources to the environment over both health and education. Such disagreements are bound to undercut our ability to evoke a sustained and widespread commitment to the common good. In the face of such pluralism, efforts to bring about the common good can only lead to adopting or promoting the views of some, while excluding others, violating the principle of treating people equally. Moreover, such efforts would force everyone to support some specific notion of the common good, violating the freedom of those who do not share in that goal, and inevitably leading to paternalism (imposing one group's preference on others), tyranny, and oppression.

A second problem encountered by proponents of the common good is what is sometimes called the "free-rider problem". The benefits that a common good provides are, as we noted, available to everyone, including those who choose not to do their part to maintain the common good. Individuals can become "free riders" by taking the benefits the common good provides while refusing to do their part to support the common good. An adequate water supply, for example, is a common good from which all people benefit. But to maintain an adequate supply of water during a drought, people must conserve water, which entails sacrifices. Some individuals may be reluctant to do their share, however, since they know that so long as enough other people conserve, they can enjoy the benefits without reducing their own consumption. If enough people become free riders in this way, the common good which depends on their support will be destroyed. Many observers believe that this is exactly what has happened to many of our common goods, such as the environment or education, where the reluctance of all person to support efforts to maintain the health of these systems has led to their virtual collapse.

The third problem encountered by attempts to promote the common good is that of individualism. Our historical traditions place a high value on individual freedom, on personal rights, and on allowing each person to "do her own thing". Our culture views society as comprised of separate independent individuals who are free to pursue their own individual goals and interests without interference from others. In this individualistic culture it is difficult, perhaps impossible, to convince people that they should sacrifice some of their freedom, some of their personal goals, and some of their self-interest, for the sake of the "common good". Our cultural traditions, in fact, reinforce the individual who thinks that she should not have to contribute to the community's common good, but should be left free to pursue her own personal ends.

Finally, appeals to the common good are confronted by the problem of an unequal sharing of burdens. Maintaining a common good often requires that particular individuals or particular groups bear costs that are much greater than those borne by others. Maintaining an unpolluted environment, for example, may require that particular firms that pollute install costly pollution control devices, undercutting profits. Making employment opportunities more equal may require that some groups, such as white males, sacrifice their own employment chances. Making the health system affordable and accessible to all may require that insurers accept lower premiums, that physicians accept lower salaries, or that those with particularly costly diseases or conditions forego the medical treatment on which their live depend. Forcing particular groups or individuals to carry such unequal burdens "for the sake of the common good", is, at least arguably, unjust. Moreover, the prospect of having to carry such heavy and unequal burdens leads such groups and individuals to resist any attempts to secure common goods.

All of these problems pose considerable obstacles to those who call for an ethic of the common good. Still, appeals to the common good ought not to be dismissed. For they urge us to reflect on broad questions concerning the kind of society we want to become and how we are to achieve that society. They also challenge us to view ourselves as members of the same community and, while respecting and valuing the freedom of individuals to pursue their own goals, to recognize and further those goals we share in common.

## Critical Thinking

1. How would you define the common good?
2. What have you done to advance the common good?
3. How should society deal with the fact that different people have different ideas about what the common good is?

# Internet References

**New American Studies Web**
www.georgetown.edu/crossroads/asw

**Social Science Information Gateway**
http://sosig.esrc.bris.ac.uk

**Sociology Web Resources**
http://www.mhhe.com/socscience/sociology/resources/index.htm

**Sociology—Study Sociology Online**
http://edu.learnsoc.org

**Sociosite**
http://www.topsite.com/goto/sociosite.net

# Unit 3

# UNIT

Prepared by: Kurt Finsterbusch, *University of Maryland, College Park*

# Problems of Poverty and Inequality

America is famous as the land of opportunity, and people from around the world have come to its shores in pursuit of the American dream. But how is America living up to this dream today? It is still a place for people to get rich, but it is also a place where people are trapped in poverty. This unit tells a number of stories of Americans dealing with advantages and disadvantages, opportunities and barriers, power, and powerlessness.

The first section of this unit deals with income inequality and the hardships of the poor. It documents that poverty is widespread in America. It explores the impacts of globalization on our economy detailing both the positive and the negative impacts. It examines the culture of poverty thesis and finds that it is a myth. The next section examines racial and ethnic issues. Racism continues to exist and one of the causes of the present strength of racism are the misperceptions embedded is a racist culture. This section also presents a discussion on LGBT rights.

*Article*          Prepared by: Kurt Finsterbusch, *University of Maryland, College Park*

# Serving No One Well: TANF Nearly Twenty Years Later

Kristin S. Seefeldt

## Learning Outcomes

*After reading this article, you will be able to:*

- Report on the immediate changes resulting from TANF.
- Discuss TANF's shortcomings.
- Describe the work requirements for receiving TANF.

*The 1996 welfare reform law transformed the nation's cash welfare system into a time-limited, work-based program. Welfare caseloads dropped by more than half, but in more recent years and in the wake of the Great Recession, relatively little research has focused on TANF program participation, particularly from the vantage point of clients and potential clients. This paper uses qualitative data from interviews with very low-income single mothers conducted in 2013. Analysis of the interview data yielded three different narratives regarding how TANF did not meet their needs: it did not help them find jobs; it did not assist those with personal and family challenges; and it failed to perform as a safety net.*

In 1996 the *nation's* cash welfare program for poor families was transformed. The entitlement program Aid to Families with Dependent Children (**AFDC**) was converted into a work-based, time-limited program, the latter aspect reflected in its name- Temporary Assistance for Needy Families (**TANF**). This transformation was part of a larger effort embodying neoliberal political tendencies that prefer market-based policy solutions for social issues as opposed to government intervention. In the neoliberalist view, the role of the welfare state is to promote behaviors that support the market by turning welfare recipients into workers. Welfare reform also reflected long-held racialized views about recipients who, these stereotypes held, were lazy,

unmarried African American women who needed to be pushed and prodded to enter the labor force

**AFDC** served 4.7 million families in 1995, but by 2010 **TANF** only served 2 million, with caseloads remaining relatively stable despite the severe economic downturn that occurred in 2008. As **TANF** neared its 20th anniversary, a number of scholars and policy makers took on the task of evaluating the program's effectiveness. A central challenge in doing so is *a lack* of shared understanding of what success would look like. For some, caseload declines are a sign that **TANF** has been successful. Additionally, employment rates among single mothers are higher than prior to welfare reform, an indication that welfare reform's supporters point to as evidence that the law's work requirements improved work effort. Finally, poverty rates for single mother families are lower now than before welfare reform. However, those who are more dubious of the law's "success" note that while employment increased, most jobs held by former recipients are very low paying, declines in poverty have not matched the large declines in the cash welfare caseload, and the number of families with extremely low income has grown These statistics, however, do not tell us about the actual experiences of those eligible for, seeking to use, and currently using **TANF** and how these individuals might view the program's success.

A large body of literature emerged in the years following welfare reform's passage which examined the law's implementation, the characteristics of those moving off the welfare rolls and those staying on, and, to a more limited degree, the dealings of clients with the welfare office. In more recent years, as **TANF** caseloads have shrunk to historically low levels, relatively little research has focused on **TANF** program participation, particularly from the vantage point of clients and potential clients. This paper attempts to fill that gap by using qualitative data from interviews with very low-income single mothers in period following the Great Recession. Analysis of the interview data yielded three different narratives regarding how **TANF** did not meet their needs.

Welfare Reform and Studies on Program Use Several important differences between **AFDC** and **TANF** are worth noting. Under **AFDC**, median state benefits were $377 a month for a family of three in **1996** (U.S. House of Representatives, 2012). Some adults were required to engage in employment and training activities in order to receive those benefits, but many recipients were exempt from such requirements. As long as a family remained income eligible and had a minor aged child, it could, in theory, continue to receive benefits. Under **TANF**, states cannot use federal dollars to provide assistance to families for more than 60 months cumulative (or less at state option), and they must meet work participation rates by placing a certain percentage of the caseload in approved work activities, such as unsubsidized employment, community service, and job search, or face financial penalties. As of 2015, 50 percent of adults receiving **TANF** are required to be participating in approved activities for 30 hours a week (20 if the parent has a young child) (Center on Budget and Policy Priorities, 2015). States can lower their participation rate if they reduce their overall **TANF** caseload from 2005 levels. **TANF** recipients who are subject to the work requirement can be sanctioned for failure to participate; depending upon the state, a sanction can result in a family's benefits being reduced or eliminated altogether. In 2010, median state **TANF** benefits stood at $424 a month, an amount that has not kept pace with inflation

Part of the impetus for reforming welfare was the growing political concern in the 1980s and early 1990s that **AFDC** caseloads were increasing at unsustainable rates. In the mid-1980s, about 3.7 million families received **AFDC** benefits. By 1992, the year of a Presidential election, that number had grown to almost 4.8 million. Some policy analysts worried that instead of using **AFDC** as a safety net of last resort, families had become "dependent" upon the program, opting out of the labor market and, since the program now predominantly served single mother families, marriage and instead relying upon a monthly welfare check. Bill Clinton ran on a platform of "ending welfare as we know it" and followed through on that pledge when he signed PRWORA in August 1996 (see Weaver, 2000 for a comprehensive accounting of the debates over welfare reform).

Welfare caseloads plummeted in the wake of the reform's implementation, although that decline had already begun prior to the law's enactment. Between 1995 and 2010 the number of families receiving cash welfare benefits declined by more than 58 percent nationally (Trisi & Pavetti, 2012). A large body of research has attempted to untangle the reasons for this sharp drop. Was it the reforms (in particular the work requirements, sanctions, and time limits), the strong economy in the late 1990s, other policy changes such as the expansion of the Earned Income Tax Credit (**EITC**), which put more money into the pockets of low wage working families, or some other set of factors? Most studies found that while the reform, the economy, and the **EITC** expansion all played roles, the cause of much of the decline has remained unexplained.

Certainly some women who left welfare did so because they became employed (or because they had an incentive to report jobs in which they were already working). Employment rates of single mothers, for example, rose from just over 60 percent in 1994 to a peak of 75 percent in 2000, along the way surpassing employment levels of married mothers. Since the economic downturn of 2001, employment rates dropped and then declined even further in the wake of the Great Recession. In 2010, 67 percent of single mothers were employed, compared to 65 percent of married mothers (U.S. Bureau of Labor Statistics, 2011). However, state-level studies of women leaving welfare in the years shortly after welfare reform found that jobs were unstable, low-paying, and without benefits such as health insurance. Although this varied by state, about one quarter to one third of families who left **TANF** in the 1990s returned at some point in the year following the initial exit. Some states and localities also instituted other practices to keep families off of **TANF**. One such practice is "diversion," or providing a lump sum of cash to a family instead of monthly cash benefits. One theory behind this practice is that some families may only need a one-time infusion of cash to solve a particular problem, such as *a car* that needs repair or a security deposit for a rental unit. Families that accept diversion payments are typically ineligible to apply for **TANF** for some period of time and are not subject to work requirements or time limits The use of lump sum payments can, in theory, keep the welfare caseload low if potential recipients are kept off the rolls, but in practice, states have not given out lump sums to large numbers of families.

Another form of diversion is requiring **TANF** applicants to search for work or comply with other program rules before being approved for benefits. This type of diversion may lead those who are most employable to forgo **TANF** if they find jobs before their application is approved. However, it might also discourage some applicants from following through with the application process. Interviews with **TANF** applicants in Wisconsin who did not complete their applications found that those with learning disabilities had difficulties with upfront job search requirements, while other challenges in their lives, such as housing problems, kept them from meeting other requirements and providing necessary.

While this group might benefit from cash assistance and from other services the welfare office could provide, keeping applicants with learning disabilities and other challenges to employment off the rolls might be a desirable outcome, if a state is concerned about meeting participation requirements. While some women formerly on welfare went to work, another group was without jobs and without cash assistance. Commonly referred to as "the disconnected," because of their disconnection from the labor market and the cash safety net, the number of single mother-headed families experiencing this phenomenon has grown over time. About one in eight low-income single mothers lacked earnings and **TANF** assistance in 1996 and 1997, but this number increased to about one in five in 2008, with almost a quarter having no earnings or **TANF** for four or more months over a year. Single mothers without earnings and **TANF** tend to have more barriers to employment. We found that for all single mothers, losing a job and not receiving **TANF**, rather than loss of **TANF** benefits without a job in place, is the reason most families go without these sources of cash. However, they also found that if a mother leaves **TANF**, she has an almost 20 percent chance of not working, as well. Health and other barriers, as well as living with other working adults, are also significant contributors to having no cash from earnings or **TANF**.

Another subset of this group are those living on less than two dollars per person per day, a level of deprivation that is often used to measure poverty in economically developing countries. As uncovered by Edin and Shaefer (2015), the number of families experiencing this phenomenon, while relatively small, has been growing over time. Families interviewed by Edin and Shaefer said they had never heard of **TANF**, or they believed that the program no longer existed. The authors document extreme hardship among this group, including homelessness, food insecurity, and sexual abuse of children.

In sum, **TANF** has transformed a cash welfare program, **AFDC**, that once served 68 out of every 100 poor families with children, to one that now only serves 27 out of 100 such. Previous studies have offered clues as to the policies and practices that may have driven the sharp downturn in **TANF** program use, while other studies have documented the fallout of welfare reform for the most disadvantaged- those without earnings and **TANF** and the deeply poor. Yet, some families are using the program, or are attempting to use **TANF**, and we know much less about how **TANF** serves these families, particularly during and after the Great Recession, a time of great economic need.

## Sample and Methodology

The analysis presented in this paper comes from qualitative interview data collected as part of a study on disconnected families. The author conducted interviews with women living in Southeast Michigan who were also participating in the Michigan Recession and Recovery Study (MRRS), conducted by

the National Poverty Center at the University of Michigan. The MRRS is representative sample of working aged adults (ages 19-50 in 2009) living in the greater Detroit metropolitan area. To qualify for participation in the study of disconnected families, respondents had to be: (1) low-income (household income below, at, or near the federal poverty line), unmarried women with at least one resident child under the age of 18; (2) not currently working for pay and not currently receiving **TANF** or federal disability benefits for themselves; or (3) if currently employed, have experienced at least six cumulative months of unemployment in the past two years, during which time they did not receive cash benefits from **TANF** or the Supplemental Security Income (**SSI**) program for themselves.

Survey data collected as part of MRRS allowed me to identify respondents who might meet these criteria. These potentially eligible MRRS respondents were notified about the study and then, if interested, they were screened for eligibility. Among the 41 who were identified through survey data as potentially eligible, 35 were screened (the other six could not be located), with 23 meeting the study eligibility criteria, and 22 completing interviews.

Participants in the study ranged in age from 27 to 51 years old, with an average age of 26. The vast majority, 18, identified as African American; one woman was white, and three identified as multi-racial. The education level of these women was quite varied. Seven had not finished high school, six were high school graduates, seven had completed some college, including one with an associate's degree, and two had bachelor's degrees or more. Only four of the 22 were working at the time of the interview. On average, women had 3.5 children, with the number of children ranging from one to seven; some of these children were adults and did not live with the respondents, although some had not yet left home.

The interviews completed with respondents were semi-structured and ranged from 60 to 120 minutes in length, lasting approximately 90 minutes on average. The interviews were audio-recorded to later produce full transcriptions. Transcripts were imported into NVivo software for text analysis. The interview guide covered a number of topics related to employment and financial well-being. For this paper, I focused on women's responses to questions about **TANF** and the welfare office, including questions about their decisions to apply (or not), their experiences with **TANF** employment programs (called Work First in Michigan), and their beliefs about the helpfulness of **TANF**, or any other responses where they talked about the welfare system. What emerged in analyzing these responses was a common thread about the ways in which **TANF** had failed to help them when they lost jobs or otherwise needed financial assistance.

# Findings

Even though the respondents in this sample were part of a study of disconnected women, all but two reported having used **TANF** at some point during their adult lives. Some had last received program benefits as long ago as 2001 or 2003 (interviews were conducted in summer **2013**) and as recently as six months before the interview took place; one woman was currently getting **TANF** at the time of the interview, after being denied benefits for more than six months. All women received other types of public assistance, such as food stamps and public medical insurance, so the entire sample had experience with the welfare office.

One of the most important goals of **TANF** was to move recipients into the labor market and off of the welfare rolls. By some accounts, **TANF** accomplished this goal, although certainly caseloads declined far more than employment rates increased and poverty decreased. Additionally, the mechanisms through which this occurred are not clear. For example, did TANF's work requirements and time limits serve as the impetus women needed to get off of the rolls? Did the program's employment services and other supports, such as childcare, provide the help women needed to get and keep jobs? And what about women who faced other challenges, such as health and mental problems? Did **TANF** meet their needs? According to nearly all of the women, **TANF** did none of these things, or if it did, the services provided were not enough to help women. Further, time limits and other requirements cut women off of assistance, even though they had not yet secured jobs and the unemployment rate remained high. As a safety net, **TANF** failed these women.

## TANF Does Not Help Find Jobs

In order to meet the work requirements in the 1996 law, states must place recipients in "work activities," which could include helping unemployed individuals find employment. For many years, Michigan operated "Work First," a job readiness and job search program that was designed to provide participants with instruction in interviewing techniques and resume preparation as well as assistance locating job openings. Local programs were given some discretion in how they structured Work First, but in general, the focus was on helping **TANF** recipients find jobs (Danziger & Seefeldt, 2000). Michigan replaced Work First with the Jobs, Education, and Training (**JET**) program in 2007. However, none of the respondents in this study used the new name, instead using the former moniker of Work First. As of 2013, **JET** has been replaced by PATH- Partnership, Accountability, Training, and Hope-, which has a greater focus on upfront assessment of client needs. Although welfare reform allows states to design their own employment programs, job search is the activity in which most non-working **TANF** recipients are engaged, indicating that *Michigan's* approach is fairly

typical. Jean, a formerly middle class mother whose economic circumstances deteriorated quickly when she left her husband, said that a job search program was not useful to someone like her, who had extensive labor market experience: "I didn't find it to be important to me, because I know how to look for a job. It was interesting in hearing other people's stories and what they *haven't* done, basically. It really *didn't* help me." The problem, as Jean saw it, was not that she needed to learn how to search for work, but rather that very few employers were hiring.

A few women questioned the value of ever going to TANF's employment program. Gina believed that she could just as easily search for work on her own, but instead she was required to come to the program every day. She was quite blunt in her assessment of the program, saying, "To me, it was a waste of time when I could do this myself, you know what I'm saying? *I shouldn't* have to keep coming here, and checking in, and signing in every day for stuff that I could be doing myself." Rose, a mother of five with a work history that included temp assignments, health care work, and fast food service jobs, reported that at times, she and her fellow participants did nothing at all. She said, "Sometimes the instructors would just not do anything. I mean, we were just sitting there, just having our own conversations. That would be for a week's time." Monica, a soft spoken young mother of four, had received **TANF** on and off since having her first child fourteen years earlier. Her view of Work First was the same: "You just sit in one classroom for eight hours a day." Gina and Monica lived in different parts of Detroit, and Rose was a suburban resident. They went to three different employment programs, yet their experiences were very similar. Some women did find aspects of Work First useful. Taurean, a pregnant single mother of two children, had the following to say about her Work First experience in 2012: "They help you look for a job, to get you prepared, and they help you with babysitting and all that. They help out a lot." However, Taurean never found a job through Work First, eventually landing a position in a factory through a connection made by a family member.

Rose believed that the support services provided by the program were very good, but unlike Taurean, she did not think the help provided with job searching was adequate. She said, "Now, them, they're helpful to a point. Now, they give you the clothes, IDs, cars, insurance ... I know they will pay for all that, no problem. The transportation to get back and forth from work, they do that with no problem. As long as they got enough people [staff], they can do that with no problem. Now, come and get the jobs, now, that's what I have a problem with, because they rarely help you with your resume, your cover letter, and your thank you letter. You got to do that yourself." Monica, when asked for her overall assessment of the employment program, said, in a deadpan manner, "I never found a job through them." Both Rose and Gina reported having been sent on job interviews through Work First, and both said that these interviews never resulted in anything. Gina said, "I was going to jobs where nobody is even getting hired, and stuff like that." Rose thought that the program misled participants about their job prospects, saying, "They tell you, 'Oh, I got a job and it's guaranteed you're gonna get hired.' You go in for the interview, and this and that, and that and this, and then they never call you back. See, that's what pisses me off. *Don't* say you're guaranteeing to get hired and then when we talk to [the employer], it's a whole other story." Rose reported that she and her fellow participants were sent on job interviews for which they were not qualified; the staff just sent everyone. "If you had the skill-if you did not have the skills, they sent you there. Then a lot of people felt like, 'Why should we go? We *ain't* got the skills.' Then [the staff] say [the employer is] not asking for skills. When you get there, it's a whole other story." Even though all of the participants were sent on the interview, no one was hired.

Michigan's economy was very slow to recover from the Great Recession, yet work requirements remained in place. The **TANF** employment program, as reported by the women in this study, did little to help them find jobs. In the face of high unemployment (Southeast Michigan's unemployment rate was around 10 percent in 2013), the prospect of welfare recipients landing a job may have been quite low, regardless of what Work First did. However, the assistance provided to women was reportedly minimal and did not match participants' skills to open jobs, such that women might have been better off looking for work on their own.

## TANF Does Not Help Those with Significant Personal Challenges

For those with significant challenges to employment, such as health limitations, ill children, and lack of reliable transportation, **TANF**, at least as it was operated in Michigan, provided no help. The individual circumstances of clients were seemingly not considered by welfare staff, and if a woman could not comply with the program's rules, she was simply terminated from the rolls and left to find other help on her own.

Ginger was one of the poorest women in this study. She had not worked since 2007 or 2008 (she could not remember the exact date), quitting her job cleaning hotel rooms after falling down a flight of stairs and breaking several bones. After the breaks healed, she was left with back and foot pain. She also reported having carpal tunnel syndrome. She had applied for disability benefits through the federal Supplemental Security Income (**SSI**) program, and had been denied, but was appealing the decision. While she was waiting for her case to work its way through the appeal process, she was receiving **TANF**. At first, her pending disability application exempted her from attending Work First. Then the state changed its policy with

respect to **SSI** applicants, and Ginger was told she needed to start going. Carless, Ginger would have needed to walk to a bus stop in order to get to the program site. Her physical limitations left her unable to do that. Rather than assist with transportation, the welfare office stopped Ginger's **TANF** benefits. Desperate for her **SSI** case to be resolved, Ginger hired a lawyer who, if Ginger's case was successful, would likely take some of the past due benefits potentially owed to her. In the meantime, Ginger lived off of a small food stamp benefit. Because she had no income, she did not have to pay rent for her public housing apartment, but she had to call upon friends to buy her items such as dish soap and toilet paper, which food stamps did not cover. And occasionally, Ginger reported, a male "friend" might ask for a sexual favor in return.

Michelle asked to be excused from Work First when her son was diagnosed with lead poisoning. His treatment required hospitalization and then numerous doctor appointments. She was told she needed to attend, and her requests to leave early were denied. She said, "They [the staff] *don't* want you to leave, and they say, 'Okay, if you go, you're out the door, and then you *can't* come back in.'" The program provided no flexibility at a time when Michelle was dealing with a challenging and serious issue. Michelle's benefits were stopped, and the only cash she had came from doing hair and from the occasional money provided by her *son's* father.

Lisa's challenge was not health-related and was one with which **TANF** and its employment program could presumably help. Lisa simply lacked the ability to get to the Work First site after she moved. She had no car and explained that in order to reach the bus that would take her from her suburban residence to Work First, she would need to walk a substantial distance. She said, "I was telling [Work First] I *didn't* have transportation. I'm not able to get back and forth like I was before, so it was hard for me. It *wasn't* really much I could do." When I asked her what Work First expected her to do, given her lack of transport, she replied, "They just [said], 'Do what you have to or do what you can,' but if *I can't* do nothing, then it is what it is basically." In the end, Lisa was cut off from **TANF** for failure to comply with the work requirements.

Providing Lisa with *a car* or some other way to get places would cost money. **TANF** funds can be used to help pay for such services (and in fact some of the women living in Detroit reported Work First did pay), however, the funding structure of **TANF** provides incentives not to do so. States receive money via a block grant, a flat amount that is not adjusted for increases in caseloads or changes in the composition of the caseload (e.g., more clients who have barriers to employment), nor for inflation. Further, the block grant is flexible in terms of what services it can pay for, and in the 1990s, many states shifted those funds away from **TANF** to other purposes, such as child care, child welfare, and other programs that serve low-income families. As revenues started to shrink, states chose to cut back on **TANF** rather than move block grant money back.

The work participation rates that states must meet may also discourage states from providing services to people like Ginger and Arlene, who faced many health challenges. As Trisi and Pavetti (2012) note, "States are more likely to meet the rate if they assist families that already have some education, skills, and/or work experience and have the best chance of either securing employment or participating in a narrowly defined set of work activities" (para. 9). That means that states may want to remove more disadvantaged recipients out of the calculation of the participation rate all together. One way to do that is by terminating their benefits.

## TANF Does Not Function as a Safety Net

**TANF** is just one of a number of programs that constitute the U.S. safety net. These programs are meant to safeguard vulnerable families from hardships that may arise from having low income or from events such as job loss. Women's narratives, however, indicate that **TANF** did not protect families from hardship, including homelessness, and it failed them at times when they needed it most- when they became unemployed and had no source of cash income.

Workers who lose their jobs through layoffs or other circumstances not of their own making may be eligible to receive Unemployment Insurance (**UI**), a program that replaces a portion of workers' wages. But not all workers are eligible for **UI** benefits; those who are fired for cause or who leave of their own volition are often ineligible, and workers must have a minimum amount of earnings and months worked to qualify. Additionally, some workers, particularly those working in low wage jobs, may not believe themselves to be eligible and may thus avoid applying. For these workers, **TANF** might serve as a replacement for **UI** during periods of job loss. Half (11) of the 22 women applied for **TANF** when they lost jobs or when their **UI** benefits ran out following a job loss, but **TANF** was not a good replacement or substitute for Unemployment Insurance. Claudette was a public employee for many years when she was downsized out of a job. She collected **UI**, but when those benefits ran out, she turned to **TANF**. At first, she said, "They denied me. And then I said, 'I never had assistance before.' You know, I mean, you all give me like $14.00 back when my daughters were younger, but I never got any money." Once on **TANF**, Claudette was subject to the state's time limit. She said, "We were on a time limit . . . She [the caseworker] told me when I got on, it would be less than 18 months or so, [I] would be cut back off. That's just what they do now." Although Claudette had been working for many years, she had received **TANF** in

the 1990s, perhaps for longer than she remembered. When her 18 months were up, Claudette's case was closed and she had to rely upon her retired mother for help paying the bills. She still had no job nine months after losing **TANF**.

. . .

None of the women who reached the **TANF** time limit had been able to find a job in the one to two years since losing **TANF**. Gina lived off of her income tax refund for as long as she could, and then she resorted to selling her plasma, a common strategy for making ends meet among the very poor. Shonda could not understand the rationale of taking away benefits from someone who did not have a job. She said, "I was upset because they took the cash away and I'm not working. To me, it seemed like *I shouldn't* be in that situation." Claudette, who was college educated, had been searching for work ever since she was laid off in 2011. She said, "I apply for jobs, but it's like no one is really hiring." She was contemplating leaving the state in order to find work.

When individuals receive help from people in their networks, such as friends and family, they are said to be drawing up their "private" safety nets. The private safety net may provide financial support in the form of cash or paying bills, and it may offer in-kind help such as providing child care for free or no cost. Private safety nets, though, may not be up to the task of adequately providing for poor families. First, the networks in which poor families are embedded are likely to contain people whose financial circumstances are similarly difficult. Kiana had been relying upon her children's father for financial support after running out of Unemployment Insurance in 2009. He paid the rent and all of her bills, while Kiana bought food with her food stamps. But her former partner had his own history of long-term unemployment, and the continued support was no guarantee, particularly given the still-recovering economy in Southeast Michigan. . . . According to study respondents, **TANF** served no one well. It did not help unemployed women secure jobs, and according to some, offered little help at *all*. It offered no assistance or flexibility to women with serious health problems, instead cutting them off of the program. And time limits were enforced with no regard to economic or individual circumstances. Because of these failures, families faced hardships such as losing housing and doubling up, or sharing living space with other families. Bills went unpaid or were paid by family members, potentially putting those who were helping at financial risk, and making women rely upon a private safety net that was unpredictable and fragile. . . .

The needs of women with serious health problems were not met through **TANF**, and perhaps it is not the role of the program to address chronic conditions like those Ginger and Arlene had. Rebecca Blank (2007) recommends the creation of a separate stream of programming for those who may not be able to work, either temporarily or permanently. These recipients would be waived from the work requirement and would be able to receive assistance until either their health or other issue resolved, or until they transitioned onto the disability rolls. Individuals who desire employment might be referred to supported work programs, where they could receive workplace accommodations and other needed assistance in order to perform their jobs. If **TANF** is able to provide employment opportunities when recipients are unable to find jobs or unable to take regular jobs, then the need for time limits, at least from the perspective of providing an incentive to work, is gone. A safety net needs to include cash assistance during times of financial need to a segment of the labor force that is much more likely to work in unstable and low paying jobs. To limit that assistance just because the recipient has accrued an arbitrary number of months on the program only hurts already vulnerable families that much more. At the very least, time limits should be suspended when unemployment is high, as it was during the Great Recession. Further, the benefit levels of **TANF** remain paltry and should be raised to more accurately account for increases in the cost of living. The Unemployment Insurance programs replaces, on average, half of a worker's previous wages. The median monthly **TANF** benefit represents only one third of what a full-time worker earning the federal minimum wage would receive.

Finally, **TANF** is in need of more accountability. Recipients are held to participation standards, and while states must meet work requirements, what they do to meet those goals is not subject to much oversight. For example, are employment programs providing meaningful activities for their participants, or, do they just have participants, "sit in one classroom for eight hours a day," as Monica noted? Before someone is removed from the rolls, whether through time limits or other reasons, are procedures in place to ensure that the termination is warranted or that the family will not face undue hardships as a result? Ultimately, an examination of how states are spending their block grant money is in order. States should not be allowed to fill revenue shortfalls with funds that are meant for some of our most vulnerable families.

Maintaining TANF's status quo has hurt many poor families. Increasing numbers of families are living on almost no income at all. More single mothers have become "disconnected" from work and from cash benefits. For the women in this study, job loss and the loss of benefits placed them in precarious situations, increasing their risk of homelessness and other hardships, or causing them to rely more heavily on their precarious private safety nets. It offered no assistance to women with serious health problems, but rather left them to wait for disability benefits that were very slow in coming. **TANF**, in its current state, serves no one well.

Acknowledgements: Data collection was funded by the U.S. Department of Health and Human Services, Administration for Children and Families. Views presented here are not those of **USDHHS-ACF**.

Kristin Seefeldt's primary research interests lie in exploring how low-income individuals understand their situations, particularly around issues related to work and economic well being.

## Critical Thinking

1. Do you agree that TANF serves no one well? Explain your answer.

2. Do you think that the work requirements are good as they are or should they be revised?

3. Should the program be altered when unemployment is high?

## Internet References

**New American Studies Web**
   www.georgetown.edu/crossroads/asw

**Social Science Information Gateway**
   http://sosig.esrc.bris.ac.uk

**Sociology Web Resources**
   http://www.mhhe.com/socscience/sociology/resources/index.htm

**Sociology—Study Sociology Online**
   http://edu.learnsoc.org

**Sociosite**
   http://www.topsite.com/goto/sociosite.net

**KRISTIN SEEFELDT**'s primary research interests lie in exploring how low-income individuals understand their situations, particularly around issues related to work and economic well-being.

*Article*                    Prepared by: Kurt Finsterbusch, *University of Maryland, College Park*

# How Should Governments Address Inequality?

## *Putting Piketty Into Practice*

Melissa S. Kearney

## Learning Outcomes

*After reading this article, you will be able to:*

- Understand the powerful theory of Piketty about income distribution.

- Understand the criticisms of Piketty's theory.

- Understand the difficulty of reversing the process that Piketty identifies.

In 2014, an unusual book topped bestseller lists around the world: *Capital in the Twenty-first Century*, an 816-page scholarly tome by the French economist Thomas Piketty that examined the massive increase in the proportion of income and wealth accruing to the world's richest people. Drawing on an unprecedented amount of historical economic data from 20 countries, Piketty showed that wealth concentration had returned to a peak not seen since the early twentieth century. Today in the United States, the top one percent of households earn around 20 percent of the nation's income, a dramatic change from the middle of the twentieth century, when income was spread more evenly and the top one percent's share hovered at around ten percent. Piketty predicted that without corrective action, the trend toward ever more concentrated income and wealth would continue, and so he called for a global tax on wealth.

Like much of the popular commentary about inequality, Piketty's book rested on an implicit moral claim-that wealth concentration beyond a certain degree violates the inherent sense of fairness on which a just society depends. But antipathy toward inequality alone cannot drive a policy agenda that will create a more egalitarian society. Critics of inequality need a compelling, evidence-based explanation for how and why the concentration of income and wealth at the top is problematic. Is this inequality the result of a purposely rigged game, or is it caused by unintentional distortions in a basically fair system? Whatever its causes, does inequality impede overall economic growth? Does it undermine widespread opportunity and upward mobility? Does it pose a threat to global capitalism and liberal democracy?

In *After Piketty*, three left-of-center economists-Heather Boushey, J. Bradford DeLong, and Marshall Steinbaumhave curated an impressive set of essays responding to Piketty's work and taking a few steps toward answering those questions. Among them are deep dives into the assumptions underlying Piketty's predictions, historical accounts of the role of slavery and gender in capitalist systems, and considerations of the relationship between concentrated wealth and political power. The essays put Piketty's arguments into a broad historical and intellectual context and highlight some noteworthy omissions that call into question his book's most dire predictions. At the end of the volume, Piketty himself weighs in. The result is an intellectual excursion of a kind rarely offered by modern economics.

The contributors tend to look backward to history or inward to economic models, which is a natural way to respond to a book that is fundamentally historical and theoretical. But to more fully answer the questions Piketty's book raised and to start crafting policies to tackle growing inequality, economists and policymakers need to know much more than they currently do about the causes and consequences of today's concentration of wealth at the top. To reduce extreme inequality's threat to economic security and upward mobility, the United States needs policies that enhance the skills and opportunities of the disadvantaged. Washington must pursue tax reform and changes to corporate-governance rules that will create more shared prosperity. But policymakers also need to avoid steps that would impede innovation and productivity.

## The Top of the Heap

In the past four decades, studies of rising inequality in the United States have typically focused on the bottom 90 percent of earners. Economists have produced rigorous evidence demonstrating how trends in technology, trade, unionization, and minimum wages have shaped the fortunes of those Americans. Global labor-market forces have pushed up the demand for highly skilled workers and have led to steadily increasing wages for those with a college education. The same forces have led to declining or stagnant wages for those with lower levels of education. And a decline in unionization rates and the fall in the real value of the minimum wage have exacerbated the downward pressures on middle- and low-wage workers.

Less well understood are the causes of the tremendous surge in income among extremely high earners, meaning the upper 1.0, 0.1, and 0.01 percent. From a policymaking point of view, the most important question is how much of the ultrarich's income reflects activity, such as technological innovation, that benefits the broader economy. The more of it that does, the greater the potential economic costs of raising taxes on the highest-income individuals. If, in contrast, the income of the biggest earners is produced by pursuits that are less broadly beneficial, such as high-frequency stock market trading, then higher taxes at the top would pose fewer economic costs. Either way, there are likely compelling reasons to raise the top income tax rates-as a way of funding public services and investing in infrastructure, for example. But policymakers would be able to make better decisions about "soaking the rich" if they had a clearer sense of the tradeoffs involved.

One of the most interesting facts uncovered by Piketty and others is that compared with the richest people and families in the early 1900s, when large fortunes often came from inherited assets, today's superrich are acquiring a larger share of their income in the form of earnings. About 60 percent of the income of the top one percent in the United States today is labor income. A number of essays in *After Piketty* mention the rise of "supersalaries" or "supermanagers": top executives of large corporations, primarily in the financial industry, who enjoy very generous compensation packages. Economists disagree, however, about whether the income earned by such executives reflects the efficient working of a market for talent, in which case their pay reflects their value, or whether the massive compensation packages result from a bargaining process that is shaped by regulations, institutions, and social norms.

In their contribution to the book, the economists Laura Tyson and Michael Spence highlight the role of technological developments in creating substantial economic rewards for those who possess specific skills and in reducing the employment security of less skilled workers. But Tyson and Spence also note that markets are imperfect and that compensation packages are not determined solely by market value. They point to a growing body of research indicating that income generated by patents and intellectual property protections and by the market power of brand names flows primarily to upper-level management and the owners of capital.

In contrast, in Piketty's view, the primary factors driving the rise in executive pay at the top are not technology or imperfect markets but eroded social norms, questionable corporate-governance practices, and declining union power. Tyson and Spence favor more research to weigh the relative impact of market forces and institutional factors but argue that either explanation provides a strong rationale for increasing the marginal income tax rate for top earners in an effort to combat income inequality.

## One for You, Two for Me

Another essential set of questions about inequality centers on whether wealth concentration negatively affects economic growth, shared prosperity, and democratic institutions. In his contribution to *After Piketty*, Mark Zandi, the chief economist at Moody's Analytics, outlines a number of ways in which it might. One such potential negative effect is reduced aggregate consumer spending. Since lower-income households have a higher propensity to spend out of their earnings than do higher-income ones, the more wealth held by high-income households, the less overall spending the economy might see. Another potential problem is that wealthy Americans tend to vote for (and lobby for) lower taxes; increased wealth concentration, then, could lead to harmful reductions in government spending on public goods such as education and infrastructure. Nevertheless, Zandi cautions that the link between income inequality and aggregate U.S. economic growth is relatively weak. "There is evidence that extreme inequality, as prevails in some parts of the world, weakens economies," he writes, "but inequality in the United States doesn't appear to be significant enough for it to make a substantial difference to the economy's prospects."

Even if the income of top earners reflects genuinely worthwhile contributions to society and does not impede economic growth, today's extreme inequality does threaten social cohesion. I used to contend that economists and policymakers need not worry about inequality and should instead focus on reducing poverty and expanding opportunity. But after years of researching the topic, I've come to believe that policymakers cannot achieve those goals without directly addressing inequality.

In the winner-take-all economy of the contemporary United States, the gap between the top and the bottom has grown so large that it undermines any reasonable notion of equal opportunity. As inequality has increased, the country has witnessed a fraying of communities and institutions and deepening divisions along socioeconomic lines. Children from high-income homes are pulling further and further ahead of their less advantaged peers in terms of education, which means it is far less likely that children born into middle- or low-income homes will experience upward economic mobility. Americans celebrate "rags to riches" stories, but the data indicate that the United States has less social mobility than most European countries. Social mobility in the United States is not yet on the decline, but if current trends continue, it will be soon.

Inequality also harms American society **by** encouraging negative perceptions of the economy and one's prospects for upward mobility. If Americans view the system as rigged against them and see economic success as out of reach, they might give up on the celebrated American ideals of hard work and meritocracy. That may already be happening. Research **I** have conducted with the economist Phillip Levine shows that young men are more likely to drop out of high school if they live in places with higher levels of income inequality, all else being equal. This is consistent with evidence produced **by** psychologists showing that beliefs about inequality negatively affect people's expectations of social mobility.

The alarmingly low rates of labor-force participation among young Americans and those of prime working age might also be driven, at least in part, by a sense of malaise shaped by today's high levels of income inequality. Labor-force participation among American men aged 25 to 54 has fallen steadily since the mid-1960s, a trend that has been sharper in the United States than in other advanced economies. In 1964, 98 percent of such prime-age men with a college degree or more participated in the work force, as did 97 percent of those with a high school degree or less. By 2015, the rate for college-educated workers had fallen only slightly, to 94 percent, but the rate among less educated men had plummeted to just 83 percent. This drop reflects market forces and technological change, to be sure, but it also suggests shifting social norms and attitudes.

## High and Not So Mighty

A growing body of evidence now indicates that inequality in the United States threatens to create intergenerational poverty traps, greatly reduce social mobility, and marginalize entire swaths of the population. Such effects are sure to have political ramifications. Piketty proposed that greater wealth inequality will increase the demand for egalitarian policy responses. But it also means that the wealthy, with their deeper-than-ever pockets, will be even better able to block such changes. Beyond that observation, Piketty doesn't have much to say about the politics of inequality in the United States or elsewhere. As the social policy expert Elisabeth Jacobs points out in her contribution to *After Piketty,* politics is both "everywhere and nowhere" in Piketty's *Capital in the Twentyfirst Century:* the problems Piketty identifies are inherently political, but he pays little attention to the crucial role that politics would play in any attempt to address them.

Unfortunately, the same criticism applies to *After Piketty.* Many of the volume's contributors assume that no matter what policy remedies for extreme inequality emerge, wealthy elites will marshal their considerable influence to maintain their position and privileges. But they do not explore those potential policies at great length, nor do they consider the precise mechanisms that would shape pushback from the elites.

*After Piketty* would also have benefited from more discussion about whether recent political events challenge the notion that elites can overcome a wave of support for more redistribution of wealth. In 2016, the Brexit vote and the American presidential election revealed the strength of populist and nationalist sentiments among voters who gleefully rejected the elite classes in both the United Kingdom and the United States. Even in the wake of such surprising outcomes, the political economy models described in *After Piketty* tend to associate rising wealth concentration with growing political power of the elite-not the rise of populism. The watershed political events of 2016 call those models into question; in both the United Kingdom and the United States, elites saw their preferred choices lose out.

## E Pluribus Unum?

When it comes to the problem of income and wealth inequality in the United States, there are no silver bullets. But policymakers have many levers available to them. The best evidence suggests that the United States could have a more progressive federal income tax code without incurring substantial economic costs. Tax reform should focus on expanding the tax base by closing loopholes and eliminating regressive features such as the mortgage-interest tax deduction, which benefits only high-income homeowners, and the carried-interest loophole, which benefits only those involved in private-equity finance.

The federal government should take the additional revenue such steps would generate and invest it in programs that would increase the country's economic potential. That would include improvements to public infrastructure, expanded access to high-quality childcare and preschool programs, and more spending on programs that assist economically disadvantaged youth. Government commitments to public universities and community colleges must be strengthened. At the same time, institutions of higher education must focus on helping their students build the skills they will need to succeed in a competitive, rapidly changing labor market. These types of investments are crucial if the United States is to remain a land of opportunity.

# Critical Thinking

1. What are some of the ways to deal with the problem of income and wealth inequality?

2. What are some of the negative consequences of increasing inequality?

3. To what extent is the fracturing of America caused by increasing inequality?

# Internet References

**New American Studies Web**
www.georgetown.edu/crossroads/asw

**Social Science Information Gateway**
http://sosig.esrc.bris.ac.uk

**Sociology Web Resources**
http://www.mhhe.com/socscience/sociology/resources/index.htm

**Sociology—Study Sociology Online**
http://edu.learnsoc.org

**Sociosite**
http://www.topsite.com/goto/sociosite.net

**MELISSA S. KEARNEY** is Professor of Economics at the University of Maryland, a Research Associate at the National Bureau of Economic Research, and a Nonresident Senior Fellow at the Brookings Institution.

*Article*         Prepared by: Kurt Finsterbusch, *University of Maryland, College Park*

# United States Welfare Programs: Myths versus Facts

There are 6 major welfare programs

KIMBERLY AMADEO

## Learning Outcomes

*After reading this article, you will be able to:*

- Assess the accomplishments of the U.S. welfare program.

- Briefly describe the six U.S. welfare programs.

- Be able to explain the differences between the welfare and entitlement programs.

Welfare programs are government subsidies to the poor. Recipients must prove their income falls below a target, which is some percentage of the federal poverty level. In 2018, that's $25,100 for a family of four.

## Welfare Programs in the United States

There are six major U.S. welfare programs. They are Temporary Assistance for Needy Families, Medicaid, Food Stamps, Supplemental Security Income, Earned Income Tax Credit, and Housing Assistance. The federal government provides the funding; the states administer them and provide additional funds.

Welfare programs are not entitlement programs; those base eligibility upon prior contributions from payroll taxes. The four major U.S. entitlement programs in the United States are Social Security, Medicare, unemployment insurance, and worker's compensation.

On April 10, 2018, President Trump signed an executive order directing federal agencies to review work requirements for many welfare programs. The programs include TANF, Medicaid, food stamps, and housing assistance. Trump wants agencies to standardize work requirements between programs and states.

For example, food stamp recipients must find a job within three months or lose their benefits. They must work at least 80 hours a month or participate in job training. But several states, such as Alaska, California, and Nevada, have opted out of the work requirement. They say unemployment rates are too high. The executive order encourages agencies to make sure all states follow the same rules.

## The Six Major U.S. Welfare Programs Myths Versus Facts

**TANF** is the Temporary Assistance for Needy Families program. Most people refer to this program as welfare. On average, TANF provided income to 2.5 million recipients in 2017. Of these, 1.9 million were children.

In 2015, TANF assisted only 23 percent of the families living in poverty. On average, a three-person family received $429 a month. Despite this help, they still live below the poverty line of $1,702 a month.

Welfare received a bad reputation due to President Reagan's 1976 presidential campaign. He portrayed the welfare queen who cheated the system to get enough benefits to drive a Cadillac. He also warned of how welfare created a cycle of poverty. As a result, 61 percent of Americans believe the government should provide jobs instead of welfare payments.

Fraud like Reagan described has been cut since 1996. That's when President Clinton created TANF out of the ashes of Aid to Families with Dependent Children. The number of families "on the dole" dropped from 10 million before welfare reform to 1.9 million in 2017.

The new requirements were the reason for this decrease. Families who receive TANF must get a job within two years. They might not get more money if they have another child. They can own no more than $2,000 in total assets. They can only receive TANF for five years or less in some states.

**Medicaid** paid for health care for 64.9 million low-income adults in 2014. The largest share, which was 50 percent, went to 29.5 million children. Next, it covered 19.2 million adults, mostly parents of these children. It pays for 40 percent of all U.S. births.

Medicaid also paid health expenses for 9.8 million blind and disabled people. The smallest category was 5.4 million low-income seniors. It paid for any health costs that Medicare didn't cover.

The Affordable Care Act increased Medicaid coverage by 28 percent. It raised the income level and allowed single adults to qualify.

**Child's Health Insurance Program**. In addition to Medicaid, 6 million children received additional benefits from CHIP. It covers hospital care, medical supplies, and tests. It also provides preventive care, such as eye exams, dental care, and regular check-ups.

**Food Stamps** is the Supplemental Nutrition Assistance Program. It gives food vouchers to 47.6 million people or 23 million households. They receive $133 a month on average. The total federal cost is $79.9 billion, of which $3.8 billion is administration.

There's an additional food stamp program for nursing mothers and young children. The Special Supplemental Food Program for Women, Infants, and Children provides food or vouchers, education, and referrals to help feed pregnant women and children up to age six. In 2017, 7.7 million people received WIC each month. Of those, more than 75 percent were children or infants. ("WIC FAQ" U.S. Department of Agriculture for 2013)

The Child Nutrition Program provides free or reduced-cost lunches to 30 million children. It costs the federal government $12 billion.

**Supplemental Security Program** provides cash to help the aged, blind, and disabled to buy food, clothing, and shelter. On average, roughly 8.4 million people receive $536 per month. Of those, 7.3 million are blind or disabled.

**Earned Income Tax Credit** is a tax credit for families with at least one child. They must earn less than $51,567 a year to qualify. In 2012, over 27 million received credits totaling $63 billion. That's a little more than $2,335 per taxpayer. EITC lifted 6.5 million people out of poverty, half of whom were children. It costs just 1 percent of the amount paid out to administer it. Unfortunately, almost one-fourth of the payments are in error. An unknown amount is fraudulent.

**Housing Assistance** is provided by 1.2 million units of public housing. The Housing Choice Voucher Program gives certificates to rent approved units. The subsidy allows them to pay no more than 30 percent of their income. Local agencies administer it to 2.2 million renters. This is the old Section 8 program. The Public Housing Agency allows some families to use the voucher to purchase a modest home.

The Low-Income Home Energy Assistance Program provides energy assistance and weatherization programs. It provides $3.4 billion in block grants to the states.

# Critical Thinking

1. How would you evaluate the appropriateness of the work requirement for welfare programs?
2. How would you change the current welfare program?
3. What are some of the myths about the U.S. welfare system?

# Internet References

**New American Studies Web**
www.georgetown.edu/crossroads/asw

**Social Science Information Gateway**
http://sosig.esrc.bris.ac.uk

**Sociology Web Resources**
http://www.mhhe.com/socscience/sociology/resources/index.htm

**Sociology—Study Sociology Online**
http://edu.learnsoc.org

**Sociosite**
http://www.topsite.com/goto/sociosite.net

*Article*    Prepared by: Kurt Finsterbusch, *University of Maryland, College Park*

# Black Pathology and the Closing of the Progressive Mind

Ta-Nehisi Coates

## Learning Outcomes

*After reading this article, you will be able to:*

- Understand the roles of both the culture of white supremacy and structural conditions in explaining the situation of blacks in the United States.

- Be able to evaluate the strength and weakness of the cultural explanation of the situation of blacks.

- Discuss the strengths of black culture.

Among opinion writers, Jonathan Chait is outranked in my esteem only by Hendrik Hertzberg. This lovely takedown of Robert Johnson is a classic of the genre, one I studied incessantly when I was sharpening my own sword. The sharpening never ends. With that in mind, it is a pleasure to engage Chait in the discussion over President Obama, racism, culture, and personal responsibility. It's good to debate a writer of such clarity—even when that clarity has failed him.

On y va.

Chait argues that I've conflated Paul Ryan's view of black poverty with Barack Obama's. He is correct. I should have spent more time disentangling these two notions, and illuminating their common roots—the notion that black culture is part of the problem. I have tried to do this disentangling in the past. I am sorry I did not do it in this instance and will attempt to do so now.

Need of moral instruction is an old and dubious tradition in America. There is a conservative and a liberal rendition of this tradition. The conservative version eliminates white supremacy as a factor and leaves the question of the culture's origin ominously unanswered. This version can never be regarded seriously. Life is short. Black life is shorter.

On y va.

The liberal version of the cultural argument points to "a tangle of pathologies" haunting black America born of oppression. This argument—which Barack Obama embraces—is more sincere, honest, and seductive. Chait helpfully summarizes:

The argument is that structural conditions shape culture, and culture, in turn, can take on a life of its own independent of the forces that created it. It would be bizarre to imagine that centuries of slavery, followed by systematic terrorism, segregation, discrimination, a legacy wealth gap, and so on did not leave a cultural residue that itself became an impediment to success.

The "structural conditions" Chait outlines above can be summed up under the phrase "white supremacy." I have spent the past two days searching that poor black people are not "holding up their end of the bargain," or that they are in ching for an era when black culture could be said to be "independent" of white supremacy. I have not found one. Certainly the antebellum period, when one third of all enslaved black people found themselves on the auction block, is not such an era. And surely we would not consider postbellum America, when freed people were regularly subjected to terrorism, to be such an era.

We certainly do not find such a period during the Roosevelt-Truman era, when this country erected a racist social safety net, leaving the NAACP to quip that the New Deal was "like a sieve with holes just big enough for the majority of Negroes to fall through." Nor do we find it during the 1940s, '50s and '60s, when African-Americans—as a matter of federal policy—were largely excluded from the legitimate housing market. Nor during the 1980s when we began the erection of a prison-industrial complex so vast that black males now comprise 8 percent of the world's entire incarcerated population.

And we do not find an era free of white supremacy in our times either, when the rising number of arrests for marijuana are mostly borne by African-Americans; when segregation drives a foreclosure crisis that helped expand the wealth gap; when big banks busy themselves baiting black people with "wealth-building seminars" and instead offering "ghetto loans" for "mud people"; when studies find that black low-wage applicants with no criminal record "fared no better than a white applicant just released from prison"; when, even after controlling for neighborhoods and crime rates, my son finds himself more likely to be stopped and frisked. Chait's theory of independent black cultural pathologies sounds reasonable. But it can't actually be demonstrated in the American record, and thus has no applicability.

What about the idea that white supremacy necessarily "bred a cultural residue that itself became an impediment to success"? Chait believes that it's "bizarre" to think otherwise. I think it's bizarre that he doesn't bother to see if his argument is actually true. Oppression might well produce a culture of failure. It might also produce a warrior spirit and a deep commitment to attaining the very things which had been so often withheld from you. There is no need for theorizing. The answers are knowable.

There certainly is no era more oppressive for black people than their 250 years of enslavement in this country. Slavery encompassed not just forced labor, but a ban on black literacy, the vending of black children, the regular rape of black women, and the lack of legal standing for black marriage. Like Chait, 19th century Northern white reformers coming South after the Civil War expected to find "a cultural residue that itself became an impediment to success."

In his masterful history, *Reconstruction,* the historian Eric Foner recounts the experience of the progressives who came to the South as teachers in black schools. The reformers "had little previous contact with blacks" and their views were largely cribbed from *Uncle Tom's Cabin.* They thus believed blacks to be culturally degraded and lacking in family instincts, prone to lie and steal, and generally opposed to self-reliance:

Few Northerners involved in black education could rise above the conviction that slavery had produced a "degraded" people, in dire need of instruction in frugality, temperance, honesty, and the dignity of labor . . . In classrooms, alphabet drills and multiplication tables alternated with exhortations to piety, cleanliness, and punctuality.

In short, white progressives coming South expected to find a black community suffering the effects of not just oppression but its "cultural residue."

Here is what they actually found:

During the Civil War, John Eaton, **who, like many whites, believed that slavery had destroyed the sense of family obligation,** was astonished by the eagerness with which former slaves in contraband camps legalized their marriage

bonds. The same pattern was repeated when the Freedmen's Bureau and state governments made it possible to register and solemnize slave unions. Many families, in addition, adopted the children of deceased relatives and friends, rather than see them apprenticed to white masters or placed in Freedmen's Bureau orphanages.

**By 1870, a large majority of blacks lived in two-parent family households, a fact that can be gleaned from the manuscript census returns but also "quite incidentally" from the Congressional Ku Klux Klan hearings, which recorded countless instances of victims assaulted in their homes, "the husband and wife in bed, and . . . their little children beside them."**

The point here is rich and repeated in American history—it was not "cultural residue" that threatened black marriages. It was white terrorism, white rapacity, and white violence. And the commitment among freed people to marriage mirrored a larger commitment to the reconstitution of family, itself necessary because of systemic white violence.

"In their eyes," wrote an official from the Freedmen's Bureau, in 1865. "The work of emancipation was incomplete until the families which had been dispersed by slavery were reunited."

White people at the time noted a sudden need in black people to travel far and wide. "The Negroes," reports one observer, "are literally crazy about traveling." Why were the Negroes "literally crazy about traveling?" Part of it was the sheer joy of mobility granted by emancipation. But there was something more: "Of all the motivations for black mobility," writes Foner, "none was more poignant than the effort to reunite families separated during slavery." reason for travel

This effort continued as late the onset of the twentieth century, when you could still find newspapers running ads like this:

During the year 1849, Thomas Sample carried away from this city, as his slaves, our daughter, Polly, and son. . . . We will give $100 each for them to any person who will assist them . . . to get to Nashville, or get word to us of their whereabouts.

Nor had the centuries-long effort to destroy black curiosity and thirst for education yielded much effect:

Perhaps the most striking illustration of the freedmen's quest for self-improvement was their seemingly unquenchable thirst for education. . . . The desire for learning led parents to migrate to towns and cities in search of education for their children, and plantation workers to make the establishment of a school-house "an absolute condition" of signing labor contracts . . .

Contemporaries could not but note the contrast **between white families seemingly indifferent to education and blacks who "toil and strive, labour and endure in order that their children 'may have a schooling'."** As one Northern educator remarked: "Is it not significant that after the lapse of

144 years since the settlement [of Beaufort, North Carolina], the Freedmen are building the first public school-house ever erected here."

"All in all," Foner concludes, "the months following the end of the Civil War were a period of remarkable accomplishment for Southern blacks." This is not especially remarkable, if you consider the time. Education, for instance, was not merely a status marker. Literacy was protection against having your land stolen or being otherwise cheated. Perhaps more importantly, it gave access to the Bible. The cultural fruits of oppression are rarely predictable merely through theorycraft. Who would predicted that oppression would make black people hungrier for education than their white peers? Who could predict the blues?

And culture is not exclusive. African-American are Americans, and have been Americans longer than virtually any other group of white Americans. There is no reason to suppose that enslavement cut African-Americans off from a broader cultural values. More likely African-Americans contributed to the creation and maintenance of those values.

The African-Americans who endured enslavement were subject to two and half centuries of degradation and humiliation. Slavery lasted twice as long as Jim Crow and was more repressive. If you were going to see evidence of a "cultural residue" which impeded success you would see it there. Instead you find black people desperate to reconstitute their families, desperate to marry, and desperate to be educated. Progressives who advocate the nineteenth-century line must specifically name the "cultural residue" that afflicts black people, and then offer evidence of it. Favoring abstract thought experiments over research will not cut it.

Progressives who advocate the nineteenth-century line must name the "cultural residue" that afflicts black people, and then offer evidence of it. Abstract thought experiments will not cut it.

Nor will pretending that old debates are somehow new. For some reason there is an entrenched belief among many liberals and conservatives that discussions of American racism should begin somewhere between the Moynihan Report and the Detroit riots. Thus Chait dates our dispute to the fights in the '70s between liberals. In fact, we are carrying on an argument that is at least a century older.

The passage of time is important because it allows us to assess how those arguments have faired. I contend that my arguments have been borne out, and the arguments of progressives like Chait and the president of the United States have not. Either Booker T. Washington was correct when he urged black people to forgo politics in favor eliminating "the criminal and loafing element of our people" or he wasn't. Either W.E.B. Du Bois was correct when he claimed that correcting "the immorality, crime and laziness among the Negroes"

should be the "first and primary" goal or he was not. The track record of progressive moral reform in the black community is knowable.

And it's not just knowable from Eric Foner. It can be gleaned from reading the entire Moynihan Report—not just the "tangle of pathologies" section—and then comparing it with Herb Gutman's *The Black Family in Slavery and Freedom*. It can be gleaned from Isabel Wilkerson's history of the Great Migration, *The Warmth of Other Suns*. One of the most important threads in this book is Wilkerson dismantling of the liberal theory of cultural degradation.

I want to conclude by examining one important element of Chait's argument—the role of the president of the United States who also happens to be a black man:

If I'm watching a basketball game in which the officials are systematically favoring one team over another (let's call them Team A and Team Duke) as an analyst, the officiating bias may be my central concern. But if I'm coaching Team A, I'd tell my players to ignore the biased officiating. Indeed, I'd be concerned the bias would either discourage them or make them lash out, and would urge them to overcome it. That's not the same as denying bias. It's a sensible practice of encouraging people to concentrate on the things they can control.

Obama's habit of speaking about this issue primarily to black audiences is Obama seizing upon his role as the most famous and admired African-American in the world to urge positive habits and behavior.

Chait's metaphor is incorrect. Barack Obama isn't the coach of "Team Negro," he is the commissioner of the league. Team Negro is very proud that someone who served on our staff has risen (for the first time in history!) to be commissioner. And Team Negro, which since the dawn of the league has endured biased officiating and whose every game is away, hopes that the commissioner's tenure among them has given him insight into the league's problems. But Team Negro is not—and should not be—confused about the commissioner's primary role.

"I'm not the president of black America," Barack Obama has said. "I'm the president of the United States of America."

Precisely.

And the president of the United States is not just an enactor of policy for today, he is the titular representative of his country's heritage and legacy. In regards to black people, America's heritage is kleptocracy—the stealing and selling of other people's children, the robbery of the fruits of black labor, the pillaging of black property, the taxing of black citizens for schools they can not attend, for pools in which they can not swim, for libraries that bar them, for universities that exclude them, for police who do not protect them, for the marking of whole communities as beyond the protection of the state and thus subject to the purview of outlaws and predators.

Obama-era progressives view white supremacy as something awful that happened in the past. I view it as one of the central organizing forces in American life.

The bearer of this unfortunate heritage feebly urging "positive habits and behavior" while his country imprisons some ungodly number of black men may well be greeted with applause in some quarters. It must never be so among those of us whose love of James Baldwin is true, whose love of Ida B. Wells is true, whose love of Harriet Tubman and our ancestors who fought for the right of family is true. In that fight America has rarely been our ally. Very often it has been our nemesis.

Obama-era progressives view white supremacy as something awful that happened in the past and the historical vestiges of which still afflict black people today. They believe we need policies—though not race-specific policies—that address the affliction. I view white supremacy as one of the central organizing forces in American life, whose vestiges and practices afflicted black people in the past, continue to afflict black people today, and will likely afflict black people until this country passes into the dust.

There is no evidence that black people are less responsible, less moral, or less upstanding in their dealings with America nor with themselves. But there is overwhelming evidence that America is irresponsible, immoral, and unconscionable in its dealings with black people and with itself. Urging African-Americans to become superhuman is great advice if you are concerned with creating extraordinary individuals. It is terrible advice if you are concerned with creating an equitable society.

The black freedom struggle is not about raising a race of hyper-moral super-humans. It is about all people garnering the right to live like the normal humans they are.

# Critical Thinking

1. How significant is the racism of white supremacy in holding back blacks today?
2. What is your view of the prospects for blacks today?
3. Why is racism still fairly strong?

# Internet References

**ACLU Criminal Justice Home Page**
www.aclu.org/crimjustice/index.html

**Human Rights and Humanitarian Assistance**
www.etown.edu/vl/humrts.html

**New American Studies Web**
www.georgetown.edu/crossroads/asw

**Sociology—Study Sociology Online**
http://edu.learnsoc.org

**Sociology Web Resources**
http://www.mhhe.com/socscience/sociology/resources/index.htm

**Sociosite**
http://www.topsite.com/goto/sociosite.net

**Socioweb**
http://www.topsite.com/goto/socioweb.com

*Article*                    Prepared by: Kurt Finsterbusch, *University of Maryland, College Park*

# When Slavery Won't Die: The Oppressive Biblical Mentality America Can't Shake

An interview with black theologian Kelly Brown Douglas on America's greatest sins.

VALERIE TARICO

## Learning Outcomes

*After reading this article, you will be able to:*

- Explain the theory "that dominant men have a right or even responsibility to enforce social hierarchy. If women or slaves or children or ethnic and religious minorities or live-stock step out of line, they must be punished to keep society in its proper order."

- Describe several areas in which iron age chattel culture plays a role.

- Describe how black young men have to behave in order not to become a victim of the oppressive mentality of people who could victimize them.

" *Y* ou rape our women and you're taking over our country. And you have to go.*" So said white supremacist Dylann Roof to black members of Emanuel AME Church in Charleston as he systematically executed nine, leaving one woman and a five-year-old child to bear witness to the slaughter.

The horror of the mass murder defies rational analysis. And yet, if we have any hope of a better future, we must analyze it—not just the circumstances or persons or events that led to this particular slaughter on this particular day, but the root attitudes and assumptions—the ancient strands of brutality and inequality that are woven into the fabric of our society.

In her article, "The Lethal Gentleman: The 'Benevolent Sexism' Behind Dylann Roof's Racism," sociologist Lisa Wade outlines how racism and sexism intersect in Roof's comments. The phrase "benevolent sexism" sounds jarring, but it is the term social scientists use when people attribute "positive traits to women that, nonetheless, justify their subordination to men:" *Women are beautiful and fragile; women are good with children; women are emotionally weak; God made woman as the perfect 'helpmeet' for man.* Roof's implication that white women need protecting from rape falls into this category.

One striking aspect of sexism and racism in Roof's statement is the sense of ownership it conveys: "Our women" in "our country" need to be protected from black men who either don't know their place or won't stay in it. White men can and should kill black men because they are having sex in our home territory with women who belong to us. We own America and we own the women who live here, and black men don't because if all was right in the world we would own them too.

The idea that women and minorities (along with children and members of other species) at some level *belong* to men of the dominant tribe can be traced all the way back to the culture and laws of the Iron Age and the concept of chattel. The term *chattel* is related to the term *cattle,* and human chattel, like cows, exist to serve their owners and must stay where they belong. In this view, dominant men have a right or even responsibility to enforce social hierarchy. If women or slaves or children or ethnic and religious minorities or livestock step out of line, they must be punished to keep society in its proper order.

I have written in the past about how Iron Age chattel culture underlies Religious Right priorities that might otherwise seem at odds: Why do the same people who oppose abortion also oppose protections and rights for children once they are born? What do opposition to marriage equality and opposition to contraception have in common? Why is the line between marriage and slavery so blurry in the Bible? How was American slavery influenced by the Iron Age worldview? Why does biblical literalism so often incline people to embrace sexual and racial inequality?

From within Christianity, Episcopal theologian and author Kelly Brown Douglas has written extensively about some of these same questions, with a particular focus on sexuality and the Black body. After the Trayvon Martin killing, she channeled her grief into a book, *Stand Your Ground: Black Bodies and the Justice of God.* In the interview that follows, Brown Douglas talks about the ancient concept of chattel, how it leads to the assumption that black bodies are "guilty, hypersexual, and dangerous," and how it underlies the slaughter, from Florida to New York to Charleston, that has left America reeling.

**Tarico:** You are the mother of a black son, so the horrendous epidemic of shootings we all have witnessed in recent years strikes very close to your heart.

**Brown Douglas:** I just couldn't shake the Trayvon Martin killing. At the time my son was 21 and I knew—as a 6' tall young man with locks that people would perceive him as a threat. My husband and I have tried to help our son understand how others perceive him as a black male. As his mother, I find myself continually reminding him that, while I will defend him to his death I don't want to defend him in his death. I have said, *If you are ever stopped by the police, even if they tell you to get on your knees, do it. A moment of humiliation could save your life.* When he's out there's not a moment that I don't fear for him, not because of anything he would do—he is a very responsible person—but because of how people might perceive him. So I am passionate about what is going on now, what is going on with our children. Somehow we have to change this world to make it safe for our children.

**Tarico:** In *Stand Your Ground,* you explore cultural values and beliefs that contribute to America's plague of racial violence including the sense of exceptionalism and manifest destiny—the idea that Anglo-Saxon European culture is fundamentally good, a light unto the world, something to be exported. When any of us has that kind of self-perception, it's hard to see ourselves as the bad guy, hard to see when we're doing harm.

**Brown Douglas:** To stop the harm, one of the first things that we have to understand is the complexity of violence. We have to understand that this Anglo-Saxon exceptionalism is inherently violent because it is unjust particularly as it suggests that certain people deserve the benefits of being treated with decency and dignity while others do not. Systems of injustice—racism, sexism, heterosexism—the ways that these systems manifest themselves systemically and structurally is violent. Anything that does harm to another is violent.

We seldom name the violence that is imbedded in the structures and systems of our society. We don't ask, where is the violence behind the violence? Yes, there are too many guns, and we should change that. But I'm speaking about the violence of injustice. Inasmuch as we don't begin to dismantle unjust discriminatory systems then we will consistently have violent eruptions that people respond to with more violence. Systemic and structural violence perpetuates a cycle of violence on all levels of society.

**Tarico:** Our handed-down cultural and religious traditions contain the concept of chattel, the idea that some people (and other species) exist for the benefit of others. Slavery is an extreme example of this. But even beyond overt slavery, you and I both write about how the residual of this concept continues to ripple down in our society.

**Brown Douglas:** When we talk about American slavery we have to talk about chattel slavery. Chattel doesn't mean simply that one person serves another, it means that one belongs to another. Black people were property. They were never meant to own their own labor or their own bodies. While I truly appreciate the way that female and black bodies intersect, the black body *came to this country as property.* When we talk about chattel in U.S. history, the only people who were considered nonhuman were those of African descent.

**Tarico:** Yes! Mercifully, by the time this country was founded, outright ownership of women was no longer the overt norm. In the Old Testament, women were literally governed by property law rather than personhood rights. A man, a father, essentially sold his daughter to another man to be a wife or slave. She was a valuable reproductive technology that produced economically valuable offspring that also belonged to the patriarch, who could beat or sell them or send them into war or even sacrifice them.

The notion of women as fully autonomous persons rather than property has taken centuries to emerge. During the American colonial era, single women could own real estate and other assets, but thanks to a legal concept called coverture, married women couldn't. "All men are created equal" really meant *men,* well, men who were white. A woman couldn't get a credit card on her own in the U.S. until 1974! When I was young, a woman couldn't obtain birth control without her husband's permission because her reproductive capacity belonged to him. Women in the South, including black women, have been of the last to get rights to control their own property and bodies. But that is a long way from literally being bought and sold in chains, as in the slave trade!

So this idea of people owning people is changing. But, damn, the process is slow. From your point of view, where do you see the residual of chattel culture in America today?

**Brown Douglas:** What we see is that some people have certain privileges because of who they are while other people are penalized because of who they are. Clearly the white male heterosexual body is the most privileged body and in as much as you lose one of those attributes you lose certain privileges. In your person you have less freedom, less right to the wages of freedom in your body. That is what we are struggling through in this country.

**Tarico:** The rape culture that we are struggling with on college campuses is rooted in the idea that men are entitled to women's bodies. Economic exploitation is rooted in the idea that might makes right, that powerful people have a right to exploit and consume the time, energy, productive capacity and reproductive capacity of the less powerful. The same could be said about environmental exploitation, that those who are most powerful have the right to exploit, consume, and take what they can; that other beings and their desires are secondary, if they matter at all.

As a theologian, you say that one way chattel culture gets justified is via "natural law" theology. What is that?

**Brown Douglas:** Natural law theology is a way of sanctifying this hierarchy of exploitation. It suggests that this wasn't just a human creation, but divine law. This was the way God designed things to be. For example, the whole idea was that God created black people as slaves not as full human beings. Slavery was legitimated specifically through Christianity.

**Tarico:** What are some echoes of natural law theology in the way that conservatives think today? How does it get translated into the modern language of the Religious Right?

**Brown Douglas:** We know that the discourse around women has been that God created women to serve men and to reproduce. Women have had to fight that battle for years, and continue to fight the battle that they were indeed not created to be subservient to men or to be reproductive machines. That is about natural law. The other way you see it is that marriage is supposed to be between a man and a woman—that's God's law according to various religious communities. Those are ways that we see "natural law" functioning in our culture today.

In racial relations, if one scanned some of the white supremacy rhetoric you see that too. Historically it is part of the rhetoric of the Klan. Today most people don't argue that in polite conversation, but we see it all the time when we place this religious canopy over discrimination. We sanctify discriminatory patterns. *If God wanted men and women to be equal, God would have created women to be different—not to be the bearers of children.* Or, *God created Adam and Eve not Adam and Steve.* Those are remnants of natural law. It functions in those places where people attempt to elevate social constructs and human laws so that they seem as if they are divine laws.

**Tarico:** I write mostly about women—about reproductive freedom and empowerment, and in our fight to create a new norm of chosen childbearing, this notion of women as chattel is hugely problematic. Specific verses from the Bible get cited to justify the GOP's assault on women. "Women will be saved through childbearing," for example. In the sphere of racial relations and justice, this notion of human chattel also gets tied in with sexuality—how black sexuality is seen, why blacks are seen as dangerous.

**Brown Douglas:** One thing that you'll notice is that marginalized oppressed people often are sexualized by the dominant narrative. You see that with LGBT people—the rhetoric is that they are indiscriminately promiscuous—as with black people and women. A couple of traditional cultural narratives come together here. In the conservative religious mindset, the only good sex is procreative sex. If you suggest that people are engaging in sexual activity for non-procreative reasons that's sinful and lustful—that's the Apostle Paul.

On top of that is this oppression narrative in which identity and sexuality get bound together. The late French philosopher Michel Foucault asked, Why is it that sexuality has become so significant in Western society that it becomes the source not just of reproduction but of truth? Why has it become the way people think of themselves and others? Foucault suggests that it is because sexuality is where the body and identity come together. If you can control the sexuality of a group of people, then you can control that.

Women are said to be driven by their passions and women's sexuality has to be controlled, and is only acceptable if it's procreative, which means men are controlling it. Sexualizing black people allowed black women to be used as breeders. It became a rationale for a black man to be lynched—because he was preying on white women. This is one way we have an overlap in how all women and black men are perceived as well as other marginalized groups. I wrote a book, *Sexuality and the Black Church,* in which I discuss this in more depth.

**Tarico:** How does this all play into a presumption of guilt? At the opening to your chapter on the Black body, you echo L. Z. Granderson's question, *Why are black murder victims put on trial?* Why *are* black murder victims put on trial?

**Brown Douglas:** Black people don't have the presumption of innocence. The concept of black people as chattel, that black people are not meant to occupy a free space and are dangerous when doing so, has been transformed into a notion of black people as criminal. If a black person has been accused of something then people assume that he or she is probably guilty, and our media representations of black people continue to reinforce this in the collective unconscious. There have been various studies which reveal that people have visceral automatic reactions to black bodies in which they see them as threatening. In one study police officers who were shown pictures of white and black men with and without guns were more likely to perceive that a black male had a gun even when he didn't and to miss a gun in the hands of a white male even when he had one. The stereotypes of the criminal black male and the angry black woman lead to the presumption of guilt.

**Tarico:** I write largely for an audience of non-theists and people who describe themselves as former Christians. Many of them look at the black community's response to an incident like the mass murder in Charleston and say, *I don't get it. How can so many Black people be Christian when Christianity has been such a tool of racial oppression against blacks? How can oppressed racial minorities embrace a sacred text that talks about chosen people and privileged blood lines?* What do you say to that?

**Brown Douglas:** That is the very question that compelled another book of mine called, *What's Faith Got to Do with It?* In the Black Christian tradition, the first time that Black people encountered God was not through their slaveholders. They knew God in freedom, as they encountered God through their African traditional religions. As black Christianity emerged during slavery, it emerged from an entirely different place than white Christianity. Black people understood that they were meant to be free, so God stood for freedom. Throughout history you see a black critique of White Christianity. The sum of the critique is this: If Christianity is used to oppress another that's not Christianity. What I ask is, How can one embrace a culture of oppression and claim to be Christian?

**Tarico:** What do you say to your own son about all of this?

**Brown Douglas:** I always told my son every morning as he was growing up, *There is no one greater than you but God and you are sacred.* I've always tried to teach him that he is not greater than anyone, that we are equal. God created us all, and the very breath we breathe comes from God—that is what makes us all sacred. Even when someone treats you as less than human, you must still affirm their humanity. I am working overtime these last two years to help him understand that, yes, this nation is racist and people do racist things but not all people are like that. And so, I try to teach him to respect people as he would respect himself, to affirm his humanity and to finds ways to affirm that of others. Most of all, I try to teach him not to get trapped in the cycle of hate because in the end, hate is self-destructive.

## Critical Thinking

1. What are the root attitudes and assumptions that lie behind some of the violence directed at blacks who do nothing to provoke it?
2. What does "benevolent sexism" mean?
3. What are various other oppressive prejudices against Blacks?

## Internet References

**New American Studies Web**
   https://blogs.commons.georgetown.edu/vkp/
**Social Science Information Gateway**
   http://www.ariadne.ac.uk/issue2/sosig
**Sociology–Study Sociology Online**
   http://edu.learnsoc.org/
**Sociology Web Resources**
   http://www.mhhe.com/socscience/sociology/resources/index.htm
**Sociosite**
   http://www.topsite.com/goto/sociosite.net
**Socioweb**
   http://www.topsite.com/goto/socioweb.com

**VALERIE TARICO** is a psychologist and writer in Seattle, Washington and the founder of Wisdom Commons. She is the author of "Trusting Doubt: A Former Evangelical Looks at Old Beliefs in a New Light" and "Deas and Other Imaginings." Her articles can be found at Awaypoint.Wordpress.com.

*Article*     Prepared by: Kurt Finsterbusch, *University of Maryland, College Park*

# Joe Biden Takes a Marriage Equality Victory Lap

On Thursday in Manhattan, the vice president looked back at the long battle—and what's next. But what really made this win inevitable was when love became the essence of marriage.

JAY MICHAELSON

## Learning Outcomes

*After reading this article, you will be able to:*

- Present the main arguments against LGBT marriages.
- Present the main arguments in favor of LGBT marriages.
- Present the legal and social action history that led to the eventual legalization of LGBT marriages.

In a way, Jane Austen won the right to same-sex marriage. Not Austen specifically, of course—though Mr. Darcy has been the object of much gay and straight adoration—but the centuries-long movement of which she is a part: the humanistic, romantic idea that love should conquer law.

Such was my impression at Thursday night's marriage equality victory lap at the swanky Cipriani New York, put on by the advocacy organization Freedom to Marry and its founder/guru, Evan Wolfson. He's the man who, more than any other individual, including Jane Austen, deserves the most credit for winning national marriage equality.

As Vice President Joe Biden, Wolfson, and others recognized, there were many, many factors that caused marriage equality to become the law of the land on June 26, 2015. But as Biden said, in a way, at the core of the movement has been a very straightforward proposition. Recalling a time when he and his father saw two men kissing, Biden said Thursday: "I looked at my Dad, and he said, 'they love each other—it's simple.'"

Of course, as Biden quickly added, the long march to marriage equality hasn't been that simple. Dozens of lawsuits have been filed, millions of philanthropic dollars spent, and a myriad of cultural moments marked, from *La Cage Aux Folles* to Ellen DeGeneres. "This is the civil rights issue of our generation," Biden told the cheering crowd. "And what you have accomplished didn't just take moral courage. It took physical courage."

That, too, is true. Recall ACT-UP activists demanding that an uncharacteristically speechless Ronald Reagan utter the word "AIDS." (It took him until September 1985, at which point 12,000 people had died.) Remember also the original transgender rioters at Stonewall and the first gay rights protest in front of the White House, in 1957, when 10 people risked their livelihoods to demand legal equality.

But what won the day, in the end, was neither constitutional legal theory nor radical societal change. It was clear at Cipriani that what won the day was—trigger alert, cynics—love.

Consider this version of the story. The arguments against same-sex marriage are many, but the majority of them insist it isn't really marriage at all but something lesser. This isn't love, it's lust, like bestiality or incest. ("Man on dog," in Rick Santorum's epitaph-worthy phrase.) Homosexuals were said to be perverts, psychological deviants, or sex fiends.

Only, gradually, it became clear that they aren't—at least, not in significantly greater number than heterosexuals.

In fact, as people got to know gays and lesbians, either personally or through the media, it turned out that most, though not all, were actually a little dull. They wanted love, equal rights, basic dignity. They wanted to live and let live.

(This outraged the non-dull gays, the radicals who wanted a movement of sexual liberation, but they turned out to be in the minority.)

Eventually, the arguments against gay marriage started to seem either mean, or abstract, or both. Sure, the Bible seems to say bad things about lascivious homosexual behavior, but that's not what Aunt Nancy and Aunt Lisa have, right?

And no one really took those abstractions about "gender complementarity" and procreation too seriously. They seemed like rationales for prejudice. How can you compare some philosophical argument with Jim Obergefell, flying his dying partner out of state so they could get married, only to have the marriage ignored by his home state of Ohio? Or with Edie Windsor?

Which is where Jane Austen comes in. If love really does conquer all—even if, in Austen, Shakespeare, and others, the lovers pay a serious price—then surely it conquers some abstract bloviating about the Bible. (Of course, it also didn't help that so many anti-gay pastors and politicians turned out to be closeted gays and so many priests turned out to be child molesters.)

And if marriage, again following Austen, is primarily about love, then how can it be denied to two consenting adults who are obviously, manifestly, in love?

I was personally involved in the marriage struggle—as a full-time activist, but playing a very bit part—from around 2008 to 2013. And I heard this firsthand from religious people, time and time again: "I used to believe it was wrong, but then my [daughter][friend][uncle] came out, and I had to think again."

I came to see victory as inexorable because there really was a truth of the matter, and it really was on our side. Our opponents were lying about our lives. If we just told the truth, we wouldn't win over everyone, but we'd win over enough.

Easy to say in 2015. But in 1983, when Evan Wolfson wrote his quixotic law review article arguing for a constitutional right to same-sex marriage, everyone thought he was crazy. As late as the 1990s, I myself thought marriage was the wrong battle to fight—too contentious, too soaked in the language of religion.

We were all wrong, and Wolfson was right.

Really, it was a two-pronged battle. The first prong was the set of cultural changes I've talked about already. The second was, indeed, a matter of law, and canny political strategy. Wolfson went state by state, winning some battles in the courts and a few in the legislature. He focused exclusively on marriage, building coalitions with willing conservatives—alienating many progressives in the process—and putting aside differences on other issues. He convinced several large LGBT organizations, each with their own interests, to coordinate their efforts.

And he made crucial legal arguments.

On Thursday in Biden's remarks, which seemed to be largely off the cuff, he pointed out that in the 1987 confirmation hearings of Robert Bork, he and the would-be Supreme Court justice had a passionate disagreement about the nature of constitutional rights. Bork, an originalist like Antonin Scalia, said the only rights guaranteed by the Constitution are those written in the Constitution. (Scalia said the same thing in his *Obergefell* dissent.)

Biden disagreed. Citing Wolfson's law review article, he said human rights are given by God and that the Constitution merely guarantees that they cannot be taken away. Exactly what those rights are—what "equal protection of the laws" means, for example—is subject to the evolution of moral and legal reasoning. Not judicial fiat, as the *Obergefell* dissenters charged, but argumentation, reason, and reflection on the ambit of human rights.

For decades after the Fourteenth Amendment was passed, Jim Crow laws oppressed those the amendment was specifically designed to protect. Were those laws really constitutional, simply because they weren't enumerated in the text of the Constitution or were present when it passed? Surely not. Surely, even if "equal protection" and "due process" meant one thing in 1868, they encompassed these later developments, as well.

Well, Biden won the battle, and Bork lost. And as the vice president pointed out, the man Reagan nominated in his place was Anthony Kennedy, the deciding vote in *Obergefell* and the author of all four major Supreme Court opinions on LGBT equality.

A cynic would say Biden just took even more credit for marriage equality—on top of the credit he already gets (and deserves) for beating his boss to the punch and saying in May 2012 that he believed that all couples, gay or straight, should be able to legally marry.

But Biden also noted that legal philosophy was never the driving force in the struggle. "The country has always been ahead of the court," he said. And he generously shared credit with the ballroom full of activists, donors, and ordinary citizens, many of whom had been fighting this battle for 30 years, well before it seemed inevitable to Johnny-Come-Latelys like me.

Biden insisted on looking forward to the next battle: anti-discrimination protection. "There are 32 states where you can get married in the morning and get fired in the afternoon," he said. "We must expose the darkness to justice."

At the same time, the reception was a kind of victory lap—combined with a retirement party for Freedom to Marry, which is admirably closing its doors, having accomplished its mission. The sponsor-provided vodka flowed freely, and Carly Rae Jepsen entertained the crowd.

I'm a pretty cynical guy, but I was honored to be among them.

# Critical Thinking

1. Why do some people believe that gay marriages will threaten heterosexual marriages?

2. How are gays the same as heterosexuals and how are they different?

3. What were Biden's main arguments against the denial of marriage rights for LGBTs?

# Internet References

**New American Studies Web**
https://blogs.commons.georgetown.edu/vkp/

**Social Science Information Gateway**
http://www.ariadne.ac.uk/issue2/sosig

**Sociology—Study Sociology Online**
http://edu.learnsoc.org/

**Sociology Web Resources**
http://www.mhhe.com/socscience/sociology/resources/index.htm

**Sociosite**
http://www.topsite.com/goto/sociosite.net

**Socioweb**
http://www.topsite.com/goto/socioweb.com

# Unit 4

# UNIT

Prepared by: Kurt Finsterbusch, *University of Maryland, College Park*

# Institutional Problems

This unit looks at the problems in four institutional areas: family, education, healthcare, and religion.

The family is the basic institution in society. Politicians and preachers are earnestly preaching this message today as though most people need to be convinced, but everyone already agrees. Nevertheless, families are having real problems, and sociologists should be as concerned as preachers. Unlike the preachers who blame couples who divorce for shallow commitment, sociologists point to additional causes such as the numerous changes in society that have had an impact on the family. For example, women have to work because many men do not make enough income to support a family adequately. So, women are working not only to enjoy a career but also out of necessity. Working women are often less dependent on their husbands. As a result, divorce can be an option for neglected or badly treated wives.

The first section in this unit examines the connection between love and power in marriage and other important relationships. The following section deals with health issues. The first examines the single price health care which has recently become a major issue. The second article asks why does health care cost so much. The third explores amazing possibilities in life extension due to scientific advances. The next section examines the general performance of public schools. Finally we look at the role of religion in America today. Its premise is that religious minorities should be protected not persecuted.

*Article*                          Prepared by: Kurt Finsterbusch, *University of Maryland, College Park*

# The American Family: An Endangered and Disappearing Species

Lynn Wardle

## Learning Outcomes

*After reading this article, you will be able to:*

- Understand the statistics that show that marriage rates have radically declined.

- Also understand why marriage rates have declined.

- Compare current patterns to marriage patterns in the past.

It is quite common to hear persons bemoaning the state of the family and of families in America. Is that just hype and rhetoric? Are American families really "disintegrating" today? Sadly, a lot of evidence seems to indicate that traditional American families are an endangered and disappearing species.

Several statistical indicia suggest that traditional families (husband and wife with children) and family life are disappearing in the United States. One major factor in the disintegration of families in America is the movement of young adults away from marriage. Nonmarital cohabitation and temporary "hooking up" have to some extent replaced marriage in some segments of the young adult population.

Citing a Pew Research Center report, The Deseret News notes that the U.S. marriage rate (percentage of persons married at age 18-32) has steadily dropped by generation from 65 percent of the Silent Generation (1960) to 48 percent of the Baby Boomer Generation (1980) to 36 percent of the Gen X Generation (1997), to just 26 percent of the Millennial Generation (2013). The decline in marriage rates in the USA has been steady and profound. Currently fewer than half as many (only 40% as many) of young Americans 18-32 have married than young Americans of the same age cohort just three generations earlier (in the "Silent" generation).

Moreover, the marriage rate is "expected to drop even further next year." A Pew Research Center report notes that:

"After decades of declining marriage rates and changes in family structure, the share of American adults who have never been married is at an historic high. In 2012, one-in-five adults ages 25 and older (about 42 million people) had never been married, according to a new Pew Research Center analysis of census data. In 1960, only about one-in-ten adults (9%) in that age range had never been married."

The percentage of American men and women ages 25 and older who have never been married has steadily risen from 1970, when it was under 10 percent for both men and women, to 23 percent of men and 17 percent of women, at present. The share of never-married has more than doubled in about four decades.

Marriage has been devalued and lost credibility in recent years. That Pew survey found that nearly as many American adults (46%) said that Society is just as well off if people have other priorities than marriage and children as do not make marriage and having children a priority, as said (50%) that Society is better off if marriage and children are given priority.

Many different factors have combined to influence the decline of marriage among young adults. "Adults are marrying later in life, and the shares of adults cohabiting and raising children outside of marriage have increased significantly. The median age at first marriage is now 27 for women and 29 for men, up from 20 for women and 23 for men in 1960." Likewise, the widespread and immature misuse and abuse of no-fault divorce has weakened the current generation of young adults' faith in marriage.

There are significant age-differences in the disintegration of marriage. Nearly the same percentage of couples who are under age 25 are living in unmarried partner households as are married couples, says U.S. Census Bureau data. U.S. Census Bureau, Current Population Survey, Annual Social and Economic Supplement, 2010. By contrast, the percentage of couples aged 35 and older who are living together in unmarried partner households is well below ten percent (10%), comprising between one-tenth and one-twentieth (or less) of the total couples in the four over-35-years-old decade-cohorts. As couples get older, they value marriage more.

The Pew Research Center also shows that the pool of unmarried men age 25-34 who have jobs has fallen steadily from 1960 (139 million) to 2012 (only 91 million). That may impact the number of marriages; women may have fewer responsible men to consider as marriage partners. That clearly influences the rate and number of marriages as another report shows that 78% of all women report that a prospective partner having "a steady job" would be "'very important' to them in choosing a spouse or partner."

Likewise, the education gap between never-married men and women age 25 and over has widened, again leaving women with fewer responsible men to consider as marriage partners.

The Pew Research Center shows that the percentage of unmarried women with a high school degree or less in 2012 was only 37 percent, while for men it was 47 percent. A higher percentage of single women than single men have obtained some college education (30%-vs-28%), a bachelor's degree (21%-vs-18%), and a post-graduate degree (11%-vs-7%). For these women today there are fewer equally qualified potential husbands.

As a result of easy no-fault divorce and its consequences, the percentage of never-married adults has dramatically increased. The Pew Research Center predicts that one in four young adults Americans today may never marry.

The growth of same-sex marriage is further evidence of the marriage crisis in the U.S. today. Same-sex marriage is legal in thirty-seven (37) of the fifty U.S. states. In two-thirds of the American states where same-sex marriage is now permitted, the legalization of same-sex marriage did not occur by any legitimate democratic or legislative process, but by the order of federal courts.

By contrast, voters voted to prohibit same-sex marriage by constitutional amendments in 31 U.S. states. The federal courts have overturned many of those.

The U.S. is out of step with most of the nations of the world regarding same-sex marriage. Currently, only seventeen nations (out of 193 sovereign nations) allow same-sex marriage – less than nine percent (only 8.8%) of the sovereign nations on earth. Within the next two years two other nations, like Ireland just recently did, are likely to permit same-sex marriage (Finland, and Slovenia).

By contrast, at least 47 nations (nearly one-quarter of all nations) have adopted constitutional language that appears to bar same-sex marriage. For example: Article 24, Constitution of Japan: "Marriage shall be based only on the mutual consent of both sexes and it shall be maintained through mutual cooperation with the equal rights of husband and wife. . . ." Likewise, Article 110, Constitution of Latvia: "The State shall protect and support marriage—a union between a man and a woman. . . ."

The issue of same-sex marriage is still open in most nations. On April 28, 2015, the Supreme Court of the United States heard oral arguments in four consolidated cases involving challenges to the marriage laws of those states which do not allow same-sex couples to marry. Chief Justice John Roberts boiled the argument down to the fundamental issue: "You're not seeking to join the institution," he said. "You're seeking to change what the institution is." The Court is likely to announce what may be a revolutionary decision about same-sex marriage this month.

Another major manifestation of the disintegration of families in America is the explosion of nonmarital childbearing and child-rearing. Those children are disadvantaged in very profound and long-lasting ways. For example, according to the recent Brooklyn Declaration (21 May 2015): Children in father-absent homes are almost four times more likely to be poor. In 2011, 12 percent of children in married-couple families were living in poverty, compared to 44 percent of children in mother-only families.

The U.S. Department of Health and Human Services states, "Fatherless children are at a dramatically greater risk of drug and alcohol abuse." There is significantly more drug use among children who do not live with their mother and father. Children of single-parent homes are more than twice as likely to commit suicide. Among children in grades 7-12 who have lived with at least one biological parent, those who experienced the divorce, separation, or a nonunion birth reported lower grade point averages than those who have always lived with both biological parents. 71 percent of high school dropouts are fatherless; fatherless children have more trouble academically, scoring poorly on tests of reading, mathematics, and thinking skills; children from father-absent homes are more likely to be truant from school, more likely to be excluded from school, more likely to leave school at age 16, and less likely to attain academic and professional qualifications in adulthood.

So, sadly, the family and families in America are disintegrating. As judicial orders are decreed and legal policy changes are enacted that re-shape the American family, we should ask how those rulings and new policies will impact the disintegration of the family in America.

# Critical Thinking

1. What effect has the women's movement had on the institution of marriage?

2. Over 60 years ago, it was very difficult to get out of a marriage. Was that better than the easy divorces of today?

3. How have children been affected by the new family structures?

# Internet References

**New American Studies Web**
www.georgetown.edu/crossroads/asw

**Social Science Information Gateway**
http://sosig.esrc.bris.ac.uk

**Sociology Web Resources**
http://www.mhhe.com/socscience/sociology/resources/index.htm

**Sociology—Study Sociology Online**
http://edu.learnsoc.org

**Sociosite**
http://www.topsite.com/goto/sociosite.net

LYNN D. WARDLE is the Bruce C. Hafen Professor of Law at Brigham Young University. He is author or editor of numerous books and law review articles mostly about family, biomedical ethics and conflict of laws policy issues. His publications present only his personal (not institutional) views.

*Article*     Prepared by: Kurt Finsterbusch, *University of Maryland, College Park*

# The Case for Single-Price Health Care

We could largely solve the cost crisis simply by making medicare prices universal.

PAUL S. HEWITT AND PHILLIP LONGMAN

## Learning Outcomes

*After reading this article, you will be able to:*

- Explain why health care prices are so high in America.
- Describe the benefits of a single payer system.
- Understand why the drug companies have so much power.

Obamacare has taken a licking but keeps on ticking. The prospect of repeal died on the Senate floor. Republican efforts to roll it back continue, but the bulk of the program is still in place and unlikely to go anywhere. Virginia appears, as of this writing, on the way to expanding Medicaid, and other states will likely follow. Thanks mostly to the Affordable Care Act's expansion of Medicaid, some eighteen million more people have health insurance today than when Obamacare went into effect, cutting the uninsured population nearly in half.

But while progress has been made on expanding access, another problem keeps getting worse: the soaring cost of health care for those who get their insurance through their employers. For these folks – who make up the majority of middle-class, working-age Americans – the ever-rising costs of premiums, deductibles, and co-pays has turned into a full-blown crisis.

Take a median-income family of four whose members are covered by a standard employer-sponsored plan. Last year, the amount that hospitals, doctors, and other providers charged to treat such a family reached an average of $26,944, according to the Milliman Medical Index – nearly $9,000 higher than in 2010, when the ACA was enacted. Families typically paid about a fifth of that difference directly in the form of increased premiums, deductibles, and co-pays. Who exactly paid how much of the rest is not certain, but it's axiomatic among economists that employees bear most if not all of the cost of employer-sponsored

health care. To employers, health insurance is just a form of employee compensation. When the cost goes up, they typically respond by cutting back on raises and other benefits.

To put this in perspective, the hit to middle-class families with employer-sponsored insurance has been roughly the same as if the government had imposed a 4.5 percent payroll tax increase beginning in 2010. No wonder, then, that four in ten adults with health insurance now say they have difficulty meeting the cost of their premiums and deductibles, according to Kaiser Family Foundation tracking polls, and another 31 percent say they have difficulty covering the cost of co-payments.

Obamacare didn't cause this crisis – in fact, relative to wages, the rate of medical inflation in the employer-provided market was substantially higher before the law. Nor is the rising cost of employer-provided health insurance the result of Obamacare forcing hospitals and other providers to shift costs on to nongovernmental, or commercial, payers, as some Republicans assert. Instead, as we shall see, it's mostly the result of monopolistic hospitals engaging in price discrimination as they exploit their increasing market power over private purchasers of health care.

But it's easy to understand why many people with commercial insurance feel that the law has made them worse off. In their experience, Congress passed the ACA and now they pay much more for health care. Adding to the grievance of many middle-class Americans is the fact that, even as their own costs have gone up and their choice of doctors has narrowed, millions more lower-income people are now paying little or nothing thanks to the expansion of Medicaid.

Fortunately, there's a straightforward way to attack this middle-class affordability problem. The Affordable Care Act dramatically tightened existing price controls on health care purchased by the federal government. It did so by setting fee schedules for how much doctors and hospitals can charge Medicare, Medicaid, and other federal health care programs for performing specific services or, in some cases, treating specific conditions. Similar price controls apply to Medicare Advantage Plans, under which private insurers are allowed to contract with providers at Medicare prices.

These cost controls save the government roughly enough money each year to fund the entire Defense Department. At a time when the price of health care paid for by commercial insurance has been increasing two to three times faster than the wages earned by most Americans, the price of health services delivered through the federal programs – which account for 37 percent of all health care bills – has actually been declining relative to the average wage.

The answer to the most pressing aspect of our health care crisis is simply to apply these cost controls to commercial plans as well. For a typical middle-class family, such a move, if enacted today, would drop the total price of health care by about a third in the first year, without having to pass any new taxes and without forcing anyone to change their health care plan. Proof of concept comes from the fact that we already do this for everyone covered by Medicare and Medicaid. You've heard of single-payer. This is the case for single-price.

To show why direct cost controls are the best fix for our broken health care system, we need to get straight on what's causing the crisis.

You might assume that Americans are just getting older and sicker – but that's not it. The increasing number of old people has accounted for only about a tenth of the rise in health care spending since the late 1990s, according to consensus estimates. And while risk factors like obesity and opioid abuse have gotten more prevalent, their effect on spending has been more than offset by other trends, especially the dramatic decline in smoking and related heart disease.

Another theory is that Americans consume too much health care. But we actually don't see more doctors, or receive more scans or surgeries, than our counterparts in other advanced countries. We spend dramatically fewer days in hospitals than we used to, and seek out less routine preventive care, thanks to the rise of high-deductible plans and narrower provider networks. Overall, the typical American's utilization of health care has been flat since the mid-1990s.

So what's driving the relentless increase in health care spending? In the words of a seminal 2003 research paper published in Health Affairs, "It's the Prices, Stupid." Study after study has found that the biggest reason Americans pay more per person for care than the residents of any other advanced country is simply that the same pill or treatment costs dramatically more in the United States.

Most people are well aware of the inflated price of prescription drugs in the U.S. But drugs account for only about 10 percent of health care spending. By far the largest source of medical inflation is the increasing cost of medical services. A report by the International Federation of Health Plans shows, for example, that in Australia, hospital and physician charges for an appendectomy typically came to around $3,800 in 2015; in the U.S., the same operation cost $16,000 on average, and often far more. Giving birth will cost you around $2,000 in Spain, but a normal delivery in the U.S. costs an average of $11,000 – and more than $18,000 in the most expensive hospitals.

For people with commercial insurance, it keeps getting worse. On the current course, by 2024, the increase in price for a typical middle-class family of four with employer coverage will be equivalent to another increase in the payroll tax – this time of 4.8 percent. That's on top of the 4.5 percent of wage income lost to medical inflation during the Obama years, and the 7.3 percent lost under George W. Bush. By 2028, the total annual health care hit will come to $44,000 per family.

## How Did This Happen?

A major, underappreciated reason is that in most markets, medical providers have merged with each other to the point that they effectively operate as local monopolies. According to the standard metric used by the Federal Trade Commission, not a single "highly competitive" hospital market remains in any region of the United States. A full 40 percent of all hospital stays now occur in areas where a single entity controls all hospitals. Another 20 percent occur in regions where only two competitors remain. The result is that when an insurer or employer wants to create a health care plan, they have to negotiate with providers who dictate their own prices.

Where health care consolidation is strongest, hospital prices run roughly 20 percent higher than in markets where some real competition remains. Since we first wrote about the phenomenon in these pages ("After Obamacare," January/February 2014), a vast literature has grown up confirming that monopoly in health care is a major factor pushing up prices for Americans not covered by Medicare or Medicaid.

What would happen if we just took the single measure of applying Medicare prices to all commercial health insurance – and did nothing else? According to a study by the Congressional Budget Office, the price for a one-day hospital stay is 89 percent higher when charged to commercial insurance plans and their customers than when a Medicare patient stays in the same bed for the same amount of time. Overall, the discounts Medicare and Medicaid receive are in the 20 to 40 percent range. Thus, if done at a stroke, the first-order effect of imposing Medicare prices universally would be to reduce the price of the health care received by a typical family by about one-third. That would translate into annual savings of about $9,000 today, and much more over time. The savings would still be substantial even if we implemented the plan in phases to ease the transition.

Wouldn't "Medicare prices for all" cause massive disruption across the health care sector? Yes, but in a good way. Importantly, hospitals that disproportionately serve low-income and elderlypatients – typically found in rural or poor, urban locations – would be the least affected. That's because they already know how to break even or even earn a surplus at Medicare and Medicaid prices. Unable to pass inflated costs along to patients with commercial insurance, they've had to learn to be more efficient.

The same is true more generally of hospitals that lack monopoly power. Studies show that hospitals with real competition in their local markets have found ways to lower costs to the point that they can get by on Medicare prices. These hospitals might even welcome a move to universal Medicare prices because it would help level the playing field with monopolistic competitors when it comes to recruiting and retaining doctors.

It would be a different story, though, for hospital systems that have been living high off their ability to extract monopoly prices from commercially insured patients. These hospitals will scream that they are already losing money on every Medicare and Medicaid patient, and that unless they are able to inflate the prices they charge commercial payers, they will go broke. But the reason they lose money on Medicare and Medicaid patients is that their costs are too high. And the reason their costs are too high is that they don't need to cut them so long as they can gouge commercial payers – which, as monopolies or near monopolies, they can. The majority of these hospitals are classified as nonprofits, so the revenue from their high prices doesn't even have to go back to shareholders. Instead, it turns into inflated salaries for administrators, lucrative contracts for specialists, and, often, giant building projects. In order to survive on Medicare prices, they would have to become much more efficient and cost conscious.

Meanwhile, going to a "Medicare prices for all" system would also help to structure the market for health insurance in ways that promote the public interest. For one, once you eliminate all the haggling and gamesmanship involved in setting different complicated fee schedules for patients on different plans, much of the administrative cost in health care vanishes. For another, since all employers would pay the same amount for health care, eliminating price discrimination would shrink the advantage large employers have when it comes to attracting workers by offering generous plans.

Moreover, large insurance companies would no longer have any advantage over smaller ones in negotiating contracts with providers. That, in turn, would encourage new companies to enter the health insurance business and actually compete over who can deliver the most value at a given price. This would mean developing plans that optimize choice, easy access, integrated care, and expanded benefits like gym memberships and

discounted drug prices. These perks are already commonly offered under Medicare Advantage Plans, which all pay the same prices for care and must therefore find more creative ways to compete for customers.

Could we be sure that all these savings would get passed on to average Americans? Provisions in the Affordable Care Act already require insurers to spend 80 to 85 percent of premium dollars on medical care, thus ensuring that the lower prices couldn't be turned into higher profits and salaries for insurance companies and their executives. That leaves open the question of whether employers would pass along savings to employees. In a truly competitive labor market, there is no reason to believe they wouldn't. But, of course, labor markets today are often noncompetitive, due to factors ranging from industry consolidation to the fading power of unions. To make sure that employers shared the savings with employees, a new law might include a requirement that existing employer-sponsored plans cut premiums, deductibles, and co-pays in line with the reductions in health care prices.

In normal markets, price controls are seldom a good idea. But health care is not a normal market. Purchasers, whether consumers, insurers, or employers, have a hard time evaluating the quality of medical services, for example. There are also all kinds of agency problems involved with so much care being purchased with other people's money, and a moral problem involved with the fact that a large and increasing share of the population can't afford to pay the price of their own health care. And that's all before you get to the problem of industry consolidation. In highly concentrated, opaque health care markets, administered prices are the only real alternative to prices dictated by the fiat of monopolists.

These are the reasons why literally every other developed country in the world uses administered prices in health care, including countries that rely on privately owned hospitals and entrepreneurial doctors. And it's why their use in the Medicare and Medicaid programs has been successful in containing cost inflation while predatory pricing prevails everywhere else in the increasingly cartelized U.S. health care sector.

Getting legislation passed to allow the federal government to set prices directly may sound far-fetched, but it's likely more politically doable than you might think. Just as Obamacare made it through Congress in part because key sectors of the health care industry came to see it as advantageous, so too with a single-price system.

Ending price discrimination would liberate insurers, employers, and other large purchasers of health care from the growing monopoly power of their "suppliers." It would also establish new opportunities for insurers to expand into local markets and take on entrenched incumbent players, including both monopolistic providers and monopolistic insurers. The single-price plan also preserves a role for a private health insurance industry, albeit one more like those found in France and Germany, where the government sets the prices and private-sector insurers compete over who can provide the best service.

Meanwhile, hospitals that have already learned how to reduce costs enough to make a living on Medicare prices would have reason to support the idea. They would stand a better chance of attracting and retaining doctors if they didn't have to match the inflated pay scales offered by monopolistic institutions living off inflated commercial prices. A major political benefit of the single-price system is that it could split the interests of providers, isolating price-gouging, monopolistic networks from smaller, community-minded hospitals and doctors. At the same time, by preserving a role for commercial insurance, it spares health care reformers from being pitted against the entire medical industrial complex. (See "How Big Medicine Can Ruin Medicare for All," November/December 2017.)

The idea of applying Medicare and Medicaid prices across the board is so compelling that it has started getting serious attention from influential policy wonks. On the conservative side, the Council for Affordable Health Coverage recently issued a white paper that calls for the expansion of Medicare prices to commercial plans. On the liberal side, Princeton's Paul Starr broached the idea in an article in the American Prospect in January. More recently, the Center of American Progress has included the idea in a policy paper.

The Starr and CAP Medicare price proposals were, however, just one small part of broader plans to achieve universal coverage – by expanding eligibility to the existing Medicare program or creating a brand-new, very expensive entitlement that would require big tax increases. Administered prices of some kind would also be a part of any single-payer plan.

But there are very strong reasons to believe that starting with price controls alone is a better idea than trying to achieve them and universal coverage in one shot. To see why, we first have to look at the potential pitfalls of more far-reaching proposals.

The most ambitious plan so far, of course, is Bernie Sanders's "Medicare for All" bill, which would shift every American onto Medicare, as the name suggests, over the course of four years. While the bill has gained momentum among prominent Democrats, it has two widely remarked-upon shortcomings. First, people who are currently satisfied with their insurance might balk at being forced into a different plan. Second, it would be terrifically expensive, requiring a major tax increase to pay for it. The Urban Institute estimated that the plan Sanders proposed during the last presidential election would increase federal spending on health care by 232 percent, or a cumulative $32 trillion by 2026. Sanders says his more recent plan could be paid for with a 7.5 percent payroll tax on employers plus a 4 percent income tax surcharge on individuals.

Medicare for All advocates make the case that, despite the sticker price, the plan will actually bring down overall health care spending by imposing lower prices on providers and saving on administration. But here's the problem: almost all of those savings will come from money that voters don't know they're currently spending. More than 150 million Americans have employer-sponsored group health care plans. They can see what they are forking out directly for premiums, deductibles, and co-pays, and they don't like it. But they are largely innocent of the far greater amounts they pay in lost wages. In a typical employer-sponsored family plan, two-thirds of the premiums are nominally paid by the employer, who in turn shifts much if not all of that cost to employees by reducing other forms of compensation. Yet few employees are aware of this reality. So selling a single-payer system involves promising to save people money on costs they don't know they pay, while at the same time telling them that they'll have to share more of their paycheck with Uncle Sam. Not easy.

Some Democrats have been trying to finesse this political reality by proposing what might be called "single-payer lite" plans. The Center for American Progress's "Medicare Extra for All" proposal is an example. Under this plan, everyone can choose between buying into Medicare or keeping their current insurance. And because the plan would impose Medicare prices universally, the price of private insurance would go down.

But that is just a part of the proposal. It would also establish a new federal health program offering enhanced benefits, including dental, vision, hearing, and maybe even coverage for long-term nursing home stays, which Medicare and standard commercial health insurance currently don't cover. Premiums would be free for people living in poverty and would be capped at no more than 10 percent of income for anyone else who wanted to join. Deductibles and co-pays would likewise be eliminated for low-income people and reduced for everyone else.

Sounds pretty good, but who would pay for it? CAP doesn't specify. Instead, it merely says that "Medicare Extra would be financed by a combination of health care savings and tax revenue options," adding that it "intends to engage an independent third party to conduct modeling simulation to determine how best to set the numerical values of the parameters."

Whatever numerical values come back, they'll be substantial and controversial. Even if the CAP plan was financed in good measure by new taxes on the super-rich, it would still involve large transfers from middle-income people, who will be at least partially financing their own benefits, to people with lower incomes, who would be paying nothing for the health care they receive.

A plan based purely on Medicare prices for all would avoid these political land mines. Ending price discrimination against people with employer-provided or other commercial insurance in one fell swoop would address the biggest concern of the largest group of voters – crucially, without asking them to make any sacrifices in the form of higher taxes. This would raise the chances of the party that passed it actually being rewarded for health care reform, rather than punished, as the Democrats were for Obamacare. Voters would quickly feel the benefits in lower premiums, deductibles, and co-pays. And that, in turn, should make them more open to efforts to extend health coverage to those that lack it.

So why not just keep it simple, at least to start? A "Medicare prices for all" plan doesn't require tax increases or involve transfers paid for by the middle class. It doesn't require Americans to give up their current health care plans. And it doesn't repeal or replace the popular features of the Affordable Care Act. But it does directly attack the middle-class affordability crisis using a proven approach that the great majority of Americans might actually support.

# Critical Thinking

1. Many Americans distrust the government playing a major role in providing health services. What are some arguments on the other side?

2. Why is health care so much less expensive in Europe than in America?

3. Why is the current health care system in crisis?

# Internet References

**Harvard Health Publishing**
https://www.health.harvard.edu/

**New American Studies Web**
www.georgetown.edu/crossroads/asw

**Social Science Information Gateway**
http://sosig.esrc.bris.ac.uk

**Sociology Web Resources**
http://www.mhhe.com/socscience/sociology/resources/index.htm

**Sociology—Study Sociology Online**
http://edu.learnsoc.org

**Sociosite**
http://www.topsite.com/goto/sociosite.net

PAUL HEWITT is an economic adviser to the Council for Affordable Health Coverage. His views do not necessarily reflect those of CAHC or its members.

PHILLIP LONGMAN is senior editor at the Washington Monthly and policy director at the Open Markets Institute.

*Article*                    Prepared by: Kurt Finsterbusch, *University of Maryland, College Park*

# Why Is Health Care So Expensive?

*Why It's So High, How It Affects Your Wallet—and Yes, What You Can Do about It*

CONSUMER REPORTS

## Learning Outcomes

*After reading this article, you will be able to:*

- Describe the per capita health care costs for the United States compared to European countries since 1980.

- Discuss some of the other adverse aspects of the U.S. health care system.

- Explain the statement of George Halvorson, former chairman of Kaiser Permanente, "Prices are made up depending on who the payer is."

Person for person, health care in the U.S. costs about twice as much as it does in the rest of the developed world. In fact, if our $3 trillion health care sector were its own country, it would be the world's fifth-largest economy.

If you have health insurance, you may think it doesn't matter because someone else is paying the bill. You'd be wrong. This country's exorbitant medical costs mean that we all pay too much for health insurance. Overpriced care also translates into fewer raises for American workers. And to top it off, we're not even getting the best care for our money.

First, be aware that even if you have insurance, it doesn't always fully protect you. Four years ago, Joclyn Krevat, a 32-year-old occupational therapist from New York City, collapsed with a rare heart condition and ended up needing an emergency heart transplant. She had it done at a hospital in her health plan's network, but no one bothered to tell her that her transplant surgeons didn't take her insurance. They billed her $70,000 and sent collection agencies and lawyers after her while she was still home recuperating. In studying the problem,

*Consumer Reports* has heard dozens of similar tales about surprise out-of-network bills. (If you have one, consider sharing it with us).

Second, higher health care costs mean higher health insurance premiums for everyone. It's Health Insurance 101: Insurance is about pooling risk. That's a good thing because it protects you against unexpected costs—but companies have to collect enough in premiums to pay for members' health expenses. The higher the expenses for the risk pool, the higher the premiums for everyone—even if you received little or none of that care.

And if you're wondering why you can't get ahead financially, blame it on the fact that health care is eating your raises. Since 2000, incomes have barely kept up with inflation and insurance premiums have more than doubled. The average employer family health plan that cost companies $6,438 per staffer in 2000 shot up to $16,351 by 2013. That's money that could have gone into your paycheck but didn't because your employer had to spend it on your health insurance instead.

The kicker: We don't get much for our money. In a 2013 Commonwealth Fund study of 11 developed countries' health care systems, the U.S. ranked fifth in quality and worst for infant mortality. We also did the worst job of preventing deaths from treatable conditions, such as strokes, diabetes, high blood pressure, and certain treatable cancers.

No wonder that when *Consumer Reports* surveyed a representative sample of 1,079 American adults, we found considerable distress about high costs. Twelve percent said they had spent more than $5,000 of their own money on medical bills (not counting prescriptions or insurance premiums) in the previous year, and 11 percent said they had medical bills they had trouble paying. Large majorities said they wanted better information about cost and quality of their health care.

# Made-up Prices and a Yen for Brand-name Hospitals

All of which brings us to the big question: Why exactly is our health care so expensive?

Health care works nothing like other market transactions. As a consumer, you are a bystander to the real action, which takes place between providers—hospitals, doctors, labs, drug companies, and device manufacturers—and the private and governmental entities that pay them. Those same providers are also pushing Americans into newer and more expensive treatments, even when there's no evidence they're any better.

"There is no such thing as a legitimate price for anything in health care," says George Halvorson, former chairman of Kaiser Permanente, the giant health maintenance organization based in California. "Prices are made up depending on who the payer is."

When Medicare is paying the bills, prices tend to be lower. That agency is by far the largest single source of revenue for most health care providers, which gives it more leverage to set prices. Private insurance companies and providers, on the other hand, bargain head-to-head over prices, often savagely. (If you see headlines in your area about such-and-such hospital leaving an insurer network, that's what's going on).

In regions with many competing providers, insurers can play them against each other to hold down prices. But where there are few providers, not so much. Providers know that, and are busily consolidating into larger groups to get more bargaining power. In your own community, you may have noticed new outpatient medical clinics sprouting up emblazoned with the name of a local hospital; that is hospitals buying up private medical practices to get more clout with insurers.

But the providers with the most clout are the brand-name medical centers, which hold special cachet for patients and are thus "must have" hospitals for many insurers. "In some markets the prestigious medical institutions can name their price," says Andrea Caballero, program director for Catalyst for Payment Reform, a national nonprofit trying to get a grip on health costs on behalf of large employers. "They may have brand names of high prestige but not necessarily deliver higher-quality care."

There are small but hopeful signs that health costs aren't growing quite as fast as they used to. Medicare's costs are stabilizing, for instance. It's too soon to tell whether that is a permanent trend.

But the "medical industrial complex" continues going for as much gold as it can, as the following examples show all too clearly.

# Outrage No. 1: Why Do Just One Test When You Can Bill for Three?

Americans usually pay for health care by the piece: so much for each office visit, X-ray, outpatient procedure, etc. That approach leads to one thing: waste. Up to 30 percent of the care provided in this country is unnecessary, according to the Congressional Budget Office. "If you have a treatment that requires three CT scans and re-engineer it to require only one, it won't happen because two CT scan places will lose a source of revenue," says George Halvorson of Kaiser Permanente. "Piecework also rewards bad outcomes. It pays a lot if you have a heart attack but very little for preventing it."

Some insurance companies are making headway against overtreatment—which is why *Consumer Reports* has prepared a list of them in collaboration with the National Committee for Quality Assurance (NCQA), a nonprofit quality measurement and accreditation organization. (Read more about health plans that help members avoid unnecessary medical care).

# Outrage No. 2: The $1,000-per-pill Hepatitis Drug

Here's a prime example of big pharma's we-charge-what-we-want syndrome: A new pill for hepatitis C has hit the market that, if taken by everyone who should take it, would cost Americans more per year than all other brand-name drugs combined. No one—not individuals, not private insurers, not Medicare—can do a thing about it. That's because here in the U.S., as long as the drug, Sovaldi, remains under patent, its owner, Gilead Sciences, can charge whatever it wants. At the moment that's $1,000 per pill, or $84,000 to $150,000 for a course of treatment.

"Drug companies charge what the market will bear, and in the United States the market will bear a lot," says Matt Salo, executive director of the National Association of Medicaid Directors, a policy group based in Washington, D.C.

Hepatitis C affects 3.2 million mostly boomer-aged Americans who got it through tainted blood transfusions (no longer a serious risk, thanks to new screening tests) and intravenous drug use. Left untreated, it can lead to liver failure and is the leading reason for liver transplants in the U.S. Older treatments were uncomfortable, took forever, came with unpleasant side effects, and didn't always work. With Sovaldi, you take the pill for a few months; it has a cure rate of about 90 percent in clinical trials.

The industry defends the price on the grounds that it's cheaper than a $500,000 liver transplant. But most people with untreated Hepatitis C never need a transplant; even after 20 years, the savings from not having to treat the disease's worst effects would offset only about 75 percent of Sovaldi's up-front costs, research suggests. Meanwhile, it would add $600 per person to the annual cost of a group health plan.

# Outrage No. 3: Pushing the New and Flashy

One way for hospitals and medical practices to make gobs of money is to push a new, trendy procedure—even if it's no better than an older one. Prime example: prostate cancer surgery. Medical science still has little idea which treatments work best for the disease, or even who really needs to be treated, because many patients have cancer so indolent that they will die of something else long before it kills them.

None of that has stopped medical marketers from persuading hospitals to spend ever larger sums of money on so-called cutting-edge prostate cancer treatments to lure patients away from competitors.

The poster child for the phenomenon is robotic surgery, which your local hospital has probably bragged about.

First introduced for prostate cancer surgery in 2001, the $2 million machine—a collection of laparoscopic instruments operated remotely—went from being used for 6 percent of prostatectomies in 2004 to 83 percent in 2014, despite little evidence that it is better than other types of surgery even though it comes with a higher price tag.

"There's marketing value in a very expensive piece of technology, such as a robot, even if it doesn't work better," says Jeffrey C. Lerner, president of the ECRI Institute, a nonprofit health technology evaluation organization. "Nobody's ever going to put up a billboard about having the best bandage."

# Three Ways You Can Help Rein in Expenses
## 1. Find Out the Real Cost of Your Treatment

More and more insurers are disclosing at least some negotiated prices to members who register with their websites. Take advantage of that feature if your health plan offers it, especially for things you can plan in advance, such as imaging tests. In a recent experiment, people scheduled for CT scans or MRIs were called and told about cheaper alternatives of equal quality; they ended up saving participating insurers an average of $220 per scan—and prompted more expensive providers to cut their prices.

## 2. If You Want the Celeb Doctor, Pay Extra

"Reference pricing" is when an insurer analyzes its past claims to set a reasonable price for a good-quality routine test or procedure and tells its customers that if they want to go to a higher-cost in-network provider, they can—but will be responsible for the difference between the reference price and the provider's price.

CalPERS, which buys health insurance for 1.3 million California state employees and retirees, set a reference price of $30,000 for routine hip and knee replacements after discovering it was paying as much as $110,000 for those procedures. In the first year, savings averaged $7,000 per patient—and several high-cost hospitals suddenly discovered that they, too, could offer $30,000 joint replacements. One caveat: This fix needs to be done carefully to make sure that quality stays high and consumers aren't caught by surprise.

## 3. Seek Out a Smaller Medical Network

You can save about 20 percent on premiums by signing up with a plan that has fewer providers than customary. Providers give the insurer a price break in exchange for fewer competitors. But before signing on, make sure that the network includes the doctors, hospitals, labs, and other services you need within a reasonable distance from your home and that they accept new patients.

# Critical Thinking

1. Why is health care so expensive in the United States?
2. What is your response to the following three facts: $37.50 for a single Tylenol in the hospital, doctor who orders an MRI because he owns the machine, $1,000 for a single pill that treats Hepatitis?
3. What is wrong with the billing system in U.S. health care?

# Internet References

**New American Studies Web**
   https://blogs.commons.georgetown.edu/vkp/
**Social Science Information Gateway**
   http://www.ariadne.ac.uk/issue2/sosig
**Sociology—Study Sociology Online**
   http://edu.learnsoc.org/
**Sociology Web Resources**
   http://www.mhhe.com/socscience/sociology/resources/index.htm
**Sociosite**
   http://www.topsite.com/goto/sociosite.net
**Socioweb**
   http://www.topsite.com/goto/socioweb.com

*Article*                    Prepared by: Kurt Finsterbusch, *University of Maryland, College Park*

# The War on Public Schools

Across the political spectrum, Americans have declared them a failure. But we've underestimated their strengths—and forgotten their purpose.

ERIKA CHRISTAKIS

## Learning Outcomes

*After reading this article, you will be able to:*

- Appreciate the pros and cons of privatization of public schools.
- Analyze your own experience in the public school system.
- Analyze how much the American public school system has changed over the past century.

PUBLIC SCHOOLS HAVE always occupied prime space in the excitable American imagination. For decades, if not centuries, politicians have made hay of their supposed failures and extortions. In 2004, Rod Paige, then George W. Bush's secretary of education, called the country's leading teachers union a "terrorist organization." In his first education speech as president, in 2009, Barack Obama lamented the fact that "despite resources that are unmatched anywhere in the world, we've let our grades slip, our schools crumble, our teacher quality fall short, and other nations outpace us."

President Donald Trump used the occasion of his inaugural address to bemoan the way "beautiful" students had been "deprived of all knowledge" by our nation's cash-guzzling schools. Educators have since recoiled at the Trump administration's budget proposal detailing more than $9 billion in education cuts, including to after-school programs that serve mostly poor children. These cuts came along with increased funding for school-privatization efforts such as vouchers. Our secretary of education, Betsy DeVos, has repeatedly signaled her support for school choice and privatization, as well as her scorn for public schools, describing them as a "dead end" and

claiming that unionized teachers "care more about a system, one that was created in the 1800s, than they care about individual students."

Few people care more about individual students than public-school teachers do, but what's really missing in this dystopian narrative is a hearty helping of reality: 21st-century public schools, with their record numbers of graduates and expanded missions, are nothing close to the cesspools portrayed by political hyperbole. This hyperbole was not invented by Trump or DeVos, but their words and proposals have brought to a boil something that's been simmering for a while—the denigration of our public schools, and a growing neglect of their role as an incubator of citizens.

Americans have in recent decades come to talk about education less as a public good, like a strong military or a noncorrupt judiciary, than as a private consumable. In an address to the Brookings Institution, DeVos described school choice as "a fundamental right." That sounds appealing. Who wouldn't want to deploy their tax dollars with greater specificity? Imagine purchasing a gym membership with funds normally allocated to the upkeep of a park.

My point here is not to debate the effect of school choice on individual outcomes: The evidence is mixed, and subject to cherry-picking on all sides. I am more concerned with how the current discussion has ignored public schools' victories, while also detracting from their civic role. Our public-education system is about much more than personal achievement; it is about preparing people to work together to advance not just themselves but society. Unfortunately, the current debate's focus on individual rights and choices has distracted many politicians and policy makers from a key stakeholder: our nation as a whole. As a result, a cynicism has taken root that suggests there is no hope for public education. This is demonstrably false. It's also dangerous.

THE IDEA THAT popular education might best be achieved privately is nothing new, of course. The Puritans, who saw education as necessary to Christian practice, experimented with the idea, and their experience is telling. In 1642, they passed a law—the first of its kind in North America—requiring that all children in the Commonwealth of Massachusetts receive an education. Puritan legislators assumed, naively, that parents would teach children in their homes; however, many of them proved unable or unwilling to rise to the task. Five years later, the legislators issued a corrective in the form of the Old Deluder Satan Law: "It being one chief project of that old deluder, Satan, to keep men from the knowledge of the Scriptures," the law intoned, "it is therefore ordered … that everie Township [of 100 households or more] in this Jurisdiction" be required to provide a trained teacher and a grammar school, at taxpayer expense.

Almost 400 years later, contempt for our public schools is common place. Americans, and especially Republicans, report that they have lost faith in the system, but notably, nearly three-quarters of parents rate their own child's school highly; it's other people's schools they worry about. Meanwhile, Americans tend to exaggerate our system's former glory. Even in the 1960s, when international science and math tests were first administered, the U.S. was never at the top of the rankings and was often near the bottom.

Not only is the idea that American test scores were once higher a fiction, but in some cases they have actually improved over time, especially among African American students. Since the early 1970s, when the Department of Education began collecting long-term data, average reading and math scores for 9- and 13-year-olds have risen significantly.

These gains have come even as the student body of American public schools has expanded to include students with ever greater challenges. For the first time in recent memory, a majority of U.S. public-school students come from low-income households. The student body includes a larger proportion than ever of students who are still learning to speak English. And it includes many students with disabilities who would have been shut out of public school before passage of the 1975 law now known as the Individuals With Disabilities Education Act, which guaranteed all children a "free appropriate public education."

The fantasy that in some bygone era U.S. test scores were higher has prevented us from acknowledging other possible explanations for America's technological, scientific, and cultural preeminence. In her 2013 book, Reign of Error, Diane Ravitch—an education historian and former federal education official who originally supported but later became a critic of

reforms like No Child Left Behind—cites surprising evidence that a nation's higher position on an international ranking of test scores actually predicted lower per capita GDP decades later, compared with countries whose test scores ranked worse. Other findings complicate the picture, but at a minimum we can say that there is no clear connection between test scores and a nation's economic success. Surely it's reasonable to ask whether some of America's success might derive not from factors measured by standardized tests, but from other attributes of our educational system. U.S. public schools, at their best, have encouraged a unique mixing of diverse people, and produced an exceptionally innovative and industrious citizenry.

Our lost faith in public education has led us to other false conclusions, including the conviction that teachers unions protect "bad apples." Thanks to articles and documentaries such as Waiting for "Superman," most of us have an image seared into our brain of a slew of know-nothing teachers, removed from the classroom after years of sleeping through class, sitting in state-funded "rubber rooms" while continuing to draw hefty salaries. If it weren't for those damned unions, or so the logic goes, we could drain the dregs and hire real teachers. I am a public-school-certified teacher whose own children attended public schools, and I've occasionally entertained these thoughts myself.

But unions are not the bogey man we're looking for. According to "The Myth of Unions' Over protection of Bad Teachers," a well-designed study by Eunice S. Han, an economist at the University of Utah, school districts with strong unions actually do a better job of weeding out bad teachers and retaining good ones than do those with weak unions. This makes sense. If you have to pay more for something, you are more likely to care about its quality; when districts pay higher wages, they have more incentive to employ good teachers (and dispense with bad ones). And indeed, many of the states with the best schools have reached that position in the company of strong unions. We can't say for sure that unions have a positive impact on student outcomes—the evidence is inconclusive. But findings like Han's certainly undermine reformers' claims.

In defending our public schools, I do not mean to say they can't be improved. But if we are serious about advancing them, we need to stop scapegoating unions and take steps to increase and improve the teaching pool. Teacher shortages are leaving many states in dire straits: The national shortfall is projected to exceed 100,000 teachers by next year.

That many top college graduates hesitate to join a profession with low wages is no great surprise. For many years, talented women had few career alternatives to nursing and teaching; this kept teacher quality artificially high. Now that women have more options, if we want to attract strong teachers, we need to pay competitive salaries. As one observer put it, if you cannot find someone to sell you a Lexus for a few dollars, that doesn't mean there is a car shortage.

Oddly, the idea of addressing our supply-and-demand problem the old-fashioned American way, with a market-based approach, has been largely unappealing to otherwise free-market thinkers. And yet raising salaries would have cascading benefits beyond easing the teacher shortage. Because salaries are associated with teacher quality, raising pay would likely improve student outcomes. Massachusetts and Connecticut have attracted capable people to the field with competitive pay, and neither has an overall teacher shortage.

Apart from raising teacher pay, we should expand the use of other strategies to attract talent, such as forgivable tuition loans, service fellowships, hardship pay for the most-challenging settings (an approach that works well in the military and the foreign service), and housing and child-care subsidies for teachers, many of whom can't afford to live in the communities in which they teach. We can also get more serious about de-larding a bureaucracy that critics are right to denounce: American public schools are bloated at the top of the organizational pyramid, with too many administrators and not enough high-quality teachers in the classroom.

WHERE SCHOOLS ARE struggling today, collectively speaking, is less in their transmission of mathematical principles or writing skills, and more in their inculcation of what it means to be an American. The Founding Fathers understood the educational prerequisites on which our democracy was based (having themselves designed it), and they had far grander plans than, say, beating the Soviets to the moon, or ensuring a literate workforce.

Thomas Jefferson, among other historical titans, understood that a functioning democracy required an educated citizenry, and crucially, he saw education as a public good to be included in the "articles of public care," despite his preference for the private sector in most matters. John Adams, another proponent of public schooling, urged, "There should not be a district of one mile square, without a school in it, not founded by a charitable individual, but maintained at the expense of the people themselves."

In the centuries since, the courts have regularly affirmed the special status of public schools as a cornerstone of the American democratic project. In its vigorous defenses of students' civil liberties—to protest the Vietnam War, for example, or not to salute the flag—the Supreme Court has repeatedly held public schools to an especially high standard precisely because they play a unique role in fostering citizens.

This role isn't limited to civics instruction; public schools also provide students with crucial exposure to people of different backgrounds and perspectives. Americans have a closer relationship with the public-school system than with any other shared institution. (Those on the right who disparagingly refer to public schools as "government schools" have obviously never been to a school-board meeting, one of the clearest examples anywhere of direct democracy in action.) Ravitch writes that "one of the greatest glories of the public school was its success in Americanizing immigrants." At their best, public schools did even more than that, integrating both immigrants and American-born students from a range of backgrounds into one citizenry.

At a moment when our media preferences, political affiliations, and cultural tastes seem wider apart than ever, abandoning this amalgamating function is a bona fide threat to our future. And yet we seem to be headed in just that direction. The story of American public education has generally been one of continuing progress, as girls, children of color, and children with disabilities (among others) have redeemed their constitutional right to push through the schoolhouse gate. But in the past few decades, we have allowed schools to grow more segregated, racially and socio economically. (Charter schools, far from a solution to this problem, are even more racially segregated than traditional public schools.)

Simultaneously, we have neglected instruction on democracy. Until the 1960s, U.S. high schools commonly offered three classes to prepare students for their roles as citizens: Government, Civics (which concerned the rights and responsibilities of citizens), and Problems of Democracy (which included discussions of policy issues and current events). Today, schools are more likely to offer a single course. Civics education has fallen out of favor partly as a result of changing political sentiment. Some liberals have come to see instruction in American values—such as freedom of speech and religion, and the idea of a "melting pot"—as reactionary. Some conservatives, meanwhile, have complained of a progressive bias in civics education.

Especially since the passage of No Child Left Behind, the class time devoted to social studies has declined steeply. Most state assessments don't cover civics material, and in too many cases, if it isn't tested, it isn't taught. At the elementary-school level, less than 40 percent of fourth-grade teachers say they regularly emphasize topics related to civics education.

So what happens when we neglect the public purpose of our publicly funded schools? The discussion of vouchers and charter schools, in its focus on individual rights, has failed to take into account American society at large. The costs of abandoning an institution designed to bind, not divide, our citizenry are high.

Already, some experts have noted a conspicuous link between the decline of civics education and young adults' dismal voting rates. Civics knowledge is in an alarming state: Three-quarters of Americans can't identify the three branches of government. Public-opinion polls, meanwhile, show a new tolerance for authoritarianism, and rising levels of anti demo-cratic and illiberal thinking. These views are found all over the ideological map, from President Trump, who recently urged the nation's police officers to rough up criminal suspects, to, iron-ically, the protesters who tried to block DeVos from entering a Washington, D.C., public school in February.

We ignore public schools' civic and integrative functions at our peril. To revive them will require good faith across the political spectrum. Those who are suspicious of public displays of national unity may need to rethink their aversion. When we neglect schools' nation-binding role, it grows hard to explain why we need public schools at all. Liberals must also work to better understand the appeal of school choice, especially for families in poor areas where teacher quality and attrition are serious problems. Conservatives and libertarians, for their part, need to muster more generosity toward the institutions that have educated our workforce and fueled our success for centuries.

The political theorist Benjamin Barber warned in 2004 that "America as a commercial society of individual consumers may survive the destruction of public schooling. America as a dem-ocratic republic cannot." In this era of growing fragmentation, we urgently need a renewed commitment to the idea that public education is a worthy investment, one that pays dividends not only to individual families but to our society as a whole.

## Critical Thinking

1. The American school system is highly criticized. Do you agree with the criticisms?
2. What are the advantages of privatization of public schools?
3. What are the economic interests at play in the privatization debate?

## Internet References

**Charter Schools - RAND Corporation**
https://www.rand.org/topics/charter-schools.html
**New American Studies Web**
www.georgetown.edu/crossroads/asw
**Social Science Information Gateway**
http://sosig.esrc.bris.ac.uk
**Sociology Web Resources**
http://www.mhhe.com/socscience/sociology/resources/index.htm
**Sociology—Study Sociology Online**
http://edu.learnsoc.org
**Sociosite**
http://www.topsite.com/goto/sociosite.net

ERIKA CHRISTAKIS is the author of *The Importance of Being Little: What Young Children Really Need From Grownups.*

*Article*                    Prepared by: Kurt Finsterbusch, *University of Maryland, College Park*

# Protecting Religious Liberty

Has That Become an Elusive Concept?

Bernard G. Prusak

## Learning Outcomes

*After reading this article, you will be able to:*

- Discuss justice from a number of perspectives.
- Discuss the extent that religion can be compatible with justice.
- Present some unresolvable conflicts between religious demands and principles of justice.

During my first year of graduate school, when I was still very wet behind the ears, I had the privilege of interviewing the philosopher John Rawls for *Commonweal* ("Politics, Religion, and the Public Good: An Interview with Philosopher John Rawls," September 25, 1998). The interview focused on Rawls's thinking about what sort of reasons one ought to present in support of laws and policies in a liberal democracy like our own, one characterized by pervasive pluralism in matters of faith and morals. Rawls defended what he called "public reason." According to him, fairness requires citizens in positions of political power to argue in terms that all other citizens can embrace. So it would be unfair—more strongly, unjust—to reject gay marriage, for example, on the basis of Scripture. It would also be unfair either to limit or to extend abortion rights on the basis of Immanuel Kant's philosophy or any other "comprehensive doctrine" (to use Rawls's terminology) that one could not reasonably expect all citizens to embrace. To be clear, Rawls's position wouldn't rule religion out of political discourse: he recognized the important part that religious language and inspiration played in the civil-rights movement, for example. But he insisted that political justifications must be based, at the end of the day, in our common political culture, embodied and articulated by the likes of Jefferson,

Madison, and Lincoln. To fail to justify laws and policies in terms that all citizens can embrace is to fail to observe the duty of civility we have toward one another.

Twenty years later, this argument is beginning to seem a little old-fashioned—as if Rawls, who died in 2002, belongs already to the same near-mythical past as Jefferson and Madison and Lincoln. How quaint his insistence on civility sounds in this tawdry age of ours! Our political culture, such as it is, has slouched from the lurid banality of the Monica Lewinsky scandal to the perpetual scandal of Donald Trump's presidency.

The conversation about religion and politics has also changed over the past twenty years. Though figures like Alabama's Roy Moore still have theocratic ambitions, the growing number of Americans who no longer identify with any religion—a trend hastened, social-science research has found, by the association of religion with reactionary politics—has made those ambitions appear ridiculous. The Evangelical right has been reduced to whispering sweet nothings into the ear of a thrice-married reality-television star who has boasted about groping women; a porn star was paid off to keep her quiet about their affair. Religion is now on the defensive.

Today, our questions about religion and politics are: Can bakers or photographers refuse to provide their services for a gay wedding on free-exercise grounds? Should employers who object on religious grounds to contraceptives or abortion be exempted from having to provide employees health insurance that covers such services? Should Catholic hospitals and physicians be allowed to refuse to perform legal, professionally sanctioned procedures to which they object? May religiously affiliated schools fire a teacher who gets pregnant out of wedlock, or a teacher who gets married to her same-sex partner? In short, why give religion special treatment under the law? Why should religious beliefs warrant accommodation when they conflict with other people's interests?

# Liberalism's Religion

Cécile Laborde, who publishes in French as well as in English, holds the Nuffield Chair in Political Theory at Oxford University. *Liberalism's Religion* is her first big book: though it's not very long, it's a major contribution to its field, likely to displace a lot of other texts from reading lists. It will command attention from political theorists, philosophers, and legal scholars for years to come.

The multiple meanings of the title reflect the book's multiple ambitions. *Liberalism's Religion* has to do with "the concept of religion at the heart of liberalism." Here "liberalism" is understood as the tradition of political thought, dating back to the seventeenth century, committed to toleration of religious differences, individual rights, and state neutrality toward what Rawls called "comprehensive doctrines." Laborde acknowledges that "liberal law is biased toward individualistic, belief-based religions"—that is, toward Protestantism. She also takes seriously the accusation that "liberal regulation of religion amounts . . . to the establishment of an alternative religion"—namely, so-called ethical individualism, a creed famously expressed in Justice Anthony Kennedy's Opinion of the Court in *Planned Parenthood v. Casey* (1992): "At the heart of liberty is the right to define one's own concept of existence, of meaning, of the universe, and of the mystery of human life." Finally, *Liberalism's Religion* insists on and explicates "the crucial point that while religion has a special place in liberal theory, it is not a uniquely special place." In this book religion is "disaggregated," to use Laborde's term. She does not try to address all its features, but only those that deserve civic respect and legal protection. In her words, "it is not sufficient simply to say 'religion is X and Y.' What is required is to identify the specific normative values that the law has reason to protect—values that make X or Y legally salient." Laborde argues that those values also belong to many "nonreligious beliefs, conceptions, and identities," with the upshot that it becomes possible "to treat religious and nonreligious individuals on the same terms, as expressions of ethical and social pluralism."

Here it is important to remember that religion is contested nowadays both from within and from without. From within, there are now so many "religions" in countries like the United States that it is increasingly hard to say what exactly counts as religion, and the demand that the law accommodate all citizens' religious beliefs appears increasingly unrealistic and imprudent. From without, there are now so many people professing no religion that it appears unfair for the law to accommodate religious beliefs in particular. Why should the beliefs of religious people be privileged in this way? Egalitarians may seek to solve this problem in two ways: either by denying that religious citizens should enjoy exemptions from generally applicable laws, or by denying that exemptions should be exclusive to

religious citizens. Brian Leiter goes the first way in *Why Tolerate Religion?* (see William Galston's review in the May 3, 2013 issue). Laborde goes the second way. For her, in a very telling line, "If exemptions are not exclusive to religion . . . then religious exemptions might be permissible."

Laborde's project might remind readers of the philosopher Charles Taylor's polemic in *A Secular Age* (2007) against what he calls "subtraction stories"—stories according to which, when religion crumbles away or is sloughed off, ideals and values that were always there, operating in the background, come to the fore, clear at last to sight. Arguably, a subtraction story is behind fifty years' worth of Supreme Court rulings on conscientious objection to military service. According to this story, what we valued in religious liberty was really liberty of conscience. Now, in this time of growing religious non-affiliation, we can begin valuing liberty of conscience directly, rather than through the proxy of religion; otherwise we privilege the consciences of the religious over the consciences of the nonreligious. In *United States v. Seeger* (1965), the Court focused on whether the objector's belief occupied in his life "a place parallel to that filled by the God of those admittedly qualifying for exemption"; in *Welsh v. United States* (1970), the Court focused on whether the objector's belief was "held with the strength of traditional religious convictions." What mattered now—and had always mattered implicitly—was not that a belief was religious but the intensity with which it was held.

Laborde acknowledges that "the *Seeger-Welsh* jurisprudence has become a point of reference for liberal egalitarian theorists, as the paradigm of accommodation extended from religious to nonreligious moral commitments." But the story she tells is more complicated. Religious liberty, she claims, cannot be redescribed without loss as liberty of conscience, for protecting liberty of conscience does "not protect all religious beliefs and practices, because religion cannot be reduced to conscience." For example, the ingestion of peyote in a Native American ceremony is not an obligation of conscience, but it is nonetheless a religious practice that arguably ought to be protected against generally applicable laws prohibiting the possession and use of hallucinogens.

The book's final two chapters stake out positions on the controversial questions in the news today concerning freedom of association and the boundaries of religious liberty. Laborde holds that "only groups that are voluntary and identificatory have rights to discriminate"—for example, in hiring and firing. An "identificatory" association is one "where individuals identify with the projects and commitments that are at the core of the association's integrity." Take a church, for instance, or a religious school. In Laborde's account, the right of such a voluntary, identificatory association to discriminate with respect to gender or sexuality is based on its "coherence interests": for the association to hang together rather than disintegrate, it must be free to live by its own standards, purposes, and commitments. Concretely, it must be free to hire ministers and teachers who satisfy the relevant criteria—perhaps church doctrine specifies the ministers must be male—and live out the relevant teachings—say, regarding same-sex relationships. What's more, an association like a church or a religious school also has "competence interests": it matters for its coherence that it be recognized as the sole competent authority to interpret its own standards, purposes, and commitments. Concretely, it is not for the state to judge whether a minister or a teacher is a good or bad fit for the association.

To this point, the argument seems unobjectionable. But then Laborde turns to what the law calls places of public accommodation, like bakeries and flower shops, which provide goods and services for the public at large. Masterpiece Cakeshop is the example in today's headlines; its owner's refusal to make a cake for a gay couple's wedding has led to a Supreme Court case. According to Laborde, public accommodations "have no relevant coherence interest that would allow them to refuse to serve all members regardless of race, gender, or sexuality." While the defining commitments of a church or religious school would be imperiled if it did not have a right to discriminate in hiring and firing, Laborde does not believe that having to serve all comers similarly imperils what a public accommodation is all about. So, for example, a Roman Catholic church that was compelled to employ a woman as a priest would run awry of Catholic doctrine and cease to be a Catholic church in good standing with Rome. A bakery compelled to serve all comers, by contrast, does not cease to be a bakery. There is just no sense in claiming it must be free to discriminate on the basis of race, gender, or sexuality lest it be untrue to its function, which is to bake.

That argument seems right, but note that it does not quite reach the point of contention in *Masterpiece Cakeshop* (which Laborde, to be clear, does not discuss). Jack Phillips does not refuse to serve gay persons all baked goods; instead, he refuses to make cakes celebrating gay weddings. Further, while there are no grounds other than racism to oppose participation in an interracial wedding, there are grounds other than homophobia to oppose participation in a same-sex wedding. Opposition to an interracial wedding can only be about the persons being wed; opposition to a same-sex wedding can be about the redefinition of the institution of marriage.

Laborde writes that "as a practice becomes more distant from the core religious practices and activities of the association, it also becomes less relevant to associational coherence," with the upshot that "religious employers cannot discriminate on religious grounds…in relation to employees not doing religious work." This claim also seems right, and it's relevant to the resistance of some Catholic colleges and universities to the formation of part-time faculty unions under the auspices of the National Labor Relations Board. But again, Laborde's argument does not quite reach the point of contention. Catholic colleges and universities like DePaul and Loyola Chicago claim that they should be recognized as having the competence to judge which employees are "doing religious work"; the NLRB claims this competence for itself. This raises the question: Who has the authority to define what counts as "religious work"? Is the question of what counts as religious itself a religious question over which religious associations have sole competence, or should they have to convince governmental bodies like the NLRB? Laborde refers to this type of dispute as a jurisdictional boundary problem—coming soon, it seems likely, to a federal court near you.

Laborde's defense of individual exemptions to generally applicable laws turns not on the rights of conscience, but on the value of integrity, which she defines as "an ideal of congruence between one's ethical commitments and one's actions." In keeping with her egalitarian premises, she argues that "the moral force of individual exemption claims lies…in their importance to individual integrity, not in their advancement of objective or collective goods such as 'religion' or 'tradition.'" In other words, for her, the question to ask is, "What kinds of commitment are so important to people that their integrity would be threatened were they prevented from acting on them?" Integrity-protecting commitments come in two kinds: those that a person feels obligated to observe (for example, a commitment not to participate in war) and those that, while not experienced as obligations, figure saliently in a person's way of life (for example, ingesting peyote in a religious ceremony). Of course, the fact that an integrity-protecting commitment is burdened by a law does not by itself mean that the burden is unfair. According to Laborde, such a law is unfair only when "there seems to be a disproportion between the aims pursued by the law and the burden it inflicts on claimants," or when "minority citizens are unable to combine the pursuit of a core societal opportunity with an [integrity-protecting commitment], whereas the equivalent opportunity set is institutionally available to the majority"—for example, denying Muslims time off from work on Fridays, when Christians enjoy time off on Sundays.

In its favor, Laborde's argument captures the logic of the U.S. Supreme Court's *Seeger-Welsh* jurisprudence while also laying the groundwork for a more capacious interpretation of religious liberty than the one put forward by the U.S. Supreme Court in the notorious case of *Employment Division v. Smith* (1990). According to Justice Antonin Scalia's Opinion of the Court, "generally applicable, religion-neutral laws that have the effect of burdening a particular religious practice need not be justified by a compelling governmental interest." Scalia feared that having to grant exemptions whenever a compelling governmental interest was not at stake "would be courting anarchy." Laborde agrees with Scalia that "religious believers have no presumptive right" to exemptions, but her argument provides principled grounds for granting exemptions in some cases.

Still, there is reason to wonder whether respect for religious liberty can be redescribed as respect for integrity without loss. According to Laborde, what we valued in religious liberty was really personal integrity all along. Now, in this age of religious pluralism and growing religious nonaffiliation, we can just value personal integrity directly, rather than through the proxy of religion. For Madison, however, it was a citizen's relationship to God in conscience—understood, roughly, as the faculty through which a person might hear God's voice and the duties it prescribes to her—that grounded the limitation on the federal government articulated in the First Amendment. As he wrote in his 1785 pamphlet titled "Memorial and Remonstrance against Religious Assessments":

The Religion…of every man must be left to the conviction and conscience of every man; and it is the right of every man to exercise it as these may dictate. This right is in its nature an unalienable right… because what is here a right towards men, is a duty towards the Creator. It is the duty of every man to render to the Creator such homage and such only as he believes to be acceptable to him. This duty is precedent, both in order of time and in degree of obligation, to the claims of Civil Society. Before any man can be considered as a member of Civil Society, he must be considered as a subject of the Governour of the Universe: And if a member of Civil Society, who enters into any subordinate Association, must always do it with a reservation of his duty to the General Authority; much more must every man who becomes a member of any particular Civil Society, do it with a saving of his allegiance to the Universal Sovereign.

In brief, any government that seeks to respect its citizens' natural rights has to recognize limits to its powers. In particular, it must seek to allow each person to practice his or her religion according to the dictates of conscience. This is because, according to Madison, a person is more than a citizen. Each of us has a dimension that transcends the temporal order and that renders us subject to an authority higher than government.

We might wonder, then, whether the claim that political authorities should avoid requiring a person to deny his or her God has the same force when it is translated into the claim that authorities should avoid requiring a person to compromise his or her integrity. It is interesting in this regard that, while in both *Seeger* and *Welsh* the Supreme Court expanded the class of conscientious-objection claims warranting accommodation,

in *Negre v. Larsen* (1971) the Court rejected the claim of a Roman Catholic who objected on faith-based grounds not to war in general, but to the war in Vietnam. Perhaps that decision is exactly what one should expect once religious liberty claims have been reduced to just one among many species of intensely held beliefs. It's hard to see why the mere intensity of a belief should give it priority over the nation's security. Perhaps Laborde's concept of integrity has more weight than that of intensely held belief; maybe "I can't go to war lest my integrity be compromised" is a more powerful argument than "I can't go to war because it's against my intensely held beliefs." But that still doesn't make it as powerful as "I can't go to war lest I violate my duty to God." In Rawls's terms, the appeal to integrity is one that all citizens can understand. Madison's defense of religious liberty, by contrast, is rooted in an increasingly foreign comprehensive doctrine.

# Critical Thinking

1. Does religion reduce freedom or support freedom?

2. Rawls theory of justice as fairness was convincing to an earlier generation but the recent generations are less accepting. Why?

3. Why are some passionate religionists extremely conservative?

# Internet References

**New American Studies Web**
www.georgetown.edu/crossroads/asw

**Social Science Information Gateway**
http://sosig.esrc.bris.ac.uk

**Sociology Web Resources**
http://www.mhhe.com/socscience/sociology/resources/index.htm

**Sociology—Study Sociology Online**
http://edu.learnsoc.org

**Sociosite**
http://www.topsite.com/goto/sociosite.net

**BERNARD G. PRUSAK** is an associate professor of philosophy and director of the McGowan Center for Ethics and Social Responsibility at King's College in Wilkes-Barre, Pennsylvania. His book *Catholic Moral Philosophy in Practice and Theory: An Introduction* was published by Paulist Press in 2016.

# Unit 5

# UNIT

Prepared by: Kurt Finsterbusch, *University of Maryland, College Park*

# Crime, Violence, and Law Enforcement

This unit deals with criminal behavior and its control by the law enforcement system. The fi rst line of defense against crime is the socialization of the young to internalize norms against harmful and illegal behavior. Thus families, schools, religious institutions, and social pressure are the major crime fighters, but they do not do a perfect job, and the police and courts have to handle their failures. Over the last half-century crime has increased, signaling for some commentators a decline in morality. If the power of norms to control criminal behavior diminishes, the role of law enforcement must increase, and that is what has happened.

The societal response to crime has been threefold: Hire more police, build more prisons, and toughen penalties for crimes. These policies by themselves can have only limited success. For example, putting a drug dealer in prison just creates an opportunity for another person to become a drug dealer. Another approach is to give potential criminals alternatives to

crime. The key factor in this approach is a healthy economy that provides many job opportunities for unemployed young men. To some extent, this has happened and has caused the crime rate to drop. Programs that work with inner-city youth might also help, but budget-tight cities are not funding many programs like this. Amid the policy debates there is one thing we can agree upon: Crime has declined significantly in the past two decades (with a slight increase recently) after rising substantially for a half century.

This unit looks at several aspects of crime, law enforcement, and terrorism. It describes many injustices in the criminal justice system such as the tendency for the poor go to jail and rich go free. Too many people are imprisoned and for too long. Many innocent people are convicted. Gun laws are often inappropriate. The Stand Your Ground law has justified murders. Many reforms are needed but are not likely to be enacted given the public mood and the government impasse.

*Article*                     Prepared by: Kurt Finsterbusch, *University of Maryland, College Park*

# Sex Slavery/Trafficking

SOROPTIMIST

## Learning Outcomes

*After reading this article, you will be able to:*

• How much money is involved in human trafficking?

• Who traffics women and girls?

• Who purchases trafficked women and girls?

## What Is Human Trafficking?

A $32 billion annual industry, modern day trafficking is a type of slavery that involves the transport or trade of people for the purpose of work. According to the U.N., about 2.5 million people around the world are ensnared in the web of human trafficking at any given time.

Human trafficking impacts people of all backgrounds, and people are trafficked for a variety of purposes. Men are often trafficked into hard labor jobs, while children are trafficked into labor positions in textile, agriculture, and fishing industries. Women and girls are typically trafficked into the commercial sex industry, that is, prostitution or other forms of sexual exploitation.

Not all slaves are trafficked, but all trafficking victims are victims of slavery. Human trafficking is a particularly cruel type of slavery because it removes the victim from all that is familiar to her, rendering her completely isolated and alone, often unable to speak the language of her captors or fellow victims.

## What Is Sex Slavery/Trafficking?

Sex trafficking or slavery is the exploitation of women and children, within national or across international borders, for the purposes of forced sex work. Commercial sexual exploitation includes pornography, prostitution, and sex trafficking of women and girls and is characterized by the exploitation of a human being in exchange for goods or money. Each year, an estimated 800,000 women and children are trafficked across international borders—though additional numbers of women and girls are trafficked within countries.

Some sex trafficking is highly visible, such as street prostitution. But many trafficking victims remain unseen, operating out of unmarked brothels in unsuspecting—and sometimes suburban—neighborhoods. Sex traffickers may also operate out of a variety of public and private locations, such as massage parlors, spas, and strip clubs.

Adult women make up the largest group of sex trafficking victims, followed by girl children, although a small percentage of men and boys are trafficked into the sex industry as well.

Human trafficking migration patterns tend to flow from East to West, but women may be trafficked from any country to another country at any given time and trafficking victims exist everywhere. Many of the poorest and most unstable countries have the highest incidences of human trafficking, and extreme poverty is a common bond among trafficking victims. Where economic alternatives do not exist, women and girls are more vulnerable to being tricked and coerced into sexual servitude. Increased unemployment and the loss of job security have undermined women's incomes and economic position. A stalled gender wage gap, as well as an increase in women's part-time and informal sector work, pushes women into poorly paid jobs and long-term and hidden unemployment, which leaves women vulnerable to sex traffickers.

## Who Traffics Women and Girls?

Organized crime is largely responsible for the spread of international human trafficking. Sex trafficking—along with its correlative elements, kidnapping, rape, prostitution, and physical abuse—is illegal in nearly every country in the world. However, widespread corruption and greed make it possible for sex trafficking to quickly and easily proliferate. Though national and international institutions may attempt to regulate and enforce antitrafficking legislation, local governments and police forces may in fact be participating in sex trafficking rings.

Why do traffickers traffic? Because sex trafficking can be extremely lucrative, especially in areas where opportunities for education and legitimate employment may be limited. According to the United Nations Office on Drugs and Crime, the greatest numbers of traffickers are from Asia, followed by Central and Southeastern Europe, and Western Europe. Crime groups involved in the sex trafficking of women and girls are also often involved in the transnational trafficking of drugs and firearms and frequently use violence as a means of carrying out their activities.

One overriding factor in the proliferation of trafficking is the fundamental belief that the lives of women and girls are expendable. In societies, where women and girls are undervalued or not valued at all, women are at greater risk for being abused, trafficked, and coerced into sex slavery. If women experienced improved economic and social status, trafficking would in large part be eradicated.

## How Are Women Trafficked?

Women and girls are ensnared in sex trafficking in a variety of ways. Some are lured with offers of legitimate and legal work as shop assistants or waitresses. Others are promised marriage, educational opportunities, and a better life. Still others are sold into trafficking by boyfriends, friends, neighbors, or even parents.

Trafficking victims often pass among multiple traffickers, moving further and further from their home countries. Women often travel through multiple countries before ending at their final destination. For example, a woman from the Ukraine may be sold to a human trafficker in Turkey, who then passes her on to a trafficker in Thailand. Along the way she becomes confused and disoriented.

Typically, once in the custody of traffickers, a victim's passport and official papers are confiscated and held. Victims are told they are in the destination country illegally, which increases victims' dependence on their traffickers. Victims are often kept in captivity and also trapped into debt bondage, whereby they are obliged to pay back large recruitment and transportation fees before being released from their traffickers. Many victims report being charged additional fines or fees while under bondage, requiring them to work longer to pay off their debts.

Human trafficking victims experience various stages of degradation and physical and psychological torture. Victims are often deprived of food and sleep, are unable to move about freely, and are physically tortured. In order to keep women captive, victims are told their families and their children will be harmed or murdered if they (the women) try to escape or tell anyone about their situation. Because victims rarely understand the culture and language of the country into which they have been trafficked, they experience another layer of psychological stress and frustration.

Often, before servicing clients, women are forcibly raped by the traffickers themselves, in order to initiate the cycle of abuse and degradation. Some women are drugged in order to prevent them from escaping. Once "broken in," sex trafficked victims can service up to 30 men a day, and are vulnerable to sexually transmitted diseases (STDs), HIV infection, and unwanted pregnancy.

## Who Purchases Trafficked Women and Girls?

Many believe that sex trafficking is something that occurs "somewhere else." However, many of the biggest trafficking consumers are developed nations, and men from all sectors of society support the trafficking industry. There is no one profile that encapsulates the "typical" client. Rather, men who purchase trafficked women are both rich and poor, Eastern and Western. Many are married and have children, and in some cases, as was reported in one New York Times article, men have sex with trafficked girls in lieu of abusing their own young children.

One reason for the proliferation of sex trafficking is because in many parts of the world there is little to no perceived stigma to purchasing sexual favors for money, and prostitution is viewed as a victimless crime. Because women are culturally and socially devalued in so many societies, there is little conflict with the purchasing of women and girls for sexual services. Further, few realize the explicit connection between the commercial sex trade, and the trafficking of women and girls, and the illegal slave trade. In western society in particular, there is a commonly held perception that women choose to enter into the commercial sex trade. However, for the majority of women in the sex trade, and specifically in the case of trafficked women and girls who are coerced or forced into servitude, this is simply not the case.

In addition, sex tourism—that is, the practice of traveling or vacationing for the purpose of having sex—is a billion dollar industry that further encourages the sexual exploitation of women and girls. Many sex tours explicitly feature young girls. The tours are marketed specifically to pedophiles who prey on young children, and men who believe that having sex with virgins or young girls will cure STDs. Often, these men spread HIV and other STDs to their young victims, creating localized disease epidemics.

# What Is the Impact of Sex Trafficking?

Trafficking has a harrowing effect on the mental, emotional, and physical well-being of the women and girls ensnared in its web. Beyond the physical abuse, trafficked women suffer extreme emotional stress, including shame, grief, fear, distrust, and suicidal thoughts. Victims often experience post-traumatic stress disorder, and with that, acute anxiety, depression, and insomnia. Many victims turn to drugs and alcohol to numb the pain.

Sex trafficking promotes societal breakdown by removing women and girls from their families and communities. Trafficking fuels organized crime groups that usually participate in many other illegal activities, including drug and weapons trafficking and money laundering. It negatively impacts local and national labor markets, due to the loss of human resources. Sex trafficking burdens public health systems. And trafficking erodes government authority, encourages widespread corruption, and threatens the security of vulnerable populations.

# What Is Soroptimist Doing to Stop Human Trafficking?

As an organization of business and professional women working to improve the lives of women and girls and local communities throughout the world, Soroptimist undertakes a number of projects that directly and indirectly help potential trafficking victims. In late 2007, the organization launched a major campaign aimed at raising awareness about the devastating practice of sex trafficking. Soroptimist club members place the cards about sex trafficking in highly visible locations including police stations, women's centers, hospitals, legal aid societies, and so on. In addition, the organization is calling on the public to do its part to end this heinous practice.

Soroptimist undertakes a number of other projects that directly and indirectly help victims and potential victims. These projects provide direct aid to women and girls—giving women economic tools and skills to achieve financial empowerment and independence:

The Live Your Dream Awards program—Soroptimist's major project—provides women who are heads of households with the resources they need to improve their education, skills, and employment prospects. By helping women to receive skill

and resource training, Soroptimist provides trafficking and potential trafficking victims with economic options.

The Soroptimist Club Grants for Women and Girls program provides Soroptimist clubs with cash grants for innovative projects benefiting women and girls. Many clubs undertake projects that directly and indirectly benefit trafficking victims: a Soroptimist club in the Philippines supports a shelter for abused women and girls escaping from sex trafficking; a club in California held a conference in support of the Western Regional Task Force to Stop Human Trafficking and a club in Chicago has held several educational events related to trafficking.

Soroptimist presents Human Trafficking Facts that Making a Difference for Women Award program honors women who work to improve the lives of women and girls. Kathryn Xian is a recent recipient. In 2004, she led a grassroots campaign against a local tour company offering Asian sex tours. She also testified at a Hawaii State House of Representatives hearing on trafficking. The hearings resulted in the passage of Act 82, which makes "promoting travel for prostitution" a Class C felony violation. Act 82 now serves as model legislation for other states. Soroptimist [strives to present] Human Trafficking Facts that make a difference in women's lives worldwide.

Soroptimist's Disaster Relief Fund provides financial assistance to regions affected by natural disasters or acts of war, with special attention paid to services benefiting women and girls. Women and girls affected by disasters are often vulnerable to traffickers.

## Critical Thinking

1. Understand the role of deception in many human trafficking cases.
2. How the human trafficking system normally operates.
3. Understand how sex trafficking affects individuals and society.

## Internet References

**Sociology—Study Sociology Online**
http://edu.learnsoc.org/
**Sociology Web Resources**
http://www.mhhe.com/socscience/sociology/resources/index.htm
**Sociosite**
http://www.topsite.com/goto/sociosite.net
**Socioweb**
http://www.topsite.com/goto/socioweb.com

*Article*                     Prepared by: Kurt Finsterbusch, *University of Maryland, College Park*

# Getting Tough on Devastating Corporate Crime

RALPH NADER

## Learning Outcomes

*After reading this article, you will be able to:*

- Understand how white-collar criminals are seldom punished for their crimes.

- Know that America is tough on crime but not white-collar crime.

- Corporate power affects laws and law enforcement and protects white-collar criminals.

Politicians looking to bolster their appeal to voters like to talk about being "tough on crime." They think this creates a winning public image. And why wouldn't it? Anyone who has ever seen an old western knows that the bandits in the black hats are bad and the lawmen in the white hats are good. Consequently, many elected officials, desperate to be perceived as White-hatters, carry the "tough on crime" banner. A result is the United States now has more incarcerated people than any other country in the world, including China and Russia. Imagine—over 2 million Americans are currently serving time in prison.

Yet despite all the tough talk from elected officials, a corporate crime wave has long swept our nation, draining people's hard-earned savings and severely harming the health and safety of millions more. The pinstripe-suit wearing perpetrators of this spree are, far more often then not, getting away scot-free. Ironically, it's many of the same politicians who say they are "tough on crime" that are collecting millions of dollars in campaign money from the biggest crooks in America. A smart politician looking to win a campaign would never knowingly accept cash from street thugs, muggers, and thieves. But corporate thugs, corporate muggers, and corporate thieves? No problem! When it comes to corporate crime, where are the heroes in the white hats?

*2.* The corporate crime wave is a result of decades of concentrated effort by big business and its lobbyists to weaken and dismantle the policing agencies responsible for keeping watch over them—a tactic that has been cleverly dubbed "deregulation," a term that effectively sidesteps any connotation of blatant wrongdoing. (See the new book *Freedom to Harm* by Thomas O. McGarity.)

It was the effects of wild "deregulation" that led to the global financial collapse in 2008 and its catastrophic effect on the world economy. In 2011, Charles Ferguson, director of the documentary film *Inside Job*, took the stage to accept his Academy Award and said: "Three years after a horrific financial crisis caused by massive fraud, not a single financial executive has gone to jail, and that's wrong." It's now two years later, and relatively nothing has changed. By comparison, in the savings and loan crisis 33 years ago, hundreds of S&L officials were convicted and sent to jail.

Grant, JPMorgan Chase and its CEO Jamie Dimon are currently in the media spotlight for their questionable dealings, resulting in billions of dollars in easily absorbed losses for the bank, yet none of its executives have been punished or charged with a crime and Dimon remains in his lofty, lucrative position. It's just another chapter in the sordid tale of big banks receiving a slap on the wrist for their excesses. The attorney General of the United States, Eric Holder, has publicly admitted that the enormous size of financial institutions has made them too difficult to prosecute. Even conservative columnist George Will wants the big banks broken up.

Once again, where are the heroes in the white hats? One of the primary issues in presenting the seriousness of the corporate crime wave is the perceived lack of physical danger from the public—after all; corporate criminals do not rob you at knifepoint in a dark alley. But corporate crime does take a physical toll. Roughly 60,000 Americans die every year from workplace-related diseases and injuries, hundreds of thousands more from medical malpractice or hospital-induced infections, tens of thousands more from air pollution and from dangerous pharmaceuticals—much of which is a direct result of corporate wrongdoing and could be prevented.

About 400,000 Americans die each year as a result of smoking-related illness, thanks to the tobacco industry, which for years covered up the harmful effects of its product and hooked youngsters with deliberate marketing. In comparison to the nearly 15,000 yearly homicide deaths in the United States, the corporate death toll is sky high.

One of the most important tools in battling corporate crime and informing the public about its long ranging and harmful effects would be the creation of comprehensive corporate crime database. Such a database, run by the Justice Department, would compile detailed statistics and data on corporate crime, searchable by name of corporation and crime committed, and produce an annual report. Such a database would make information on corporate crime easily available to both law enforcement and the media and would place the issue of patterns and costs of corporate crime on the table for national discourse.

So far, all attempts to create such a public record of corporate crime have been met with little enthusiasm or action from the major political parties and successive Attorneys General, including the current AG Eric Holder. In late 2010, as Chair of the House Judiciary Committee, and again in 2011, Rep. John Conyers (D-Mich.) introduced The Corporate Crime Database Act that aimed to establish such a database. (Alongside it, Conyers also introduced the Dangerous Products Warning Act, which would make it a crime for a corporate official to knowingly place a dangerous product into the stream of commerce.) Neither bill gained any traction at all in Congress.

Further steps need to be taken as well. There should be more funding for the Justice Department's tiny corporate crime division, so that they have the prosecutorial tools and resources to adequately go after violators. Congress needs to take steps so that companies that commit corporate crime are not on the federal dole—taxpayer money should never be used to buy goods and services from corporate criminals. It's time to crack down on corporate tax avoidance—a worker on the minimum wage should not be paying more in sheer federal tax dollars than a large, very profitable corporation like General Electric. Going further, shareholders should have the final say in corporate governance, with the right to approve major business decisions and executive compensation—similar to the referendum recently passed in Switzerland. After all, it's the shareholders—not the executives—who ultimately pay the fines when wrongdoing is discovered.

Most importantly, the obsolete and weak federal corporate crime laws need to be upgraded for the times, toughened and clearly defined. Congress and President Obama have to seek law and order for crime in the suites. For rampant, corporate crime is going to continue unless we start punishing and deterring these violations that devastate so many innocent people.

## Critical Thinking

1. Would you say that producing and promoting cigarettes is a crime?
2. What kind of criminals give campaign contributions?
3. Are the evils in the criminal justice system likely to be fixed?

## Internet References

**Sociology—Study Sociology Online**
http://edu.learnsoc.org/
**Sociology Web Resources**
http://www.mhhe.com/socscience/sociology/resources/index.htm
**Sociosite**
http://www.topsite.com/goto/sociosite.net
**Socioweb**
http://www.topsite.com/goto/socioweb.com
**White-collar Crime**
https://www.nytimes.com/column/white-collar-watch

# Rough Justice

How America became over-policed.

Mychal Denzel Smith

## Learning Outcomes

*After reading this article, you will be able to:*

- Understand why the police are seen as more virtuous than they may be.

- Discuss how the shooting of Michael Brown in 2016 has greatly affected the public view of the police.

- Comment on the assertion that Americans largely revere police, who are endowed with the authority to use violence in defense of the people against the "bad guys."

IN POP CULTURE, representations of police have tended with few exceptions to start with the vision of a righteous force on the side of the people. In the 1950s, *Dragnet* showed Sergeant Joe Friday solving crimes with a cool professionalism. In the ongoing *Law & Order* franchise, detectives often trample civil liberties in pursuit of New York City's most vile criminals. Any violation of rights that occurs in the course of this work results only from the relentless pursuit of truth and justice. "Hollywood's police stories," the film critic Alyssa Rosenberg has written, "have reinforced myths about cops and the work of policing."

In the early 2000s, *The Wire* made itself more compelling than any other police drama by assuming that policing—not just the people who do the job but also the institutional demands of the job—is flawed. Examining systems—schools, government, media, and, above all, law enforcement—and their impact on a decaying city, even as it captured compelling characters and told human stories, *The Wire* made a major innovation by putting police at the center of the show without assuming they were heroes. "If you're gonna be authentic, you've gotta be authentic," the actor Wendell Pierce, who played the detective

Bunk Moreland, told an audience at Columbia University in 2016. This commitment, especially to portraying the shortcomings of the police, won fans among policing's fiercest critics.

Yet there was one aspect of *The Wire*'s depiction of police that I always hoped was fabricated. Several times during the show someone is referred to as "natural police." It is meant as the highest form of praise: The characters Lester Freamon and Jimmy McNulty, portrayed as detective-work savants, possess an innate curiosity that helps with complicated problem-solving, as well as a tenacious relationship to truth-finding, and an easy way with people. If this is what it is to be "natural police," we are back at the idea that police are inherently virtuous, even as the show constantly dug into the ways in which they were not. Calling someone "natural police" implies that policing is itself natural, and necessary, when it is anything but.

**THE FIRST MODERN** police force—the London Metropolitan Police—was established by Sir Robert Peel in 1829. He developed his ideas about law and order, Alex S. Vitale writes in his book *The End of Policing*, when he was "managing the British colonial occupation of Ireland and seeking new forms of social control . . . in the face of growing insurrections, riots, and political uprisings." The "Peace Preservation Force" was meant to serve as a less expensive alternative to the British army, which had previously been tasked with quelling Irish resistance. Appointed home secretary in 1822, Vitale writes, Peel would run the London Metropolitan Police along the same lines. Although the group claimed political neutrality, its main functions were "to protect property, quell riots, put down strikes and other industrial actions, and produce a disciplined industrial work force."

Boston adopted the London model in 1838, and New York established a formal police force in 1844. (This, it would seem, is what Attorney General Jeff Sessions was referring to when he invoked the "Anglo-American heritage of law enforcement.")

But well before then, cities in the southern United States, such as New Orleans, Savannah, and Charleston, "had paid full-time officers who wore uniforms, were accountable to local civilian officials, and were connected to a broader criminal justice system," Vitale writes. These police officers were charged with preventing slave revolts. They had the authority to go onto private property to make sure enslaved people were not harboring weapons or conducting meetings, and they enforced laws against black literacy.

The motto "to protect and to serve"—adopted by the Los Angeles Police Department in 1955 and later used by others around the country—has been a highly effective public relations tool for the police, as it obscures the main function of their work, which since its inception has been to act in an adversarial manner toward the wider community. "Police often think of themselves as soldiers in a battle with the public," Vitale writes, "rather than guardians of public safety." This has held true through the last century and up to the present: in the Memorial Day Massacre of 1937, in which the Chicago police killed ten protesters during a steelworkers' strike; in the raid of the Stonewall Inn in 1969; in the killing of Stephon Clark, a 22-year-old black man whom the Sacramento police shot at 20 times on March 18, 2018, in his grandmother's backyard. No matter what other responsibilities police have assumed, they have consistently inflicted violence on the most marginalized people in society and maintained the economic, political, and social dominance of the ruling class.

Vitale's book does not give a comprehensive history of the police but rather examines the implications of that history for American police today. Only after the killing of Michael Brown in Ferguson, Missouri, in 2014, did police reform became one of the most pressing and hotly debated domestic political issues in the country. Even that debate started, like all those Hollywood narratives, around a faulty assumption that police are essential to safe and secure communities. "Understand, our police officers put their lives on the line for us every single day," President Obama said after a grand jury decided not to bring charges against Darren Wilson, the officer who killed Michael Brown. "They've got a tough job to do to maintain public safety and hold accountable those who break the law."

Critiques of police violence are often tempered by assertions that the police provide a necessary peacekeeping force to guard against crime and ensure that criminals are brought to justice. In reality, the police in Ferguson actually operated as an armed collection agency: They targeted black citizens at traffic stops and imposed fines that became an integral part of the city's budget. When residents protested police violence, they were met with tanks, tear gas, and arrests. The police, as James Baldwin once put it, are "simply the hired enemies of this population."

**AND YET, AMERICANS** have made police the primary problem-solving institution in our society. When we profess a moral objection to something, say sex work or drug use, we criminalize it and charge the police with stamping it out. When we fail to care for people's basic needs, and more and more people become homeless, we criminalize their means of survival and suggest the police "clean up the streets." When we cut resources for mental health care, the only people left to respond to a crisis are the police, and they tend to use the means they have been most proficiently trained to use—violence—as their first response.

Americans largely revere police, who are endowed with the authority to use violence in defense of the people against the "bad guys." *Which* Americans revere the police depends on which Americans are viewed as the "bad guys" and are therefore subject to that violence. Perhaps the "bad guy" is Arab (and therefore a terrorist), or Latinx (and therefore illegal), or a "lone wolf" (read: white) gunman who fires an automatic weapon into a crowd of people. As the past few years have shown, the "bad guys" are often presumed to be black. Although black people make up only 13 percent of the population, 31 percent of people killed by police in 2012 were black. That figure, which dropped to 25 percent in 2017, remains disproportionate. But these well-publicized injustices have not dented the general population's confidence in police—which remains highest among white people.

One of the hallmarks of Donald Trump's political rise has been his ability to tap into a persistent sense that only the police can protect the population from any number of threats, and that their most violent methods are the most effective ones. He famously began his presidential campaign by claiming that Mexico was sending drugs, crime, and rapists over the southern border, dredging up racist tropes that further inflamed white Americans' sense of insecurity. Very early into his presidency, he acted on his promise to ban Muslims from entering the country, playing to the post–September 11 fear of the Muslim terrorist—even though there exists no evidence that Muslims are particularly likely to commit such devastatingly violent acts.

In speeches during the past year, Trump has actively encouraged police violence. In an address delivered before law enforcement officers at Suffolk County Community College in Brentwood, Long Island, he said: "You see these thugs being thrown into the back of a paddy wagon—you just see them thrown in, rough—I said, please don't be too nice. Like when you guys put somebody in the car and you're protecting their head, you know, the way you put their hand over? Like, don't hit their head, and they've just killed somebody—don't hit their head. I said, you can take the hand away, OK?" In a later speech, in which he talked about eradicating the MS-13 street gang, he celebrated an increase of military-grade weaponry being sent to local police forces.

Most perceived threats to Americans' safety—urban gun violence, foreign terrorist attacks, immigrant crime waves—result, in fact, from American policies or are created wholly out of our imaginations. "Having an enemy is important not only to define our identity but also to provide us with an obstacle against which to measure our system of values, and, in seeking to overcome it, to demonstrate our own worth," Umberto Eco wrote in a 2009 essay. "So when there is no enemy, we have to invent one."

**IN AMERICA, WE** have created many enemies, and it is their creation that Elaine Tyler May takes up in her book *Fortress America: How We Embraced Fear and Abandoned Democracy.* The years immediately following World War II are her starting point, since she identifies this as the moment when "fear increased far out of proportion to any real threat" in the United States. From the advent of the Cold War, with its concerns over "nuclear attack from abroad and communist subversion at home," to a focus in the 1960s and '70s on "other presumed dangers, especially crime and social unrest," she traces how a growing preoccupation with vigilance and safety shaped American culture and prompted millions of people to invest in "security measures that did not make them any safer."

One such example is bomb shelters. The bombing of Pearl Harbor had shaken Americans' confidence in the country's natural defense system—the oceans to its east and west—and as both the United States and the Soviet Union increased their nuclear capability, the threat of an attack at home loomed large. "For our own protection," California Governor Earl Warren said in 1951, "all Californians must realize, and realize quickly, that the danger is here, the task of preparation is great, and the time may be shorter than we think." With the federal government unable to offer much in the way of security, people began constructing amateur bunkers, turning to their own backyards for a sense of protection. Of course these shelters would have been insufficient in the event of a nuclear strike, but that didn't stop a government body endorsing them.

Not all families, however, were able to construct these shelters. Only suburban dwellers had the means or the space, and only white families were suburban families at this time, as redlining practices in housing ensured no black person was able to purchase one of these suburban homes. "By promoting suburban homes as essential for civil defense," May writes, "the government underscored that the white middle-class nuclear family represented not only the 'normal' American family, but also the family most deserving of protection from external and internal threats." Even antagonism toward the Soviet Union served to reinforce black people's status as second-class citizens within the states.

The fear of communism, meanwhile, contributed to the impoverishment of urban areas. From the 1940s, city policymakers and real estate agents found common ground, both campaigning against funding for public housing in urban areas,

the former dismissing it as socialism, while the latter stood to lose profits. In fact, in Los Angeles, "a 1952 ordinance against 'socialist projects' virtually outlawed public housing." As white flight diverted tax dollars to the suburbs, municipalities saw their budgets shrink and struggled to provide maintenance and improvement in urban areas. The draining of resources from cities, where largely black populations were residing, brought the unsurprising effect of an increase in violent crime. This, in turn, led to social unrest and what some would call riots but are perhaps more accurately described as rebellions.

Instead of attracting policy solutions, American cities became the focus of more fear. A 1961 headline in the *Los Angeles Examiner* even integrated rising crime into larger Cold War anxieties, warning that teen violence was "as bad as [the] h-bomb." In his bid for the presidency in 1968, Alabama Governor George Wallace promised to "help make it possible for you and your families to walk the streets of our cities in safety." Politicians like Sam Yorty in Los Angeles and Frank Rizzo in Philadelphia ran for office on racist ideas around crime and promises to restore "law and order." And law and order, we know, meant only more policing and more police violence.

**AS THE TITLE** of Vitale's book suggests, he proposes the "end of policing," or rather the end of the way the United States currently does policing. At times he makes gestures toward abolishing the police altogether, but ultimately he does not embrace the idea. "Policing needs to be reformed," he says instead. "The culture of the police must be changed so that it is no longer obsessed with the use of threats and violence to control the poor and socially marginal." Yet, he adds, "as long as the basic mission of police remains unchanged, none of these reforms will be achievable."

While most of the book is dedicated to describing the consequences of over-policing, Vitale does suggest alternatives to the current order. Many of the solutions would involve the decriminalization or legalization of what are now nonviolent crimes, such as sex work and the possession and sale of drugs. Because economic distress lies at the root of many forms of violence, he also recommends rerouting resources toward programs that would eliminate poverty, joblessness, and homelessness—a vision similar to the platform laid out by the Movement for Black Lives and also adopted by the Democratic Socialists of America. Vitale proposes that "trained civilian responders should be the default preference" for responding to situations in which people who suffer from mental illnesses have a breakdown that potentially poses a threat to others—and he advocates for a significant public investment in mental health care. In cases of violent crime, Vitale favors restorative justice practices that move away from punitive measures and toward those "that demand that people take meaningful responsibility for their actions and work to change them."

These are the kinds of societal reforms that could make America less dependent on police. To get there would require a shift in public opinion and a marshaling of the political will. As a country, we would have to decide once and for all that the harm police do is too great a price for the limited protection they promise. We would have to recognize the root causes of the problems we have been deploying police to address, and instead of increasing the number of armed officers and the quantity of deadly weapons at their disposal, we would need to direct our attention toward closing the gap in various forms of inequality.

"Everyone wants to live in safe communities," Vitale writes, "but when individuals and communities look to the police to solve their problems they are in essence mobilizing the machinery of their own oppression." Unless Americans can reconceptualize safety, taking away its racist connotations and recognizing that we are safer not with more guns and violence but with adequate food, clothing, housing, education, health care, jobs, and income for all, we are doomed to continue calling the police for rescue from every conceivable threat, real or imagined. The myth of their goodness will feed the delusion of our security. We will create a sense of the natural in which they fit right in. We already have.

# Critical Thinking

1. What is the proper role of the police?
2. How do you evaluate the statement that the police "have consistently inflicted violence on the most marginalized people in society and maintained the economic, political, and social dominance of the ruling class"?
3. Where does democracy come into police work?

# Internet References

**New American Studies Web**
www.georgetown.edu/crossroads/asw

**Prison Reform - RAND Corporation**
https://www.rand.org/topics/prison-reform.html

**Social Science Information Gateway**
http://sosig.esrc.bris.ac.uk

**Sociology Web Resources**
http://www.mhhe.com/socscience/sociology/resources/index.htm

**Sociology—Study Sociology Online**
http://edu.learnsoc.org

**Sociosite**
http://www.topsite.com/goto/sociosite.net

*Article* Prepared by: Kurt Finsterbusch, *University of Maryland, College Park*

# Public Safety, Public Justice

First, we must acknowledge previous failure; and then we must go on to change our criminal justice philosophy
and the relevant laws to reflect common sense and current worldwide knowledge and experience.

Daniel Rose

## Learning Outcomes

*After reading this article, you will be able to:*

- Describe the ideal law enforcement system and compare it
  to the American system.
- Compare American law enforcement to law enforcement in
  other developed nations.
- Explain why "The Punishment Imperative" is a social disaster for the lower class and the economy.

The term "crisis" is represented in written Chinese by the
characters for "danger" and "opportunity." This accurately describes the state of tension between America's
racial and ethnic minorities and the police, as well as between
our criminal justice system and a growing portion of the American public. The "danger" from destructive action stimulated by
irresponsible demagogues is clear; the "opportunity" for constructive and positive action on legitimate civilian grievances is
also. Sadly, the latter gets polemic but little well-reasoned and
constructive thought.

Healing social rifts, diminishing tensions and increasing confidence in those who legally control violence in our society are
national priorities, and we must take the long view. Yes, we must
respect our police and look to them for protection; and yes, police
practices—lawful and constitutional—should merit respect. And
we clearly need: A) more accountable and effective leadership
in our courts, prisons and police departments and more accountability for the few "bad eggs" in uniform; B) more effective use
of prisoners' time during incarceration, including basic education
and vocational training; and C) much improvement in our scan-
dalously over-crowded and decrepit prisons.

But 40 years of criminal justice abuses must also be faced.

When it comes to incarceration, America has an unenviable
record, with just 5% of the world's population but nearly 25%
of the world's prisoners. Our prisoner recidivism rates are mul-
tiples of those of all other developed nations, and our death penalties for adults and life imprisonment for juveniles are at rates
unheard of in other advanced countries. Many knowledgeable
observers regard the U.S. criminal justice system as a national
disgrace crying out for reform.

In addition, African-American imprisonment rates are six
times that of Caucasians, while former Black "stop and frisk"
rates in New York were indefensibly high. The statistics on
Black/police interactions are heartbreaking; these problems
also can no longer be ignored.

America's surging mass incarceration rates and huge black/
white imprisonment disparities began in the 1960's, when
increased drug use and open disrespect for the police accompanied youthful political dissent and social upheaval.

In 1964, Presidential candidate Barry Goldwater announced,
"The abuse of law and order in this country is going to be
an issue; at least I am going to make it one." In 1971, President Nixon declared a "War on Drugs." The number of people behind bars for non-violent drug offenses increased
from 50,000 in 1960 to over 400,000 in 1997. Nationwide,
the prison population skyrocketed eightfold since 1970 to
2.4 million today.

"Doubling the conviction rate in this country will do more
to cure crime in America than quadrupling the funds for Hubert
Humphrey's war on poverty," declared President Nixon, inau-
gurating a national period of severe mandatory sentences, zero
tolerance, longer and harsher prison sentences and curtailment
of rehabilitation services for prisoners. The infamous Rockefeller drug laws were introduced in 1973.

"Getting tough on crime" was bi-partisan. Jimmy Carter (formerly Governor of Georgia, one of the most repressive states in the nation) was an advocate. Bill Clinton pushed the Violent Crime Control and Law Enforcement Act of 1994, which stimulated the largest all-time expansion of imprisonment.

With fervor similar to that which accompanied alcoholic Prohibition (1920–1933), to reduce crime, America embarked on what has been called "The Punishment Imperative," now widely acknowledged to be a social disaster for the poor and uneducated and an annual $50 billion economic fiasco for state and city governments.

Where do we go from here? First, we must acknowledge previous failure; and then we must go on to change our criminal justice philosophy and the relevant laws to reflect common sense and current worldwide knowledge and experience.

As have all other advanced countries, we must replace punishment and isolation with crime prevention and prisoner rehabilitation as our criminal justice goals for protecting our society, with incarceration a tool to be used appropriately. And we must understand the relationship to crime of illiteracy and lack of basic education, mental health problems and lack of employment, along with gun laws that make our public the world's most armed.

Thoughtful discussion by an engaged public and calls for action should focus on:

## Youthful Offenders
Non-violent youthful first offenders should not be incarcerated in cells with hardened criminals, where they are raped or forced to join gangs for protection. Incarcerated in separate facilities and protected from sexual abuse by inmates and prison staff, they should be tested for their ability to read, write and count; if deficient, they should be kept in remedial class until they learn. Ideally, they should also be given vocational training so on release they can earn a living. The possibilities of earlier parole for "good performance" should be explored.

## The Mentally Disabled
Over half of those in U.S. prisons and jails have mental health problems, many of them serious. An estimated 15% should be in mental hospitals, or when released, not permitted to carry guns (and assassinate New York policemen).

## Former Prisoners
Those who are released after prison should be prepared and encouraged to return to normal civilian life, without the severe limitation, restrictions and handicaps that only America requires for former inmates. Today, former prisoners are denied

Pell grants for education, access to public housing, the right to vote, even the possibility of enlisting in the armed forces, and their prior records make future employment difficult. Unlike other countries, we unwittingly encourage them to return to a life of crime.

## Hardened Criminals
Repeat career criminals who have demonstrated their inability to take part in normal society should be isolated in prison, for our benefit if not for theirs.

## Supervision of Police and Prisons
Armed and violent criminals are a menace to our society and a life-threatening challenge to police who must deal with them. No one should underestimate the courage and heroism of those who, for our protection, put themselves in harm's way. But there are ground rules.

"The deep-seated culture of violence directed against adolescents" (reported by the U.S. Attorney about New York's Rikers Island), the vicious and unprovoked beatings of prisoners by gangs of guards in Los Angeles County jails, (F.B.I. reports describe the level of violence and brutality there as "astonishing"); New York's "stop and frisk" practices, which until recently stopped young Black and Hispanic men without provocation, demanded they empty their pockets and, if marijuana was found, charged them with the serious crime of "public display of narcotics"—all are examples of abusive police power that must be examined, reported, reconsidered and reformed.

## Police and the Community
It is in everyone's best interests to have a comfortable working relationship between the police and the community—based on mutual understanding, trust and respect. Lack of public safety on inner city streets and in schools—and attention to the horrendously high rate of Black-on-Black homicide—must be addressed openly. (Martin Luther King, Jr. said that the highest form of maturity is the ability to be self-critical.) The problems are obvious, but free, open and continuing communication between the police and elected public officials, clergy, educators and local organization leaders is the place to start.

## Public Defenders
More effective legal defense provisions and legal aid should be made available to help the poor in their self-defense battle against established authorities, perhaps by volunteer lawyers.

## Special Narcotics Courts

Some observers believe that narcotics crime should be dealt with by special courts and procedures, and that distinctions should be maintained between marijuana (increasingly legalized) and hard drugs like heroin and cocaine. This merits investigation and public discussion.

## Rethink State Grand Jury Systems

The Grand Jury System appears to work well on the Federal level but much less well on the State, where local prosecutors—working closely with the police and often over-protective of them—have undue influence. This April, Wisconsin passed the nation's first law requiring a team of at least two investigations from an outside agency to lead reviews of deaths due to police killings, and a public report must be made if criminal charges are not filed. Other states are following suit.

## Conclusion:

i) Prevention of crime and ii) the successful rehabilitation of former prisoners are the goals of the criminal justice systems in all other advanced countries, where certainty of punishment rather than severity is advocated, and where long isolation is less for punishment than to protect the public from those likely to be violent. Their success is manifest in their lower crime rates and very much lower prisoner recidivism rates, fewer broken homes and fewer socially-devastated communities.

Not rocket science, but common sense is what we require on these difficult questions, where fairness and prudence are joint concerns.

Last year only four countries accounted for nearly all executions worldwide: China, Iran, Saudi Arabia and the United States. There are today more than 41,000 people serving life without parole in the U.S. compared to 59 in Australia, 41 in England and 37 in the Netherlands; and those countries are safer than we are. We must ask why.

The "public safety" and "public justice" all other advanced nations have achieved we can have as well—if we will it.

## Critical Thinking

1. What changes in law enforcement would do the most to improve police-community relations?

2. Why did the prison population skyrocket eightfold since 1970 to 2.4 million today?

3. What are some of the major problems of the American prison system?

## Internet References

**New American Studies Web**
https://blogs.commons.georgetown.edu/vkp/

**Social Science Information Gateway**
http://www.ariadne.ac.uk/issue2/sosig

**Sociology—Study Sociology Online**
http://edu.learnsoc.org/

**Sociology Web Resources**
http://www.mhhe.com/socscience/sociology/resources/index.htm

**Sociosite**
http://www.topsite.com/goto/sociosite.net

**Socioweb**
http://www.topsite.com/goto/socioweb.com

*Article*          Prepared by: Kurt Finsterbusch, *University of Maryland, College Park*

# This Man Was Sentenced to Die in Prison for Shoplifting a $159 Jacket: This Happens More Than You Think

ED PILKINGTON

## Learning Outcomes

*After reading this article, you will be able to:*

- Understand the U.S. criminal justice system and how it works.

- Analyze the thesis that the U.S. criminal justice system is too punitive.

- Understand why crazy laws are not removed.

At about 12.40 P.M. on 2 January 1996, Timothy Jackson took a jacket from the Maison Blanche department store in New Orleans, draped it over his arm, and walked out of the store without paying for it. When he was accosted by a security guard, Jackson said: "I just needed another jacket, man."

A few months later Jackson was convicted of shoplifting and sent to Angola prison in Louisiana. That was 16 years ago. Today he is still incarcerated in Angola, and will stay there for the rest of his natural life having been condemned to die in jail. All for the theft of a jacket, worth $159.

Jackson, 53, is one of 3,281 prisoners in America serving life sentences with no chance of parole for nonviolent crimes. Some, like him, were given the most extreme punishment short of execution for shoplifting; one was condemned to die in prison for siphoning petrol from a truck; another for stealing tools from a tool shed and yet another for attempting to cash a stolen cheque.

"It has been very hard for me," Jackson wrote to the American Civil Liberties Union (ACLU) as part of its new report on life without parole for nonviolent offenders. "I know that for my crime I had to do some time, but a life sentence for a jacket value at $159. I have met people here whose crimes are a lot badder with way less time."

Senior officials at Angola prison refused to allow the *Guardian* to speak to Jackson, on grounds that it might upset his victims—even though his crime was victimless. But his sister Loretta Lumar did speak to the *Guardian*. She said that the last time she talked by phone with her brother he had expressed despair. "He told me, 'Sister, this has really broke my back. I'm ready to come out.'"

Lumar said that she found her brother's sentence incomprehensible. "This doesn't make sense to me. I know people who have killed people, and they get a lesser sentence. That doesn't make sense to me right there. You can take a life and get 15 or 16 years. He takes a jacket worth $159 and will stay in jail forever. He didn't kill the jacket!"

The ACLU's report, *A Living Death*, chronicles the thousands of lives ruined and families destroyed by the modern phenomenon of sentencing people to die behind bars for nonviolent offences. It notes that contrary to the expectation that such a harsh penalty would be meted out only to the most serious offenders, people have been caught in this brutal trap for sometimes the most petty causes.

Ronald Washington, 48, is also serving life without parole in Angola, in his case for shoplifting two Michael Jordan jerseys from a Foot Action sportswear store in Shreveport, Louisiana, in 2004. Washington insisted at trial that the jerseys were reduced in a sale to $45 each—which meant that their combined value was below the $100 needed to classify the theft as a felony; the prosecution disagreed, claiming they were on sale for $60 each, thus surpassing the $100 felony minimum and opening him up to a sentence of life without parole.

"I felt as though somebody had just taken the life out of my body," Washington wrote to the ACLU about the moment he learnt his fate. "I seriously felt rejected, neglected, stabbed right through my heart."

He added: "It's a very lonely world, seems that nobody cares. You're never ever returning back into society. And whatever you had or established, its now useless, because you're being buried alive at slow pace."

Louisiana, where both Washington and Jackson are held, is one of nine states where prisoners are serving life without parole sentences for nonviolent offences (other states with high numbers are Alabama, Florida, Mississippi, Oklahoma, and South Carolina). An overwhelming proportion of those sentences—as many as 98 percent in Louisiana—were mandatory: in other words judges had no discretion but to impose the swingeing penalties.

The warden of Angola prison, Burl Cain, has spoken out in forthright terms against a system that mandates punishment without any chance of rehabilitation. He told the ACLU: "It's ridiculous, because the name of our business is 'corrections'—to correct deviant behaviour. If I'm a successful warden and I do my job and we correct the deviant behaviour, then we should have a parole hearing. I need to keep predators in these big old prisons, not dying old men."

The toll is not confined to the state level: most of those nonviolent inmates held on life without parole sentences were given their punishments by the federal government. More than 2,000 of the 3,281 individuals tracked down on these sentences by the ACLU are being held in the federal system. Overall, the ACLU has calculated that taxpayers pay an additional $1.8 billion to keep the prisoners locked up for the rest of their lives.

## "It Doesn't Have to Be This Way"

Until the early 1970s, life without parole sentences were virtually unknown. But they exploded as part of what the ACLU calls America's "late-twentieth-century obsession with mass incarceration and extreme, inhumane penalties."

The report's author Jennifer Turner states that today, the United States is "virtually alone in its willingness to sentence nonviolent offenders to die behind bars." Life without parole for non-violent sentences has been ruled a violation of human rights by the European Court of Human Rights. The UK is one of only two countries in Europe that still metes out the penalty at all, and even then only in 49 cases of murder.

Even within America's starkly racially charged penal system, the disparities in nonviolent life without parole are stunning. About 65 percent of the prisoners identified nationwide by the ACLU are African American. In Louisiana, that proportion rises to 91 percent, including Jackson and Washington, who are both black.

The United States has the highest incarceration rate in the world, with 2.3 million people now in custody, with the war on drugs acting as the overriding push-factor. Of the prisoners serving life without parole for nonviolent offences nationwide, the ACLU estimates that almost 80 percent were for drug-related crimes.

Again, the offences involved can be startlingly petty. Drug cases itemised in the report include a man sentenced to die in prison for having been found in possession of a crack pipe; an offender with a bottle cap that contained a trace of heroin that was too small to measure; a prisoner arrested with a trace amount of cocaine in their pocket too tiny to see with the naked eye; a man who acted as a go-between in a sale to an undercover police officer of marijuana—street value $10.

Drugs are present in the background of Timothy Jackson's case too. He was high when he went to the Maison Blanche store, and he says that as a result he shoplifted "without thinking." Paradoxically, like many of the other prisoners on similar penalties, the first time he was offered drug treatment was after he had already been condemned to spend the rest of his life in jail.

The theft of the $159 jacket, taken in isolation, carries today a six-month jail term. It was combined at Jackson's sentencing hearing with his previous convictions—all for nonviolent crimes including a robbery in which he took $216—that brought him under Louisiana's brutal "four-strikes" law by which it became mandatory for him to be locked up and the key thrown away.

The ACLU concludes that it does not have to be this way—suitable alternatives are readily at hand, including shorter prison terms and the provision of drug treatment and mental health services. The organisation calls on Congress, the Obama administration and state legislatures to end the imposition of mandatory life without parole for nonviolent offenders and to require resentencing hearings for all those already caught in this judicial black hole.

A few months after Timothy Jackson was put away for life, a Louisiana appeals court reviewed the case and found it "excessive," "inappropriate," and "a prime example of an unjust result." Describing Jackson as a "petty thief," the court threw out the sentence.

The following year, in 1998, the state's supreme court gave a final ruling. "This sentence is constitutionally excessive in that it is grossly out of proportion to the seriousness of the offence," concluded Judge Bernette Johnson. However, she found that the state's four strikes law that mandates life without parole could only be overturned in rare instances, and as a result she reinstated the sentence—putting Jackson back inside his cell until the day he dies.

"I am much older and I have learned a lot about myself," Jackson wrote to the ACLU from that cell. "I am sorry for the crime that I did, and I am a changed man."

Jackson expressed a hope that he would be granted his freedom when he was still young enough to make something of his life and "help others." But, barring a reform of the law, the day of his release will never come.

## Critical Thinking

1. Laws and law enforcement are supposed to establish justice. In reality it establishes both justice and injustice. Why?

2. It seems that the most poignant cases of the miscarriage of justice applies to poor people. Why?

3. Pilkington argues against overpunishment. Discuss cases of underpunishment and explain the differences.

# Internet References

**ACLU Criminal Justice Home Page**
www.aclu.org/crimjustice/index.html

**Human Rights and Humanitarian Assistance**
www.etown.edu/vl/humrts.html

**New American Studies Web**
www.georgetown.edu/crossroads/asw

**Sociology—Study Sociology Online**
http://edu.learnsoc.org

**Sociology Web Resources**
http://www.mhhe.com/socscience/sociology/resources/index.htm

**Sociosite**
http://www.topsite.com/goto/sociosite.net

**Socioweb**
http://www.topsite.com/goto/socioweb.com

Pilkington, Ed, "Over 3,000 US prisoners serving life without parole for non-violent crimes," theguardian.com, November 13, 2013. Copyright Guardian News & Media Ltd 2013.

*Article*                    Prepared by: Kurt Finsterbusch, *University of Maryland, College Park*

# The Price of Justice

State and local governments are plundering the poor.

PETER EDELMAN

## Learning Outcomes

*After reading this article, you will be able to:*

- Explain the horrible injustices foisted on the poor by fraudulent law enforcement systems.

- Comment on the current efforts at judicial policy reform and their chance for success.

- Analyze the facts/feelings associated with the many poor who have been victimized by these injustices.

Vera Cheeks, a resident of Bainbridge, Georgia, was ticketed for rolling through a stop sign in 2014. The judge hit her with a $135 fine and ordered her to pay it in full immediately. Cheeks said that she was unemployed and caring for her terminally ill father, so the judge gave her three months to pay up, during which time she'd be on "probation." He sent her to a room behind the courtroom, where a long line of people—all of them African-American—were waiting to pay money to a woman behind a desk. "It was like the twilight zone, totally mind-boggling," Cheeks recalls.

The woman behind the desk told Cheeks that she had to sign a paper indicating that she had been placed on probation and now owed $267—the fine plus $105 for the (for-profit) probation company that would be monitoring her, as well as $27 for the Georgia Crime Victims Emergency Fund. When Cheeks refused to agree to the so-called probation and the additional sums, the woman—who, it turned out, worked for the probation company—told her that the judge would put her in jail for five days. Cheeks still refused, and finally the woman demanded a $50 payment on the spot if Cheeks wanted to avoid being jailed. Cheeks's fiancé raised the money by pawning her engagement

ring and Weed Eater lawn machine. That avoided the crisis for the moment, but Cheeks was told she would still be jailed if she was late on even one payment.

Cheeks went home furious. She says that people in town knew something was wrong, but they were all too scared to do anything. She Googled for three hours and found her way to Sarah Geraghty of the Southern Center for Human Rights, who used Cheeks's case to challenge the threat of jail by private probation companies looking to extract exorbitant fines and fees from people who can't afford them. Geraghty resolved Cheeks's issue—and used the case to end Bainbridge's illegal money-collecting scheme—by pointing out that incarcerating people unable to pay a fine was unconstitutional.

Cheeks was fortunate. She found a lawyer (and a great one at that) and was forced neither to pay an excessive fine nor go to jail when she couldn't afford it. But many poor Americans aren't so lucky. While most people in this country believe that debtors' prisons are a thing of the past, Americans are in jail by the thousands for no other reason than being unable to pay a fine and its accompanying fees—which is unconstitutional, in many instances. Yet even when jail doesn't ensue, the courts' policy of garnishing wages and seizing tax refunds creates a prison of another kind. An estimated 10 million people currently owe a collective $50 billion in court debt.

Meanwhile, even more people are locked up pending trial on low-level misdemeanors or violations because they can't afford the bail set for them. Altogether, roughly 500,000 people are in jails across the country simply because they are poor. These men and women haven't been found guilty of any crime. Rather, most of them have merely been accused of low-level infractions that shouldn't be crimes at all and that often don't carry jail time. One result is that many low-income people plead guilty just to get out even if they are innocent, leaving them with a lifetime of collateral consequences. (For more on this, see "The Injustice of Cash Bail," by Bryce Covert, in the November 6 issue of *The Nation*.)

The criminalization of poverty has metastasized into other areas as well. We see it in the use of police officers as the front line of discipline in schools serving low-income students, leading to criminal records for behavior that could be dealt with in the principal's office. We see it in the vigorous prosecution of vagrancy laws against the homeless. We see it in rules that bar ex-offenders from living in public housing. And we see it in the heartless practice of evicting poor women from their homes for calling 911 "too often," even when they're reporting domestic abuse. For far too many people, to be poor in 2017 is to live under the constant threat of incarceration for no other reason than poverty itself.

Many of these practices began with the Reagan-era anti-tax revolution and expanded during the Clinton era. States and local governments, starved for revenues, turned to their own residents—especially low-income people of color—to subsidize everything from courts and prisons to private probation companies, piling on higher and higher fines and fees. Oklahoma, for instance, assesses 15 possible fees, including a law-library fee and a forensic-science improvement assessment, for minor infractions like failing to mow high grass and weeds or drinking a beer on the front porch. Between 1996 and 2013, Florida added more than 20 new fees. The Justice Department's report on Ferguson, Missouri, which revealed a system geared more toward gouging residents than public safety, opened the eyes of many to what is going on. But most people still don't appreciate that Ferguson is everywhere in America today.

There is, however, a rising response. Across the country, a growing movement is pushing back, using everything from law to legislation to policy to dismantle the vicious circle of debt and incarceration that traps so many poor people.

Lawyers have been at the forefront of this push. These are attorneys like Thomas Harvey of ArchCity Defenders and Alec Karakatsanis of Civil Rights Corps, who in 2015 sued the city of Jennings, Missouri, just to the east of Ferguson, and succeeded in emptying the jail of its mistreated population. They also obtained $4.75 million for almost 2,000 people who had been locked up for a combined total of 8,300 days.

Around the same time, Karakatsanis, along with Sam Brooke of the Southern Poverty Law Center, won the release from jail of 60 people in Montgomery, Alabama, and the termination of the city's debtors'-prison policy. Also in 2015, the ACLU joined forces with a private law firm to rescue Jayne Fuentes, who had been forced to labor on a local work crew to pay off her debts, from this unconstitutional treatment in Benton County, Washington. They also obtained a settlement that ended the county's debtors'-prison system.

Litigation to abolish cash bail is also making headway. Karakatsanis won an enormous victory in Harris County, Texas, which includes Houston, where he challenged the widespread mistreatment of people during their arraignment. Federal Judge Lee Rosenthal accompanied her ruling with a 193-page opinion holding, essentially, that it is unconstitutional to assess excessive bail, since it creates two separate and unequal criminal-justice systems: one for the wealthy and another for the poor. The case is now under review in the Fifth Circuit Court of Appeals and has the potential to affect policy across the country.

Meanwhile, a new wave of policy reform has begun. State judicial leaders have taken a strong stance against high fines and fees and their consequences. They speak out publicly and lobby personally. Many legislators still claim that their cities and counties need the money, but elected officials are joining with chief justices and outside advocates to create change in states like California and Texas, to name just two.

Policy reform on bail is making progress, too. Based on careful research, states including Kentucky, New Jersey, Maryland, and New Mexico have adopted a methodology that helps determine whether an accused person will be a flight risk or pose a danger outside of jail. Not surprisingly, bail bondsmen and underwriters have been waging a fierce resistance to these changes. When bail reform was pending in Maryland, intense lobbying by both bail and insurance interests nearly killed it. More recently, bail-industry representatives filed two cases in New Jersey contending that the state's reform is unconstitutional.

Still, the fight continues, including against some of the most entrenched structures. Rikers Island is a sprawling jail complex in New York City that holds people who have not been convicted of any crime, simply because they cannot afford bail. These include people like Kalief Browder, a young man who killed himself in 2015 after spending three years in Rikers without ever being convicted of a crime. After an intense grassroots campaign, Mayor Bill de Blasio has said that the city will close the complex, marking a profound victory. But the stated time frame for doing so is painfully long.

And so the effort to decriminalize poverty continues. As hundreds of thousands of people molder in jails for the simple "crime" of being poor, we must all call out the legislative irresponsibility that finances the courts on the backs of the poor, and we must stand up to the bail bondsmen and their underwriters, as well as the private prison industry and the correction officers' union, which all profit off the misery of low-income people in a system where injustice reigns. Justice demands it.

# Critical Thinking

1. Do you agree with Edelman's description of the "Criminalization of poverty?" Explain your answer.

2. Some debtors' prisons have been closed. Why and how?

# Internet References

**New American Studies Web**
www.georgetown.edu/crossroads/asw

**Social Science Information Gateway**
http://sosig.esrc.bris.ac.uk

**Sociology Web Resources**
http://www.mhhe.com/socscience/sociology/resources/index.htm

**Sociology—Study Sociology Online**
http://edu.learnsoc.org

**Sociosite**
http://www.topsite.com/goto/sociosite.net

**PETER EDELMAN** is a professor at the Georgetown University Law Center and the author of *Not a Crime to Be Poor*.

*Article*    Prepared by: Kurt Finsterbusch, *University of Maryland, College Park*

# Statement for the Record: Worldwide Threat Assessment of the US Intelligence Community

JAMES R. CLAPPER

## Learning Outcomes

*After reading this article, you will be able to:*

- Describe the trends in cyber attacks and the types and severity of likely attacks.

- Describe the report's analysis of current terrorism and its danger to America.

- Present its analysis of the threat of weapons of mass destruction to America.

## Introduction

Chairman McCain, Ranking Member Reed, Members of the Committee, thank you for the invitation to offer the United States Intelligence Community's 2015 assessment of threats to US national security. My statement reflects the collective insights of the Intelligence Community's extraordinary men and women, whom I am privileged and honored to lead. We in the Intelligence Community are committed every day to provide the nuanced, multidisciplinary intelligence that policymakers, warfighters, and domestic law enforcement personnel need to protect American lives and America's interests anywhere in the world.

Information available as of February 13, 2015 was used in the preparation of this assessment.

## Global Threats
### Cyber
### Strategic Assessment

Cyber threats to US national and economic security are increasing in frequency, scale, sophistication, and severity of impact.

The ranges of cyber threat actors, methods of attack, targeted systems, and victims are also expanding. Overall, the unclassified information and communication technology (ICT) networks that support US Government, military, commercial, and social activities remain vulnerable to espionage and/or disruption. However, the likelihood of a catastrophic attack from any particular actor is remote at this time. Rather than a "Cyber Armageddon" scenario that debilitates the entire US infrastructure, we envision something different. We foresee an ongoing series of low-to-moderate level cyber attacks from a variety of sources over time, which will impose cumulative costs on US economic competitiveness and national security.

- A growing number of computer forensic studies by industry experts strongly suggest that several nations—including Iran and North Korea—have undertaken offensive cyber operations against private sector targets to support their economic and foreign policy objectives, at times concurrent with political crises.

**Risk.** Despite ever-improving network defenses, the diverse possibilities for remote hacking intrusions, supply chain operations to insert compromised hardware or software, and malevolent activities by human insiders will hold nearly all ICT systems at risk for years to come. In short, the cyber threat cannot be eliminated; rather, cyber risk must be managed. Moreover, the risk calculus employed by some private sector entities does not adequately account for foreign cyber threats or the systemic interdependencies between different critical infrastructure sectors.

**Costs.** During 2014, we saw an increase in the scale and scope of reporting on malevolent cyber activity that can be measured by the amount of corporate data stolen or deleted, personally identifiable information (PII) compromised, or remediation costs incurred by US victims. For example:

- After the 2012–13 distributed denial of service (DDOS) attacks on the US financial sector, JPMorgan Chase (JPMorgan) announced plans for annual cyber security expenditures of $250 million by the end of 2014. After the company suffered a hacking intrusion in 2014, JPMorgan's CEO said he would probably double JPMorgan's annual computer security budget within the next five years.
- The 2014 data breach at Home Depot exposed information from 56 million credit/debit cards and 53 million customer email addresses. Home Depot estimated the cost of the breach to be $62 million.
- In 2014, unauthorized computer intrusions were detected on the networks of the Office of Personnel Management (OPM) as well as its contractors, US Investigations Services (USIS) and KeyPoint Government Solutions. The two contractors were involved in processing sensitive PII related to national security clearances for Federal Government employees.
- In August 2014, the US company, Community Health Systems, informed the Securities and Exchange Commission that it believed hackers "originating from China" had stolen PII on 4.5 million individuals.

**Attribution.** Although cyber operators can infiltrate or disrupt targeted ICT networks, most can no longer assume that neither their activities will remain undetected nor can they assume that if detected, they will be able to conceal their identities. Governmental and private sector security professionals have made significant advances in detecting and attributing cyber intrusions.

- In May 2014, the US Department of Justice indicted five officers from China's Peoples' Liberation Army on charges of hacking US companies.
- In December 2014, computer security experts reported that members of an Iranian organization were responsible for computer operations targeting US military, transportation, public utility, and other critical infrastructure networks.

**Deterrence.** Numerous actors remain undeterred from conducting economic cyber espionage or perpetrating cyber attacks. The absence of universally accepted and enforceable norms of behavior in cyberspace has contributed to this situation. The motivation to conduct cyber attacks and cyber espionage will probably remain strong because of the relative ease of these operations and the gains they bring to the perpetrators. The result is a cyber environment in which multiple actors continue to test their adversaries' technical capabilities, political

resolve, and thresholds. The muted response by most victims to cyber attacks has created a permissive environment in which low-level attacks can be used as a coercive tool short of war, with relatively low risk of retaliation. Additionally, even when a cyber attack can be attributed to a specific actor, the forensic attribution often requires a significant amount of time to complete. Long delays between the cyber attack and determination of attribution likewise reinforce a permissive environment.

### Threat Actors

Politically motivated cyber attacks are now a growing reality, and foreign actors are reconnoitering and developing access to US critical infrastructure systems, which might be quickly exploited for disruption if an adversary's intent became hostile. In addition, those conducting cyber espionage are targeting US government, military, and commercial networks on a daily basis. These threats come from a range of actors, including: (1) nation states with highly sophisticated cyber programs (such as Russia or China), (2) nations with lesser technical capabilities but possibly more disruptive intent (such as Iran or North Korea), (3) profit-motivated criminals, and (4) ideologically motivated hackers or extremists. Distinguishing between state and non-state actors within the same country is often difficult—especially when those varied actors actively collaborate, tacitly cooperate, condone criminal activity that only harms foreign victims, or utilize similar cyber tools.

**Russia.** Russia's Ministry of Defense is establishing its own cyber command, which—according to senior Russian military officials—will be responsible for conducting offensive cyber activities, including propaganda operations and inserting malware into enemy command and control systems. Russia's armed forces are also establishing a specialized branch for computer network operations.

- Computer security studies assert that unspecified Russian cyber actors are developing means to access industrial control systems (ICS) remotely. These systems manage critical infrastructures such as electric power grids, urban mass-transit systems, air-traffic control, and oil and gas distribution networks. These unspecified Russian actors have successfully compromised the product supply chains of three ICS vendors so that customers download exploitative malware directly from the vendors' websites along with routine software updates, according to private sector cyber security experts.

**China.** Chinese economic espionage against US companies remains a significant issue. The "advanced persistent threat" activities continue despite detailed private sector reports, public indictments, and US demarches, according to a computer security study. China is an advanced cyber actor; however, Chinese hackers often use less sophisticated cyber tools to access targets. Improved cyber defenses would require hackers to use more sophisticated skills and make China's economic espionage more costly and difficult to conduct.

**Iran.** Iran very likely values its cyber program as one of many tools for carrying out asymmetric but proportional retaliation against political foes, as well as a sophisticated means of collecting intelligence. Iranian actors have been implicated in the 2012–13 DDOS attacks against US financial institutions and in the February 2014 cyber attack on the Las Vegas Sands casino company.

**North Korea.** North Korea is another state actor that uses its cyber capabilities for political objectives. The North Korean Government was responsible for the November 2014 cyber attack on Sony Pictures Entertainment (SPE), which stole corporate information and introduced hard drive erasing malware into the company's network infrastructure, according to the FBI. The attack coincided with the planned release of a SPE feature film satire that depicted the planned assassination of the North Korean president.

**Terrorists.** Terrorist groups will continue to experiment with hacking, which could serve as the foundation for developing more advanced capabilities. Terrorist sympathizers will probably conduct lowlevel cyber attacks on behalf of terrorist groups and attract attention of the media, which might exaggerate the capabilities and threat posed by these actors.

## *Integrity of Information*

Most of the public discussion regarding cyber threats has focused on the confidentiality and availability of information; cyber espionage undermines confidentiality, whereas denial-of-service operations and datadeletion attacks undermine availability. In the future, however, we might also see more cyber operations that will change or manipulate electronic information in order to compromise its integrity (i.e., accuracy and reliability) instead of deleting it or disrupting access to it. Decisionmaking by senior government officials (civilian and military), corporate executives, investors, or others will be impaired if they cannot trust the information they are receiving.

- Successful cyber operations targeting the integrity of information would need to overcome any institutionalized checks and balances designed to prevent the manipulation of data, for example, market monitoring and clearing functions in the financial sector.

## *Counterintelligence*

We assess that the leading state intelligence threats to US interests in 2015 will continue to be Russia and China, based on their capabilities, intent, and broad operational scopes. Other states in South Asia, the Near East, and East Asia will pose increasingly sophisticated local and regional intelligence threats to US interests. For example, Iran's intelligence and security services continue to view the United States as a primary threat and have stated publicly that they monitor and counter US activities in the region.

Penetrating the US national decisionmaking apparatus and Intelligence Community will remain primary objectives for foreign intelligence entities. Additionally, the targeting of national security information and proprietary information from US companies and research institutions dealing with defense, energy, finance, dual-use technology, and other areas will be a persistent threat to US interests.

Non-state entities, including transnational organized criminals and terrorists, will continue to employ human, technical, and cyber intelligence capabilities that present a significant counterintelligence challenge. Like state intelligence services, these non-state entities recruit sources and perform physical and technical surveillance to facilitate their illegal activities and avoid detection and capture.

The internationalization of critical US supply chains and service infrastructure, including for the ICT, civil infrastructure, and national security sectors, increases the potential for subversion. This threat includes individuals, small groups of "hacktivists," commercial firms, and state intelligence services.

Trusted insiders who disclose sensitive US Government information without authorization will remain a significant threat in 2015. The technical sophistication and availability of information technology that can be used for nefarious purposes exacerbates this threat.

## *Terrorism*

Sunni violent extremists are gaining momentum and the number of Sunni violent extremist groups, members, and safe havens is greater than at any other point in history. These groups challenge local and regional governance and threaten US allies, partners, and interests. The threat to key US allies and partners will probably increase, but the extent of the increase will depend on the level of success that Sunni violent extremists achieve in seizing and holding territory, whether or not attacks on local regimes and calls for retaliation against the West are accepted by their key audiences, and the durability of the US-led coalition in Iraq and Syria.

Sunni violent extremists have taken advantage of fragile or unstable Muslim-majority countries to make territorial advances, seen in Syria and Iraq, and will probably continue to do so. They also contribute to regime instability and internal conflict by engaging in high levels of violence. Most will be unable to seize and hold territory on a large scale, however, as long as local, regional, and international support and resources are available and dedicated to halting their progress. The increase in the number of Sunni violent extremist groups also will probably be balanced by a lack of cohesion and authoritative leadership. Although the January 2015 attacks against Charlie Hebdo in Paris is a reminder of the threat to the West, most groups place a higher priority on local concerns than on attacking the so-called far enemy—the United States and the West—as advocated by core al-Qa'ida.

Differences in ideology and tactics will foster competition among some of these groups, particularly if a unifying figure or group does not emerge. In some cases, groups—even if hostile to each other— will ally against common enemies. For example, some Sunni violent extremists will probably gain support from like-minded insurgent or anti-regime groups or within disaffected or disenfranchised communities because they share the goal of radical regime change.

Although most homegrown violent extremists (HVEs) will probably continue to aspire to travel overseas, particularly to Syria and Iraq, they will probably remain the most likely Sunni violent extremist threat to the US homeland because of their immediate and direct access. Some might have been inspired by calls by the Islamic State of Iraq and the Levant (ISIL) in late September for individual jihadists in the West to retaliate for US-led airstrikes on ISIL. Attacks by lone actors are among the most difficult to warn about because they offer few or no signatures.

If ISIL were to substantially increase the priority it places on attacking the West rather than fighting to maintain and expand territorial control, then the group's access to radicalized Westerners who have fought in Syria and Iraq would provide a pool of operatives who potentially have access to the United States and other Western countries. Since the conflict began in 2011, more than 20,000 foreign fighters—at least 3,400 of whom are Westerners—have gone to Syria from more than 90 countries.

## Weapons of Mass Destruction and Proliferation

Nation-states' efforts to develop or acquire weapons of mass destruction (WMD), their delivery systems, or their underlying technologies constitute a major threat to the security of the United States, its deployed troops, and allies. Syrian regime use of chemical weapons against the opposition further demonstrates that the threat of WMD is real. The time when only a few states had access to the most dangerous technologies is past. Biological and chemical materials and technologies, almost always dual-use, move easily in the globalized economy, as do personnel with the scientific expertise to design and use them. The latest discoveries in the life sciences also diffuse rapidly around the globe.

## Iran Preserving Nuclear Weapons Option

We continue to assess that Iran's overarching strategic goals of enhancing its security, prestige, and regional influence have led it to pursue capabilities to meet its civilian goals and give it the ability to build missile-deliverable nuclear weapons, if it chooses to do so. We do not know whether Iran will eventually decide to build nuclear weapons.

We also continue to assess that Iran does not face any insurmountable technical barriers to producing a nuclear weapon, making Iran's political will the central issue. However, Iranian implementation of the Joint Plan of Action (JPOA) has at least temporarily inhibited further progress in its uranium enrichment and plutonium production capabilities and effectively eliminated Iran's stockpile of 20 percent enriched uranium. The agreement has also enhanced the transparency of Iran's nuclear activities, mainly through improved International Atomic Energy Agency (IAEA) access and earlier warning of any effort to make material for nuclear weapons using its safeguarded facilities.

We judge that Tehran would choose ballistic missiles as its preferred method of delivering nuclear weapons, if it builds them. Iran's ballistic missiles are inherently capable of delivering WMD, and Tehran already has the largest inventory of ballistic missiles in the Middle East. Iran's progress on space launch vehicles—along with its desire to deter the United States and its allies—provides Tehran with the means and motivation to develop longer-range missiles, including intercontinental ballistic missiles (ICBMs).

## North Korea Developing WMD-Applicable Capabilities

North Korea's nuclear weapons and missile programs pose a serious threat to the United States and to the security environment in East Asia. North Korea's export of ballistic missiles and associated materials to several countries, including Iran and Syria, and its assistance to Syria's construction of a nuclear reactor, destroyed in 2007, illustrate its willingness to proliferate dangerous technologies.

In 2013, following North Korea's third nuclear test, Pyongyang announced its intention to "refurbish and restart" its nuclear facilities, to include the uranium enrichment facility at Yongbyon, and to restart its graphite-moderated plutonium production reactor that was shut down in 2007. We assess that North Korea has followed through on its announcement by expanding its Yongbyon enrichment facility and restarting the reactor.

North Korea has also expanded the size and sophistication of its ballistic missile forces, ranging from close-range ballistic missiles to ICBMs, while continuing to conduct test launches.

In 2014, North Korea launched an unprecedented number of ballistic missiles.

Pyongyang is committed to developing a long-range, nuclear-armed missile that is capable of posing a direct threat to the United States and has publicly displayed its KN08 road-mobile ICBM twice. We assess that North Korea has already taken initial steps toward fielding this system, although the system has not been flight-tested.

Because of deficiencies in their conventional military forces, North Korean leaders are focused on developing missile and WMD capabilities, particularly building nuclear weapons. Although North Korean state media regularly carries official statements on North Korea's justification for building nuclear weapons and threatening to use them as a defensive or retaliatory measure, we do not know the details of Pyongyang's nuclear doctrine or employment concepts. We have long assessed that, in Pyongyang's view, its nuclear capabilities are intended for deterrence, international prestige, and coercive diplomacy.

## China's Expanding Nuclear Forces

The People's Liberation Army's (PLA's) Second Artillery Force continues to modernize its nuclear missile force by adding more survivable road-mobile systems and enhancing its silo-based systems. This new generation of missiles is intended to ensure the viability of China's strategic deterrent by providing a second strike capability. In addition, the PLA Navy continues to develop the JL-2 submarine-launched ballistic missile (SLBM) and might produce additional JIN-class nuclear-powered ballistic missile submarines. The JIN-class submarines, armed with JL-2 SLBMs, will give the PLA Navy its first longrange, sea-based nuclear capability. We assess that the Navy will soon conduct its first nuclear deterrence patrols.

## Russia's New Intermediate-Range Cruise Missile

Russia has developed a new cruise missile that the United States has declared to be in violation of the Intermediate-Range Nuclear Forces (INF) Treaty. In 2013, Sergei Ivanov, a senior Russian administration official, commented in an interview how the world had changed since the time the INF Treaty was signed 1987 and noted that Russia was "developing appropriate weapons systems" in light of the proliferation of intermediate- and shorter-range ballistic missile technologies around the world. Similarly, as far back as 2007, Ivanov publicly announced that Russia had tested a ground-launched cruise missile for its Iskander weapon system, whose range complied with the INF Treaty "for now." The development of a cruise missile that is inconsistent with INF, combined with these statements about INF, calls into question Russia's commitment to this treaty.

## WMD Security in Syria

In June 2014, Syria's declared (CW) stockpile was removed for destruction by the international community. The most hazardous chemical agents were destroyed aboard the MV CAPE RAY as of August 2014. The United States and its allies continue to work closely with the Organization for the Prohibition of Chemical Weapons (OPCW) to verify the completeness and accuracy of Syria's Chemical Weapons Convention (CWC) declaration. We judge that Syria, despite signing the treaty, has used chemicals as a means of warfare since accession to the CWC in 2013. Furthermore, the OPCW continues to investigate allegations of chlorine use in Syria.

## Space and Counterspace

Threats to US space systems and services will increase during 2015 and beyond as potential adversaries pursue disruptive and destructive counterspace capabilities. Chinese and Russian military leaders understand the unique information advantages afforded by space systems and services and are developing capabilities to deny access in a conflict. Chinese military writings highlight the need to interfere with, damage, and destroy reconnaissance, navigation, and communication satellites. China has satellite jamming capabilities and is pursuing antisatellite systems. In July 2014, China conducted a nondestructive antisatellite missile test. China conducted a previous destructive test of the system in 2007, which created long-lived space debris. Russia's 2010 Military Doctrine emphasizes space defense as a vital component of its national defense. Russian leaders openly assert that the Russian armed forces have antisatellite weapons and conduct antisatellite research. Russia has satellite jammers and is pursuing antisatellite systems.

## Transnational Organized Crime

Transnational Organized Crime (TOC) is a global, persistent threat to our communities at home and our interests abroad. Savvy, profit-driven criminal networks traffic in drugs, persons, wildlife, and weapons; corrode security and governance; undermine legitimate economic activity and the rule of law; cost economies important revenue; and undercut U.S. development efforts.

## Drug Trafficking

Drug trafficking will remain a major TOC threat to the United States. Mexico is the largest foreign producer of US-bound marijuana, methamphetamines, and heroin, and the conduit for the overwhelming majority of US-bound cocaine from South America. The drug trade also undermines US interests abroad, eroding stability in parts of Africa and Latin America; Afghanistan accounts for 80 percent of the world's opium production.

Weak Central American states will continue to be the primary transit area for the majority of US-bound cocaine. The Caribbean is becoming an increasingly important secondary transit area for US- and European-bound cocaine. In 2013, the world's capacity to produce heroin reached the second highest level in nearly 20 years, increasing the likelihood that the drug will remain accessible and inexpensive in consumer markets in the United States, where heroin-related deaths have surged since 2007. New psychoactive substances (NPS), including synthetic cannabinoids and synthetic cathinones, pose an emerging and rapidly growing global public health threat. Since 2009, US law enforcement officials have encountered more than 240 synthetic compounds. Worldwide, 348 new psychoactive substances had been identified, exceeding the number of 234 illicit substances under international controls.

## Criminals Profiting from Global Instability

Transnational criminal organizations will continue to exploit opportunities in ongoing conflicts to destabilize societies, economies, and governance. Regional unrest, population displacements, endemic corruption, and political turmoil will provide openings that criminals will exploit for profit and to improve their standing relative to other power brokers.

## Corruption

Corruption facilitates transnational organized crime and vice versa. Both phenomena exacerbate other threats to local, regional, and international security. Corruption exists at some level in all countries; however, the symbiotic relationship between government officials and TOC networks is particularly pernicious in some countries. One example is Russia, where the nexus among organized crime, state actors, and business blurs the distinction between state policy and private gain.

## Human Trafficking

Human trafficking remains both a human rights concern and a challenge to international security. Trafficking in persons has become a lucrative source of revenue—estimated to produce tens of billions of dollars annually. Human traffickers leverage corrupt officials, porous borders, and lax enforcement to ply their illicit trade. This exploitation of human lives for profit continues to occur in every country in the world—undermining the rule of law and corroding legitimate institutions of government and commerce.

## Wildlife Trafficking

Illicit trade in wildlife, timber, and marine resources endangers the environment, threatens rule of law and border security in fragile regions, and destabilizes communities that depend on wildlife for biodiversity and ecotourism. Increased demand for ivory and rhino horn in Asia has triggered unprecedented increases in poaching in Africa. Criminal elements, often in collusion with corrupt government officials or security forces, are involved in poaching and movement of ivory and rhino horn across Africa. Poaching presents significant security challenges for militaries and police forces in African nations, which often are outgunned by poachers and their allies. Illegal, unreported, and unregulated fishing threatens food security and the preservation of marine resources. It often occurs concurrently with forced labor in the fishing industry.

## Theft of Cultural Properties, Artifacts, and Antiquities

Although the theft and trafficking of cultural heritage and art are traditions as old as the cultures they represent, transnational organized criminals are acquiring, transporting, and selling valuable cultural property and art more swiftly, easily, and stealthily. These criminals operate on a global scale without regard for laws, borders, nationalities, or the significance of the treasures they smuggle.

# Economics and Natural Resources

The global economy continues to adjust to and recover from the global financial crisis that began in 2008; economic growth since that period is lagging behind that of the previous decade. Resumption of sustained growth has been elusive for many of the world's largest economies, particularly in European countries and Japan. The prospect of diminished or forestalled recoveries in these developed economies as well as disappointing growth in key developing countries has contributed to a readjustment of energy and commodity markets.

## Energy and Commodities

Energy prices experienced sharp declines during the second half of 2014. Diminishing global growth prospects, OPEC's decision to maintain its output levels, rapid increases in unconventional oil production in Canada and the United States, and the partial resumption of some previously sidelined output in Libya and elsewhere helped drive down prices by more than half since July, the first substantial decline since 2008–2009. Lower-priced oil and gas will give a boost to the global economy, with benefits enjoyed by importers more than outweighing the costs to exporters.

## Macroeconomic Stability

Extraordinary monetary policy or "quantitative easing" has helped revive growth in the United States since the global financial crisis. However, this recovery and the prospect of higher returns in the United States will probably continue to draw investment capital from the rest of the world, where weak growth has left interest rates depressed.

Global output improved slightly in 2014 but continued to lag the growth rates seen before 2008. Since 2008, the worldwide GDP growth rate has averaged about 3.2 percent, well below its 20-year, pre-GFC average of 3.9 percent. Looking ahead, prospects for slowing economic growth in Europe and China do not bode well for the global economic environment.

Economic growth has been inconsistent among developed and developing economies alike. Outside of the largest economies—the United States, the EU, and China—economic growth largely stagnated worldwide in 2014, slowing to 2.1 percent. As a result, the difference in growth rates of developing countries and developed countries continued to narrow—to 2.6 percentage points. This gap, smallest in more than a decade, underscores the continued weakness in emerging markets, whose previously much higher average growth rates helped drive global growth.

# Human Security
## Critical Trends Converging

Several trends are converging that will probably increase the frequency of shocks to human security in 2015. Emerging infectious diseases and deficiencies in international state preparedness to address them remain a threat, exemplified by the epidemic spread of the Ebola virus in West Africa. Extremes in weather combined with public policies that affect food and water supplies will probably exacerbate humanitarian crises. Many states and international institutions will look to the United States in 2015 for leadership to address human security issues, particularly environment and global health, as well as those caused by poor or abusive governance.

Global trends in governance are negative and portend growing instability. Poor and abusive governance threatens the security and rights of individuals and civil society in many countries throughout the world. The overall risk for mass atrocities—driven in part by increasing social mobilization, violent conflict, and a diminishing quality of governance—is growing. Incidents of religious persecution also are on the rise. Legal restrictions on NGOs and the press, particularly those that expose government shortcomings or lobby for reforms, will probably continue.

## Infectious Disease Continues to Threaten Human Security Worldwide

Infectious diseases are among the foremost health security threats. A more crowded and interconnected world is increasing the opportunities for human and animal diseases to emerge and spread globally. This has been demonstrated by the emergence of Ebola in West Africa on an unprecedented scale. In addition, military conflicts and displacement of populations with loss of basic infrastructure can lead to spread of disease. Climate change can also lead to changes in the distribution of vectors for diseases.

- The Ebola outbreak, which began in late 2013 in a remote area of Guinea, quickly spread into neighboring Liberia and Sierra Leone and then into dense urban transportation hubs, where it began spreading out of control. Gaps in disease surveillance and reporting, limited health care resources, and other factors contributed to the outpacing of the international Community's response in West Africa. Isolated Ebola cases appeared outside of the most affected countries—notably in Spain and the United States—and the disease will almost certainly continue in 2015 to threaten regional economic stability, security, and governance.

- Antimicrobial drug resistance is increasingly threatening global health security. Seventy percent of known bacteria have acquired resistance to at least one antibiotic that is used to treat infections, threatening a return to the pre-antibiotic era. Multidrug-resistant tuberculosis has emerged in China, India, Russia, and elsewhere. During the next twenty years, antimicrobial drug-resistant pathogens will probably continue to increase in number and geographic scope, worsening health outcomes, straining public health budgets, and harming US interests throughout the world.

- MERS, a novel virus from the same family as SARS, emerged in 2012 in Saudi Arabia. Isolated cases migrated to Southeast Asia, Europe, and the United States. Cases of highly pathogenic influenza are also continuing to appear in different regions of the world. HIV/AIDS and malaria, although trending downward, remain global health priorities. In 2013, 2.1 million people were newly infected with HIV and 584,000 were killed by malaria, according to the World Health Organization. Diarrheal diseases like cholera continue to take the lives of 800,000 children annually.

- The world's population remains vulnerable to infectious diseases because anticipating which pathogen might spread from animals to humans or if a human virus will take a more virulent form is nearly impossible. For example, if a highly pathogenic avian influenza virus like H7N9 were to become easily transmissible among humans, the outcome could be far more disruptive than the great influenza pandemic of 1918. It could lead to global economic losses, the unseating of governments, and disturbance of geopolitical alliances.

## Extreme Weather Exacerbating Risks to Global Food and Water Security

Extreme weather, climate change, and public policies that affect food and water supplies will probably create or exacerbate humanitarian crises and instability risks. Globally averaged surface temperature rose approximately 0.8 degrees Celsius (about 1.4 degrees Fahrenheit) from 1951 to 2014; 2014 was warmest on earth since recordkeeping began. This rise in temperature has probably caused an increase in the intensity and frequency of both heavy precipitation and prolonged heat waves and has changed the spread of certain diseases. This trend will probably continue. Demographic and development trends that concentrate people in cities—often along coasts—will compound and amplify the impact of extreme weather and climate change on populations. Countries whose key systems—food, water, energy, shelter, transportation, and medical—are resilient will be better able to avoid significant economic and human losses from extreme weather.

- Global food supplies will probably be adequate for 2015 but are becoming increasingly fragile in Africa, the Middle East, and South Asia. The risks of worsening food insecurity in regions of strategic importance to the United States will increase because of threats to local food availability, lower purchasing power, and counterproductive government policies. Price shocks will result if extreme weather or disease patterns significantly reduce food production in multiple areas of the world, especially in key exporting countries.

- Risks to freshwater supplies—due to shortages, poor quality, floods, and climate change—are growing. These problems hinder the ability of countries to produce food and generate energy, potentially undermining global food markets and hobbling economic growth. Combined with demographic and economic development pressures, such problems will particularly hinder the efforts of North Africa, the Middle East, and South Asia to cope with their water problems. Lack of adequate water might be a destabilizing factor in countries that lack the management mechanisms, financial resources, political will, or technical ability to solve their internal water problems.

- Some states are heavily dependent on river water controlled by upstream nations. When upstream water infrastructure development threatens downstream access to water, states might attempt to exert pressure on their neighbors to preserve their water interests. Such pressure might be applied in international forums and also includes pressing investors, nongovernmental organizations, and donor countries to support or halt water infrastructure projects. Some countries will almost certainly construct and support major water projects. Over the longer term, wealthier developing countries will also probably face increasing water-related social

disruptions. Developing countries, however, are almost certainly capable of addressing water problems without risk of state failure. Terrorist organizations might also increasingly seek to control or degrade water infrastructure to gain revenue or influence populations.

### Increase in Global Instability Risk

Global political instability risks will remain high in 2015 and beyond. Mass atrocities, sectarian or religious violence, and curtailed NGO activities will all continue to increase these risks. Declining economic conditions are contributing to risk of instability or internal conflict.

- Roughly half of the world's countries not already experiencing or recovering from instability are in the "most risk" and "significant risk" categories for regime-threatening and violent instability through 2015.

- Overall international will and capability to prevent or mitigate mass atrocities will probably diminish in 2015 owing to reductions in government budgets and spending.

- In 2014, about two dozen countries increased restrictions on NGOs. Approximately another dozen also plan to do so in 2015, according to the International Center for Nonprofit Law.

## Critical Thinking

1. What is the basic message of the 2015 Report of the U.S. Intelligence Community on its worldwide threat assessment?

2. What is being done and can yet be done about cyber attacks?

3. Does this report reassure you or increase your fears?

## Internet References

**New American Studies Web**
   https://blogs.commons.georgetown.edu/vkp/
**Social Science Information Gateway**
   http://www.ariadne.ac.uk/issue2/sosig
**Sociology—Study Sociology Online**
   http://edu.learnsoc.org/
**Sociology Web Resources**
   http://www.mhhe.com/socscience/sociology/resources/index.htm
**Sociosite**
   http://www.topsite.com/goto/sociosite.net
**Socioweb**
   http://www.topsite.com/goto/socioweb.com

Clapper, James R. "Statement for the Record: Worldwide Threat Assessment of the US Intelligence Community," Office of the Director of National Intelligence, February 2015.

*Article*                    Prepared by: Kurt Finsterbusch, *University of Maryland, College Park*

# Low-Tech Terrorism

BRUCE HOFFMAN

## Learning Outcomes

*After reading this article, you will be able to:*

- Understand the dangers of cyberterrorism.

- Describe how the United States can combat cyberterrorism.

Among the more prescient analyses of the terrorist threats that the United States would face in the twenty-first century was a report published in September 1999 by the US Commission on National Security/21st century, better known as the Hart-Rudman commission. Named after its cochairs, former senators Gary Hart and Warren Rudman, and evocatively titled *New World Coming,* it correctly predicted that mass-casualty terrorism would emerge as one of America's preeminent security concerns in the next century. "Already," the report's first page lamented, "the traditional functions of law, police work, and military power have begun to blur before our eyes as new threats arise." It added, "Notable among these new threats is the prospect of an attack on US cities by independent or state-supported terrorists using weapons of mass destruction."

Although hijacked commercial aircraft deliberately flown into high-rise buildings were not the weapons of mass destruction that the commission had in mind, the catastrophic effects that this tactic achieved—obliterating New York City's World Trade Center, slicing through several of the Pentagon's concentric rings and killing nearly 3,000 people—indisputably captured the gist of that prophetic assertion.

The report was also remarkably accurate in anticipating the terrorist organizational structures that would come to dominate the first dozen or so years of the new century. "Future terrorists will probably be even less hierarchically organized, and yet better networked, than they are today. Their diffuse nature will make them more anonymous, yet their ability to coordinate

mass effects on a global basis will increase," the commission argued. Its vision of the motivations that would animate and subsequently fuel this violence was similarly revelatory. "The growing resentment against Western culture and values in some parts of the world," along with "the fact that others often perceive the United States as exercising its power with arrogance and self-absorption," was already "breeding a backlash" that would both continue and likely evolve into new and more insidious forms, the report asserted.

Some of the commission's other visionary conclusions now read like a retrospective summary of the past decade. "The United States will be called upon frequently to intervene militarily in a time of uncertain alliances," says one, while another disconsolately warns that "even excellent intelligence will not prevent all surprises." Today's tragic events in Syria were also anticipated by one statement that addressed the growing likelihood of foreign crises "replete with atrocities and the deliberate terrorizing of civilian populations."

Fortunately, the report's most breathless prediction concerning the likelihood of terrorist use of weapons of mass destruction (WMD) has not come to pass. But this is not for want of terrorists trying to obtain such capabilities. Indeed, prior to the October 2001 US-led invasion of Afghanistan, Al Qaeda had embarked upon an ambitious quest to acquire and develop an array of such weapons that, had it been successful, would have altered to an unimaginable extent our most basic conceptions about national security and rendered moot debates over whether terrorism posed a potentially existential threat.

But just how effective have terrorist efforts to acquire and use weapons of mass destruction actually been? The September 11, 2001, attacks were widely noted for their reliance on relatively low-tech weaponry—the conversion, in effect, of airplanes into missiles by using raw physical muscle and box cutters to hijack them. Since then, efforts to gain access to WMD have been unceasing. But examining those efforts results in some surprising conclusions. While there is no cause for complacency, they do suggest that terrorists face some inherent constraints that will be difficult for them to overcome. It is easier to proclaim the threat of mass terror than to perpetrate it.

The terrorist attacks on September 11 completely recast global perceptions of threat and vulnerability. Long-standing assumptions that terrorists were more interested in publicity than in killing were dramatically swept aside in the rising crescendo of death and destruction. The butcher's bill that morning was without parallel in the annals of modern terrorism. Throughout the entirety of the twentieth century no more than 14 terrorist incidents had killed more than a 100 people, and until September 11 no terrorist operation had ever killed more than 500 people in a single attack. Viewed from another perspective, more than twice as many Americans perished within those excruciating 102 minutes than had been killed by terrorists since 1968—the year widely accepted as marking the advent of modern, international terrorism.

So massive and consequential a terrorist onslaught naturally gave rise to fears that a profound threshold in terrorist constraint and lethality had been crossed. Renewed fears and concerns were in turn generated that terrorists would now embrace an array of deadly nonconventional weapons in order to inflict even greater levels of death and destruction than had occurred that day. Attention focused specifically on terrorist use of WMD, and the so-called Cheney Doctrine emerged to shape America's national-security strategy. The doctrine derived from former vice president Dick Cheney's reported statement that "if there's a one percent chance that Pakistani scientists are helping Al Qaeda build or develop a nuclear weapon, we have to treat it as a certainty in terms of our response." What the "one percent doctrine" meant in practice, according to one observer, was that "even if there's just a one percent chance of the unimaginable coming due, act as if it's a certainty." Countering the threat of nonconventional-weapons proliferation—whether by rogue states arrayed in an "axis of evil" or by terrorists who might acquire such weapons from those same states or otherwise develop them on their own—thus became one of the central pillars of the Bush administration's time in office.

In the case of Al Qaeda, at least, these fears were more than amply justified. That group's interest in acquiring a nuclear weapon reportedly commenced as long ago as 1992—a mere four years after its creation. An attempt by an Al Qaeda agent to purchase uranium from South Africa was made either late the following year or early in 1994 without success. Osama bin Laden's efforts to obtain nuclear material nonetheless continued, as evidenced by the arrest in Germany in 1998 of

a trusted senior aide named Mamdouh Mahmud Salim, who was attempting to purchase enriched uranium. And that same year, the Al Qaeda leader issued a proclamation in the name of the "International Islamic Front for Fighting the Jews and Crusaders." Titled "The Nuclear Bomb of Islam," the proclamation declared that "it is the duty of Muslims to prepare as much force as possible to terrorize the enemies of God." When asked several months later by a Pakistani journalist whether Al Qaeda was "in a position to develop chemical weapons and try to purchase nuclear material for weapons," bin Laden replied: "I would say that acquiring weapons for the defense of Muslims is a religious duty."

Bin Laden's continued interest in nuclear weaponry was also on display at the time of the September 11 attacks. Two Pakistani nuclear scientists named Sultan Bashiruddin Mahmood and Abdul Majeed spent three days that August at a secret Al Qaeda facility outside Kabul. Although their discussions with bin Laden, his deputy Ayman al-Zawahiri and other senior Al Qaeda officials also focused on the development and employment of chemical and biological weapons, Mahmood—the former director for nuclear power at Pakistan's Atomic Energy Commission—claimed that bin Laden's foremost interest was in developing a nuclear weapon.

The movement's efforts in the biological-warfare realm, however, were far more advanced and appear to have begun in earnest with a memo written by al-Zawahiri on April 15, 1999, to Muhammad Atef, then deputy commander of Al Qaeda's military committee. Citing articles published in *Science,* the *Journal of Immunology* and the *New England Journal of Medicine,* as well as information gleaned from authoritative books such as *Tomorrow's Weapons, Peace or Pestilence* and *Chemical Warfare,* al-Zawahiri outlined in detail his thoughts on the priority to be given to developing a biological-weapons capability.

One of the specialists recruited for this purpose was a US-trained Malaysian microbiologist named Yazid Sufaat. A former captain in the Malaysian army, Sufaat graduated from the California State University in 1987 with a degree in biological sciences. He later joined Al Gamaa al-Islamiyya (the "Islamic Group"), an Al Qaeda affiliate operating in Southeast Asia, and worked closely with its military operations chief, Riduan Isamuddin, better known as Hambali, and with Hambali's own Al Qaeda handler, Khalid Sheikh Mohammed—the infamous KSM, architect of the September 11 attacks.

In January 2000, Sufaat played host to two of the 9/11 hijackers, Khalid al-Midhar and Nawaf Alhazmi, who stayed in his Kuala Lumpur condominium. Later that year, Zacarias Moussaoui, the alleged "twentieth hijacker," who was sentenced in 2006 to life imprisonment by a federal district court in Alexandria, Virginia, also stayed with Sufaat. Under KSM's direction, Hambali and Sufaat set up shop at an Al Qaeda camp in Kandahar, Afghanistan, where their efforts focused on the weaponization of anthrax. Although the two made some progress, biowarfare experts believe that on the eve of September 11 Al Qaeda was still at least two to three years away from producing a sufficient quantity of anthrax to use as a weapon.

Meanwhile, a separate team of Al Qaeda operatives was engaged in a parallel research-and-development project to produce ricin and chemical-warfare agents at the movement's Derunta camp, near the eastern Afghan city of Jalalabad. As one senior US intelligence officer who prefers to remain anonymous explained, "Al Qaeda's WMD efforts weren't part of a single program but rather multiple compartmentalized projects involving multiple scientists in multiple locations."

The Derunta facility reportedly included laboratories and a school that trained handpicked terrorists in the use of chemical and biological weapons. Among this select group was Kamal Bourgass, an Algerian Al Qaeda operative who was convicted in British courts in 2004 and 2005 for the murder of a British police officer and of "conspiracy to commit a public nuisance by the use of poisons or explosives." The school's director was an Egyptian named Midhat Mursi—better known by his Al Qaeda nom de guerre, Abu Kebab—and among its instructors were a Pakistani microbiologist and Sufaat. When US military forces overran the camp in 2001, evidence of the progress achieved in developing chemical weapons as diverse as hydrogen cyanide, chlorine and phosgene was discovered. Mursi himself was killed in 2008 by a missile fired from a U.S. Predator drone.

Mursi's death dealt another significant blow to Al Qaeda's efforts to develop nonconventional weapons—but it did not end them. In fact, as the aforementioned senior US intelligence officer recently commented, "Al Qaeda's ongoing procurement efforts have been well established for awhile now . . . They haven't been highlighted in the U.S. media, but that isn't the same as it not happening." In 2010, for instance, credible intelligence surfaced that Al Qaeda in the Arabian Peninsula—widely considered the movement's most dangerous and capable affiliate—was deeply involved in the development of ricin, a bioweapon made from castor beans that the FBI has termed the third most toxic substance known, behind only plutonium and botulism.

Then, in May 2013, Turkish authorities seized two kilograms of sarin nerve gas—the same weapon used in the 1995 attack on the Tokyo subway system—and arrested 12 men linked to Al Qaeda's Syrian affiliate, Al Nusra Front. Days later, another set of sarin-related arrests was made in Iraq of Al Qaeda operatives based in that country who were separately overseeing the production of sarin and mustard blistering agents at two or more locations.

Finally, Israel admitted in November 2013 that for the past three years it had been holding a senior Al Qaeda operative whose expertise was in biological warfare. "The revelations over his alleged biological weapons links," one account noted of the operative's detention, "come amid concerns that Al Qaeda affiliates in Syria are attempting to procure bioweapons—and may already have done so."

Indeed, Syria's ongoing civil war and the prominent position of two key Al Qaeda affiliates—Al Nusra Front and the Islamic State of Iraq and the Levant—along with other sympathetic jihadi entities in that epic struggle, coupled with the potential access afforded to Bashar al-Assad's chemical-weapons stockpiles, suggest that we have likely not heard the last of Al Qaeda's ambitions to obtain nerve agents, poison gas and other harmful toxins for use as mass-casualty weapons.

Nonetheless, a fundamental paradox appears to exist so far as terrorist capabilities involving chemical, biological and nuclear weapons are concerned. As mesmerizingly attractive as these nonconventional weapons remain to Al Qaeda and other terrorist organizations, they have also mostly proven frustratingly disappointing to whoever has tried to use them. Despite the extensive use of poison gas during World War I, for instance, this weapon accounted for only 5 percent of all casualties in that conflict. Reportedly, it required some 60 pounds of mustard gas to produce even a single casualty. Even in more recent times, chemical weapons claimed the lives of less than 1 percent (500) of the 600,000 Iranians who died in the Iran-Iraq war. The Japanese cult Aum Shinrikyo succeeded in killing no more than 13 people in its attack on the Tokyo underground in 1995. And, five years earlier, no fatalities resulted from a Tamil Tigers assault on a Sri Lankan armed forces base in East Kiran that employed chlorine gas. In fact, the wind changed and blew the gas back into the Tigers' lines, thus aborting the attack.

Biological weapons have proven similarly difficult to deploy effectively. Before and during World War II, the Imperial Japanese Army carried out nearly a dozen attacks using a variety of germ agents—including cholera, dysentery, bubonic plague, anthrax and paratyphoid, disseminated through both air and water—against Chinese forces. Not once did these weapons decisively affect the outcome of a battle. And, in the 1942 assault on Chekiang, 10,000 Japanese soldiers themselves became ill, and nearly 2,000 died, from exposure to these agents. "The Japanese program's principal defect, a problem to all efforts so far," the American terrorism expert David Rapoport concluded, was "an ineffective delivery system."

The challenges inherent in using germs as weapons are borne out by the research conducted for more than a decade by Seth Carus, a researcher at the National Defense University.

Carus has assembled perhaps the most comprehensive database of the use of biological agents by a wide variety of adversaries, including terrorists, government operatives, ordinary criminals and the mentally unstable. His exhaustive research reveals that no more than a total of 10 people were killed and less than a 1,000 were made ill as a result of about 200 incidents of bioterrorism or biocrime. Most of which, moreover, entailed the individual poisoning of specific people rather than widespread, indiscriminate attacks.

The formidable challenges of obtaining the material needed to construct a nuclear bomb, along with the fabrication and dissemination difficulties involving the use of noxious gases and biological agents, perhaps account for the operational conservatism long observed in terrorist tactics and weaponry. As politically radical or religiously fanatical as terrorists may be, they nonetheless to date have overwhelmingly seemed to prefer the tactical assurance of the comparatively modest effects achieved by the conventional weapons with which they are familiar, as opposed to the risk of failure inherent in the use of more exotic means of death and destruction. Terrorists, as Brian Jenkins famously observed in 1985, thus continue to "appear to be more imitative than innovative." Accordingly, what innovation does occur tends to take place in the realm of the clever adaptation or modification of existing tactics—such as turning hijacked passenger airliners into cruise missiles—or in the means and methods used to fabricate and detonate explosive devices, rather than in the use of some new or dramatically novel weapon.

Terrorists have thus functioned mostly in a technological vacuum: either aloof or averse to the profound changes that have fundamentally altered the nature of modern warfare. Whereas technological progress has produced successively more complex, lethally effective, and destructively accurate weapons systems that are deployed from a variety of air, land, sea—and space—platforms, terrorists continue to rely, as they have for more than a century, on the same two basic "weapons systems": the gun and the bomb. Admittedly, the guns used by terrorists today have larger ammunition capacities and more rapid rates of fire than the simple revolver the Russian revolutionary Vera Zasulich used in 1878 to assassinate the governor-general of St. Petersburg. Similarly, bombs today require smaller amounts of explosives that are exponentially more powerful and more easily concealed than the sticks of TNT with which the Fenian dynamiters terrorized London more than a century ago. But the fact remains that the vast majority of terrorist incidents continue to utilize the same two attack modes.

Why is this? There are perhaps two obvious explanations: ease and cost. Indeed, as Leonardo da Vinci is said to have observed in a completely different era and context, "Simplicity is the ultimate sophistication." The same can be said about *most* terrorist—and insurgent—weapons and tactics today.

Improvised explosive devices (IED) and bombs constructed of commercially available, readily accessible homemade materials now account for the lion's share of terrorist—and insurgent—attacks. The use of two crude bombs packed in ordinary pressure cookers that killed three people and injured nearly 300 others at last April's Boston Marathon is among the more recent cases in point. Others include the succession of peroxide-based bombs that featured in the July 2005 suicide attacks on London transport, the 2006 plot to blow up seven American and Canadian airliners while in flight from Heathrow Airport to various destinations in North America, and the 2009 attempt to replicate the London transport bombings on the New York City subway system.

The account of the construction of the bombs intended for the New York City attack presented in the book *Enemies Within* vividly illustrates this point. Written by two Pulitzer Prize-winning journalists, Matt Apuzzo and Adam Goldman, the book describes how the would-be bomber, an Afghanistan-born, permanent U.S. resident named Najibullah Zazi, easily purchased the ingredients needed for the device's construction and then, following the instructions given to him by his Al Qaeda handlers in Pakistan, created a crude but potentially devastatingly lethal weapon:

> For weeks he'd been visiting beauty supply stores, filling his carts with hydrogen peroxide and nail polish remover. At the Beauty Supply Warehouse, among the rows of wigs, braids, and extensions, the manager knew him as Jerry. He said his girlfriend owned hair salons. There was no reason to doubt him.

> On pharmacy shelves, in the little brown plastic bottles, hydrogen peroxide is a disinfectant, a sting-free way to clean scrapes. Beauty salons use a more concentrated version to bleach hair or activate hair dyes. At even higher concentrations, it burns the skin. It is not flammable on its own, but when it reacts with other chemicals, it quickly releases oxygen, creating an environment ripe for explosions. . . . Even with a cheap stove, it's easy to simmer water out of hydrogen peroxide, leaving behind something more potent. It takes time, and he had plenty of that.

Preparing the explosive initiator was only slightly more complicated, but considerably more dangerous. Hence, Zazi had to be especially careful. "He added the muriatic acid and watched as the chemicals crystallized," the account continues:

> The crystals are known as triacetone triperoxide, or TATP. A spark, electrical current, even a bit of friction can set off an explosion. . . .

The white crystal compound had been popular among Palestinian terrorists. It was cheap and powerful, but its instability earned it the nickname "Mother of Satan". . . .

When he was done mixing, he rinsed the crystals with baking soda and water to make his creation more stable. He placed the finished product in a wide-rimmed glass jar about the size of a coffee tin and inspected his work. There would be enough for three detonators. Three detonators inside three backpacks filled with a flammable mixture and ball bearings—the same type of weapon that left 52 dead in London in 2005. . . .

He was ready for New York.

These types of improvised weapons are not only devastatingly effective but also remarkably inexpensive, further accounting for their popularity. For example, the House of Commons Intelligence and Security Committee, which investigated the 2005 London transport attacks, concluded that the entire operation cost less than £8,000 to execute. This sum included the cost of a trip to Pakistan so that the cell leader and an accomplice could acquire the requisite bomb-making skills at a secret Al Qaeda training camp in that country's North-West Frontier Province; the purchase of all the needed equipment and ingredients once they were back in Britain; the rental of an apartment in Leeds that they turned into a bomb factory; car rentals and the purchase of cell phones; and other incidentals.

The cost-effectiveness of such homemade devices—and their appeal to terrorists—is of course not new. Decades ago, the Provisional Irish Republican Army (PIRA) demonstrated the disproportionate effects and enormous damage that crude, inexpensive homemade explosive devices could achieve. In what was described as "the most powerful explosion in London since World War II," a PIRA fertilizer bomb made with urea nitrate and diesel fuel exploded outside the Baltic Exchange in April 1992, killing three people, wounding 90 others, leaving a 12-foot-wide crater—and causing $1.25 billion in damage. Exactly a year later, a similar bomb devastated the nearby Bishops Gate, killing one person and injuring more than 40 others. Estimates put the damage of that blast at $1.5 billion.

Long a staple of PIRA operations, in the early 1990s fertilizer had cost the group on average 1 percent of a comparable amount of plastic explosive. Although after adulteration fertilizer is admittedly far less powerful than plastic explosives, it also tends to cause more damage than plastic explosives because the energy of the blast is more sustained and less controlled.

Similarly, the homemade bomb used in the first attack on New York's World Trade Center in 1993—consisting of urea nitrate derived from fertilizer but enhanced by three canisters of hydrogen gas to create a more powerful fuel-air explosion—produced a similarly impressive return on the terrorists' investment. The device cost less than $400 to construct. Yet, it not only killed six people, injured more than a 1,000 others and gouged a 180-foot-wide crater six stories deep, but also caused an estimated $550 million in damages and lost revenue to the businesses housed there. The seaborne suicide-bomb attack seven years later on the USS *Cole,* a U.S. Navy destroyer anchored in Aden, Yemen, reportedly cost Al Qaeda no more than $10,000 to execute. But, in addition to claiming the lives of 17 American sailors and wounding 39 others, it cost the U.S. Navy $250 million to repair the damage caused to the vessel.

This trend toward the increased use of IEDS has had its most consequential and pernicious effects in Iraq and Afghanistan during our prolonged deployments there. As Andrew Bacevich, a retired U.S. Army officer and current Boston University professor, has written, "No matter how badly battered and beaten, the 'terrorists'" on these and other recent battlefields were not "intimidated, remained unrepentant, and kept coming back for more, devising tactics against which forces optimized for conventional combat did not have a ready response." He adds, "The term invented for this was 'asymmetric conflict,' loosely translated as war against adversaries who won't fight the way we want them to."

In Iraq and Afghanistan, both terrorists and insurgents alike have waged low-risk wars of attrition against American, British, allied and host military forces using a variety of IEDS with triggering devices as simple as garage-door openers, cordless phones and car key fobs to confound, if not hobble, among the most technologically advanced militaries in the history of mankind. "The richest, most-trained army got beat by dudes in manjammies and A.K.'s," an American soldier observed to a *New York Times* reporter of one such bloody engagement in Afghanistan five years ago.

Indeed, terrorists and insurgents in both Afghanistan and Iraq have demonstrated the effectiveness of even poorly or modestly armed nonstate adversaries in confronting superior, conventional military forces and waging a deadly war of attrition designed in part to undermine popular support and resolve back home for these prolonged deployments. Equally worrisome, these battle environments have become spawning grounds for continued and future violence: real-life training camps for jihadis and hands-on laboratories for the research and development of new and ever more deadly terrorist and insurgent tactics and techniques. "How do you stop foes who kill with devices built for the price of a pizza?" was the question posed by a *Newsweek* cover story about IEDS in 2007. "Maybe the question is," it continued, "can you stop them?"

At one point, IEDS were responsible for nearly two-thirds of military fatalities caused by terrorists and insurgents in Iraq and a quarter of the military fatalities in Afghanistan. According to one authoritative account, there was an IED incident every 15 minutes in Iraq during 2006. And, after the number of IED attacks had doubled in Afghanistan during 2009, this tactic accounted for three-quarters of military casualties in some areas.

These explosive devices often were constructed using either scavenged artillery or mortar shells, with military or commercial ordnance, or from entirely homemade ingredients. They were then buried beneath roadways, concealed among roadside refuse, hidden in animal carcasses or telephone poles, camouflaged into curbsides or secreted along the guard rails on the shoulders of roadways, put in boxes, or disguised as rocks or bricks strewn by the side of the road. As military vehicle armor improved, the bomb makers adapted and adjusted to these new force-protection measures and began to design and place IEDS in elevated positions, attaching them to road signs or trees, in order to impact the vehicles' unarmored upper structure.

The method of detonation has also varied as United States, allied and host forces have adapted to insurgent tactics. Command-wire detonators were replaced by radio-signal triggering devices such as cell phones and garage-door openers. These devices were remote wired up to 100 meters from the IED detonator to obviate jamming measures. More recently, infrared lasers have been used as explosive initiators. One or more artillery shells rigged with blasting caps and improvised shrapnel (consisting of bits of concrete, nuts, bolts, screws, tacks, ball bearings, etc.) have been the most commonly used, but the makeshift devices have also gradually become larger as multinational forces added more armor to their vehicles, with evidence from insurgent propaganda videos of aviation bombs of 500 lb. being used as IEDS. In some cases, these improvised devices are detonated serially—in "daisy chain" explosions—designed to mow down quick-reaction forces converging on the scene following the initial blast and first wave of casualties.

By 2011, the U.S. Defense Department had spent nearly $20 billion on IED countermeasures—including new technologies, programs, and enhanced and constantly updated training. A "massive new military bureaucracy" had to be created to oversee this effort and itself was forced to create "unconventional processes for introducing new programs," as a 2010 New America Foundation report put it. Yet, as the British Army found in its war against Jewish terrorists in Palestine 70 years ago, there is no easy or lasting solution to this threat, IED attacks had in fact become so pervasive in Palestine that in December 1946 British Army headquarters in Jerusalem issued a meticulously detailed 35-page pamphlet, complete

with photographs and diagrams, describing these weapons, their emplacement and their lethal effects. Even so, as military commanders and civilian authorities alike acknowledged at the time, IEDS were then as now virtually impossible to defend against completely.

Perhaps the most novel and innovative use of IEDS, however, has been when they have been paired with toxic chemicals. Much as the Iraq conflict has served as a proving ground for other terrorist weapons and tactics, it has also served this purpose with chemical weapons. Between 2007 and 2010, more than a dozen major truck-bomb attacks occurred in Iraq involving conventional explosions paired with chlorine gas.

The most serious incident, however, was one that was foiled by Jordanian authorities in April 2004. It involved the toxic release of chemicals into a crowded urban environment and was orchestrated by the late Abu Musab al-Zarqawi, the founder and leader of Al Qaeda in Iraq. The Amman plot entailed the use of some 20 tons of chemicals and explosives to target simultaneously the prime minister's office, the General Intelligence Department's headquarters and the U.S. embassy. Although the main purpose of the coordinated operations was to conduct forced-entry attacks by suicide bombers against these three heavily protected, high-value targets, an ancillary intention is believed to have been the infliction of mass casualties on the surrounding areas by the noxious chemical agents deliberately released in the blasts. An estimated 80,000 people, Jordanian authorities claim, would have been killed or seriously injured in the operation.

The above attacks in Iraq and the foiled incident in Amman all underscore the potential for terrorists to attack a domestic industrial chemical facility with a truck bomb or other large explosive device, with the purpose of triggering the release of toxic chemicals. In this respect, the effects of prior industrial accidents involving chemicals may exert a profound influence over terrorists. In 2005, for instance, a train crash and derailment in South Carolina released some 60 tons of liquefied chlorine into the air, killing nine people and injuring 250 others. Considerably more tragic, of course, was the 1984 disaster at a Union Carbide chemical facility in Bhopal, India. Some 40 tons of methyl isocyanate were accidentally released into the environment and killed nearly 4,000 people living around the plant. Methyl isocyanate is one of the more toxic chemicals used in industry, with a toxicity that is only a few percent less than that of sarin.

The war on terrorism today generates little interest and even less enthusiasm. A decade of prolonged military deployments to Iraq and Afghanistan has drained both the treasuries and willpower of the United States, Great Britain, and many other countries, as well as the ardor and commitment that attended the commencement of this global struggle over a dozen years ago. The killings of leading Al Qaeda figures such as bin Laden and Anwar al-Awlaki—along with some 40 other senior commanders and hundreds of the group's fighters—have sufficiently diminished the threat of terrorism to our war-weary, economically preoccupied nations.

But before we simply conclude that the threat from either Al Qaeda or terrorism has disappeared, it would be prudent to pause and reflect on the expansive dimensions of Al Qaeda's WMD research-and-development efforts—and also to consider the continuing developments on the opposite end of the technological spectrum that have likewise transformed the threat against conventionally superior militaries and even against superpowers. Like it or not, the war on terrorism continues, abetted by the technological advances of our adversaries and thus far mercifully countered by our own technological prowess—and all the more so by our unyielding vigilance.

# Critical Thinking

1. What kind of damages can cyberterrorists cause?
2. How can the United States defend against cyberterrorists?
3. Could cyberterrorism cause society to literally break down?

# Internet References

**ACLU Criminal Justice Home Page**
www.aclu.org/crimjustice/index.html

**Human Rights and Humanitarian Assistance**
www.etown.edu/vl/humrts.html

**New American Studies Web**
www.georgetown.edu/crossroads/asw

**Sociology—Study Sociology Online**
http://edu.learnsoc.org

**Sociology Web Resources**
http://www.mhhe.com/socscience/sociology/resources/index.htm

**Sociosite**
http://www.topsite.com/goto/sociosite.net

**Socioweb**
http://www.topsite.com/goto/socioweb.com

**Terrorism Research Center**
www.terrorism.com

BRUCE HOFFMAN is a contributing editor to *The National Interest,* a senior fellow at the U.S. Military Academy's Combating Terrorism Center, and a professor and director of the Center for Security Studies at Georgetown University.

# Unit 6

# UNIT

Prepared by: Kurt Finsterbusch, *University of Maryland, College Park*

# Problems of Population, Environment, Resources, and the Future

This unit focuses on problems of the future (mostly from a worldwide perspective) and covers topics such as present population and environmental trends, problems with new technologies, and prospects for the future.

Some scholars are very concerned about the worsening state of the environment, and others are confident that technological developments will solve most of these problems. Because the debate is about the future, neither view can be proved or disproved. Nevertheless, it is important to look at the factors that are causing environmental decline and increasing the demands on the environment. One factor is population growth, so future demographics and their implications must be assessed. Another required assessment is a survey of the many environmental

problems that need to be addressed. Especially important are food production problems and the current and potential impacts of global warming.

A key issue in predicting the future is how future technology will change conditions and prospects. One author in this unit argues that technology and innovation will save the planet. Many futurists, however, are not so optimistic. There have been many positive trends in the past century, and many of these are expected to continue, but there have been some negative trends, and they might increase. Especially worrisome are trends in economic and political power and in ideologies that may be creating a world that Americans fear.

*Article*          Prepared by: Kurt Finsterbusch, *University of Maryland, College Park*

# How Will We Feed the New Global Middle Class?

Charles C. Mann

## Learning Outcomes

*After reading this article, you will be able to:*

- Answer Mann's question: "In 2050 . . . can everyone eat without destroying the earth?"

- Understand both apocalyptic environmentalism and techno-optimism and possibly choose between them.

- Describe how the new plant varieties postponed environmental collapse.

**I**n 2050 the world population will be 10 billion. Can everyone eat without destroying the Earth?

All parents remember the moment when they first held their children—the tiny crumpled face, an entire new person, emerging from the hospital blanket. I extended my hands and took my daughter in my arms. I was so overwhelmed that I could hardly think. Afterward I wandered outside so that mother and child could rest. It was three in the morning, late February in New England. There was ice on the sidewalk and a cold drizzle in the air. As I stepped from the curb, a thought popped into my head: When my daughter is my age, almost 10 billion people will be walking the Earth. I stopped mid-stride. I thought, How is that going to work? In 1970, when I was in high school, about one out of every four people was hungry-"undernourished," to use the term preferred today by the United Nations. Today the proportion has fallen to roughly one out of 10. In those four-plus decades, the global average life span has, astoundingly, risen by more than 11 years; most of the increase occurred in poor places.

Hundreds of millions of people in Asia, Latin America, and Africa have lifted themselves from destitution into something like the middle class. This enrichment has not occurred evenly or equitably: Millions upon millions are not prosperous. Still, nothing like this surge of well-being has ever happened before. No one knows whether the rise can continue, or whether our current affluence can be sustained.

Today the world has about 7.6 billion inhabitants. Most demographers believe that by about 2050, that number will reach 10 billion or a bit less. Around this time, our population will probably begin to level off. As a species, we will be at about "replacement level": On average, each couple will have just enough children to replace themselves. All the while, economists say, the world's development should continue, however unevenly. The implication is that when my daughter is my age, a sizable percentage of the world's 10 billion people will be middle-class.

Like other parents, I want my children to be comfortable in their adult lives. But in the hospital parking lot, this suddenly seemed unlikely. Ten billion mouths, I thought. Three billion more middle-class appetites. How can they possibly be satisfied? But that is only part of the question. The full question is: How can we provide for everyone without making the planet uninhabitable?

## Bitter Rivals

While my children were growing up, I took advantage of journalistic assignments to speak about these questions, from time to time, with experts in Europe, Asia, and the Americas. As the conversations accumulated, the responses seemed to fall into two broad categories, each associated (at least in my mind) with one of two people, both of them Americans who lived in the 20th century. The two people were barely acquainted and had little regard for each other's work. But they were largely responsible for the creation of the basic intellectual blueprints that institutions around the world use today for understanding our environmental dilemmas. Unfortunately, their blueprints offer radically different answers to the question of survival.

The two people were William Vogt and Norman Borlaug.

Vogt, born in 1902, laid out the basic ideas for the modern environmental movement. In particular, he founded what the Hampshire College population researcher Betsy Hartmann has called "apocalyptic environmentalism"—the belief that unless humankind drastically reduces consumption and limits population, it will ravage global ecosystems. In best-selling books and powerful speeches, Vogt argued that affluence is not our greatest achievement but our biggest problem. If we continue taking more than the Earth can give, he said, the unavoidable result will be devastation on a global scale. Cut back! Cut back! was his mantra. Borlaug, born 12 years after Vogt, has become the emblem of "techno-optimism"—the view that science and technology, properly applied, will let us produce a way out of our predicament. He was the best-known figure in the research that in the 1960s created the Green Revolution, the combination of high-yielding crop varieties and agronomic techniques that increased grain harvests around the world, helping to avert tens of millions of deaths from hunger. To Borlaug, affluence was not the problem but the solution. Only by getting richer and more knowledgeable can humankind create the science that will resolve our environmental dilemmas. Innovate! Innovate! was his cry.

Both men thought of themselves as using new scientific knowledge to face a planetary crisis. But that is where the similarity ends.

For Borlaug, human ingenuity was the solution to our problems. One example: By using the advanced methods of the Green Revolution to increase per-acre yields, he argued, farmers would not have to plant as many acres, an idea researchers now call the "Borlaug hypothesis." Vogt's views were the opposite: The solution, he said, was to use ecological knowledge to get smaller. Rather than grow more grain to produce more meat, humankind should, as his followers say, "eat lower on the food chain," to lighten the burden on Earth's ecosystems. This is where Vogt differed from his predecessor, Robert Malthus, who famously predicted that societies would inevitably run out of food because they would always have too many children. Vogt, shifting the argument, said that we may be able to grow enough food, but at the cost of wrecking the world's ecosystems.

I think of the adherents of these two perspectives as "Wizards" and "Prophets." Wizards, following Borlaug's model, unveil technological fixes; Prophets, looking to Vogt, decry the consequences of our heedlessness.

Borlaug and Vogt traveled in the same orbit for decades, but rarely acknowledged each other. Their first and only meeting, in the mid-1940s, led to disagreement—immediately afterward, Vogt tried to get Borlaug's work shut down. So far as I know, they never spoke afterward. Each referred to the other's ideas

in public addresses, but never attached a name. Instead, Vogt rebuked the anonymous "deluded" scientists who were actually aggravating our problems. Borlaug branded his opponents "Luddites."

Both men are dead now, but the dispute between their disciples has only become more vehement. Wizards view the Prophets' emphasis on cutting back as intellectually dishonest, indifferent to the poor, even racist (because most of the world's hungry are non Caucasian). Following Vogt, they say, is a path toward regression, narrowness, poverty, and hunger—toward a world where billions live in misery despite the scientific knowledge that could free them. Prophets sneer that the Wizards' faith in human resourcefulness is unthinking, ignorant, even driven by greed (because refusing to push beyond ecological limits will cut into corporate profits). High-intensity, Borlaug-style industrial farming, Prophets say, may pay off in the short run, but in the long run will make the day of ecological reckoning hit harder.

The ruination of soil and water by heedless overuse will lead to environmental collapse, which will in turn create worldwide social convulsion. Wizards reply: That's exactly the global humanitarian crisis we're preventing! As the finger pointing has escalated, conversations about the environment have turned into dueling monologues, each side unwilling to engage with the other.

Which might be all right, if we weren't discussing the fate of our children.

## The Roads to Hell

Vogt entered history in 1948, when he published Road to Survival, the first modern we're-all-going-to-hell book. It contained the foundational argument of today's environmental movement: carrying capacity. Often called by other names—"ecological limits," "planetary boundaries"—carrying capacity posits that every ecosystem has a limit to what it can produce. Exceed that limit for too long and the ecosystem will be ruined. As human numbers increase, Road to Survival said, our demands for food will exceed the Earth's carrying capacity. The results will be catastrophic: erosion, desertification, soil exhaustion, species extinction, and water contamination that will, sooner or later, lead to massive famines. Embraced by writers like Rachel Carson (the author of Silent Spring and one of Vogt's friends) and Paul Ehrlich (the author of The Population Bomb), Vogt's arguments about exceeding limits became the wellspring of today's globe spanning environmental movement—the only enduring ideology to emerge from the past century.

When Road to Survival appeared, Borlaug was a young plant pathologist working in a faltering program to improve Mexican agriculture. Sponsored by the Rockefeller Foundation, the project focused on helping the nation's poor corn farmers. Borlaug was in Mexico for a small side project that involved wheat—or rather, black stem rust, a fungus that is wheat's oldest and worst predator (the Romans made sacrifices to propitiate the god of stem rust). Cold usually killed stem rust in the United States, but it was constantly present in warmer Mexico, and every spring winds drove it across the border to reinfect U.S. wheat fields.

The sole Rockefeller researcher working on wheat, Borlaug was given so little money that he had to sleep in sheds and fields for months on end. But he succeeded by the mid-'50s in breeding wheat that was resistant to many strains of rust. Not only that, he then created wheat that was much shorter than usual—what became known as "semi-dwarf" wheat. In the past, when wheat was heavily fertilized, it had grown so fast that its stalks became spindly and fell over in the wind. The plants, unable to pull themselves erect, had rotted and died. Borlaug's shorter, stouter wheat could absorb large doses of fertilizer and channel the extra growth into grain rather than roots or stalk. In early tests, farmers sometimes harvested literally 10 times as much grain from their fields. Yields climbed at such a rate that in 1968 a USAID official called the rise the Green Revolution, thus naming the phenomenon that would come to define the 20th century.

The Green Revolution had its most dramatic effects in Asia, where in 1962 the Rockefeller Foundation and the Ford Foundation opened the International Rice Research Institute (IRRI) in the Philippines. At the time, at least half of Asia lived in hunger and want; farm yields in many places were stagnant or falling. Governments that had only recently thrown off colonialism were battling communist insurgencies, most notably in Vietnam. U.S. leaders believed the appeal of communism lay in its promise of a better future. Washington wanted to demonstrate that development occurred best under capitalism. IRRI'S hope was that top research teams would transform Asia by rapidly introducing modern rice agriculture—"a Manhattan Project for food," in the historian Nick Cullather's phrase.

Following Borlaug's lead, IRRI researchers developed new, high-yielding rice varieties. These swept through Asia in the '70s and '80s, nearly tripling rice harvests. More than 80 percent of the rice grown in Asia today originated at IRRI. Even though the continent's population has soared, Asian men, women, and children consume an average of 30 percent more calories than they did when IRRI was founded. Seoul and Shanghai, Jaipur and Jakarta; shining skyscrapers, pricey hotels, traffic-jammed streets ablaze with neon—all were built atop a foundation of laboratory-bred rice.

Were the Prophets disproved? Was carrying capacity a chimera? No. As Vogt had predicted, the enormous jump in productivity led to enormous environmental damage: drained aquifers, fertilizer runoff, aquatic dead zones, and degraded and waterlogged soils. Worse in a human sense, the rapid increase in productivity made rural land more valuable.

Suddenly it was worth stealing—and rural elites in many places did just that, throwing poor farmers off their land. The Prophets argued that the Green Revolution would merely postpone the hunger crisis; it was a one-time lucky break, rather than a permanent solution. And our rising numbers and wealth mean that, just as the Prophets said, our harvests will have to jump again—a second Green Revolution, the Wizards add.

Even though the global population in 2050 will be just 25 percent higher than it is now, typical projections claim that farmers will have to boost food output by 50 to 100 percent. The main reason is that increased affluence has always multiplied the demand for animal products such as cheese, dairy, fish, and especially meat—and growing feed for animals requires much more land, water, and energy than producing food simply by growing and eating plants. Exactly how much more meat tomorrow's billions will want to consume is unpredictable, but if they are anywhere near as carnivorous as today's Westerners, the task will be huge.

And, Prophets warn, so will the planetary disasters that will come of trying to satisfy the world's desire for burgers and bacon: ravaged landscapes, struggles over water, and land grabs that leave millions of farmers in poor countries with no means of survival.

What to do? Some of the strategies that were available during the first Green Revolution aren't anymore. Farmers can't plant much more land, because almost every accessible acre of arable soil is already in use. Nor can the use of fertilizer be increased; it is already being overused everywhere except some parts of Africa, and the runoff is polluting rivers, lakes, and oceans. Irrigation, too, cannot be greatly expanded—most land that can be irrigated already is. Wizards think the best course is to use genetic modification to create more-productive crops. Prophets see that as a route to further overwhelming the planet's carrying capacity. We must go in the opposite direction, they say: use less land, waste less water, stop pouring chemicals into both.

### William Vogt

It is as if humankind were packed into a bus racing through an impenetrable fog. Somewhere ahead is a cliff: a calamitous reversal of humanity's fortunes. Nobody can see exactly where it is, but everyone knows that at some point the bus will have to turn. Problem is, Wizards and Prophets disagree about which way to yank the wheel. Each is certain that following the other's ideas will send the bus over the cliff. As they squabble, the number of passengers keeps rising.

## The Story of Nitrogen

Almost everybody eats every day, but too few of us give any thought to how that happens. If agricultural history were required in schools, more people would know the name of Justus von

Liebig, who in the mid içth century established that the amount of nitrogen in the soil controls the rate of plant growth. Historians of science have charged Liebig with faking his data and stealing others' ideas—accurately, so far as I can tell. But he was also a visionary who profoundly changed the human species' relationship with nature.

Smarmy but farsighted, Liebig imagined a new kind of agriculture: farming as a branch of chemistry and physics. Soil was just a base with the physical attributes necessary to hold roots. Pour in nitrogen-containing compounds—factory-made fertilizer—and gigantic harvests would automatically follow. In today's terms, Liebig was taking the first steps toward chemically regulated industrial agriculture—an early version of Wizardly thought.

But there was no obvious way to manufacture the nitrogenous substances that feed plants. That technology was provided before and during the First World War by two German chemists, Fritz Haber and Carl Bosch. Their subsequent Nobel Prizes were richly deserved: The Haber-Bosch process, as it is called, was arguably the most consequential technological innovation of the 20th century.

Today the Haber-Bosch process is responsible for almost all of the world's synthetic fertilizer. A little more than 1 percent of the world's industrial energy is devoted to it. "That 1 percent," the futurist Ramez Naam has noted, "roughly doubles the amount of food the world can grow." The environmental scientist Vaclav Smil has estimated that nitrogen fertilizer from the Haber-Bosch process accounts for "the prevailing diets of nearly 45% of the world's population." More than 3 billion men, women, and children—an incomprehensibly vast cloud of hopes, fears, memories, and dreams—owe their existence to two obscure German chemists.

Hard on the heels of the gains came the losses. About 40 percent of the fertilizer applied in the past 60 years was not absorbed by plants. Instead, it washed away into rivers or seeped into the air in the form of nitrous oxides. Fertilizer flushed into water still fertilizes: It boosts the growth of algae, weeds, and other aquatic organisms. When these die, they fall to the floor of the river, lake, or ocean, where microbes consume their remains. So rapidly do the microbes grow on the manna of dead algae and weeds that their respiration drains oxygen from the lower depths, killing off most other life. Nitrogen from Midwestern farms flows down the Mississippi to the Gulf of Mexico every summer, creating an oxygen desert that in 2016 covered almost 7,000 square miles. The next year a still larger dead zone—23,000 square miles—was mapped in the Bay of Bengal, off the east coast of India.

Rising into the air, nitrous oxides from fertilizers is a major cause of pollution. High in the stratosphere, it combines with and neutralizes the planet's ozone, which guards life on the surface by blocking cancer-causing ultraviolet rays. Were it not

for climate change, suggests the science writer Oliver Morton, the spread of nitrogen's empire would probably be our biggest ecological worry.

Passionate resistance to that empire sprang up even before Haber and Bosch became Nobel laureates. Its leader was an English farm boy named Albert Howard (1873-1947), who spent most of his career as British India's official imperial economic botanist. Individually and together, Howard and his wife, Gabrielle, a Cambridge-educated plant physiologist, spent their time in India breeding new varieties of wheat and tobacco, developing novel types of plows, and testing the results of providing oxen with a super healthy diet. By the end of the First World War, they were convinced that soil was not simply a base for chemical additives. It was an intricate living system that required a wildly complex mix of nutrients in plant and animal waste: harvest leftovers, manure. The Howards summed up their ideas in what they called the Law of Return: "the faithful return to the soil of all available vegetable, animal, and human wastes." We depend on plants, plants depend on soil, and soil depends on us. Howard's 1943 Agricultural Testament became the founding document of the organic movement.

Wizards attacked Howard and Jerome I. Rodale—a hard-scrabble New York-born entrepreneur, publisher, playwright, gardening theorist, and food experimenter who publicized Howard's ideas through books and magazines—as charlatans and crackpots. It is true that their zeal was inspired by a near-religious faith in a limit-bound natural order. But when Howard lauded the living nature of the soil, he was referring to the community of soil organisms, the dynamic relations between plant roots and the earth around them, and the physical structure of humus, which stickily binds together soil particles into airy crumbs that hold water instead of letting it run through. All of this was very real, and all of it was unknown when Liebig shaped the basic ideas behind chemical agriculture. The claim Howard made in his many books and speeches that industrial farming was depopulating the countryside and disrupting an older way of life was accurate, too, though his opponents disagreed with him about whether this was a bad thing. Nowadays the Prophets' fears about industrial agriculture's exhausting the soil seem prescient: A landmark 2011 study from the United Nations' Food and Agriculture Organization concluded that up to a third of the world's cropland is degraded.

At first, reconciling the two points of view might have been possible. One can imagine Borlaugian Wizards considering manure and other natural soil inputs, and Vogtian Prophets willing to use chemicals as a supplement to good soil practice. But that didn't happen. Hurling insults, the two sides moved further apart. They set in motion a battle that has continued into the 21st century—and become ever more intense with the ubiquity of genetically modified crops. That battle is not just between two philosophies, two approaches to technology, two ways of thinking how best to increase the food supply for a growing population. It is about whether the tools we choose will ensure the survival of the planet or hasten its destruction.

# "Not One of Evolution's Finest Efforts"

All the while that Wizards were championing synthetic fertilizer and Prophets were denouncing it, they were united in ignorance: Nobody knew why plants were so dependent on nitrogen. Only after the Second World War did scientists discover that plants need nitrogen chiefly to make a protein called rubisco, a prima donna in the dance of interactions that is photosynthesis.

In photosynthesis, as children learn in school, plants use energy from the sun to tear apart carbon dioxide and water, blending their constituents into the compounds necessary to make roots, stems, leaves, and seeds. Rubisco is an enzyme that plays a key role in the process. Enzymes are biological catalysts. Like jaywalking pedestrians who cause automobile accidents but escape untouched, enzymes cause biochemical reactions to occur but are unchanged by those reactions. Rubisco takes carbon dioxide from the air, inserts it into the maelstrom of photosynthesis, then goes back for more. Because these movements are central to the process, photosynthesis walks at the speed of rubisco.

Alas, rubisco is, by biological standards, a sluggard, a lazybones, a couch potato. Whereas typical enzyme molecules catalyze thousands of reactions a second, rubisco molecules deign to involve themselves with just two or three a second. Worse, rubisco is inept. As many as two out of every five times, rubisco fumblingly picks up oxygen instead of carbon dioxide, causing the chain of reactions in photosynthesis to break down and have to restart, wasting energy and water. Years ago I talked with biologists about photosynthesis for a magazine article. Not one had a good word to say about rubisco. "Nearly the world's worst, most incompetent enzyme," said one researcher. "Not one of evolution's finest efforts," said another. To overcome rubisco's lassitude and maladroitness, plants make a lot of it, requiring a lot of nitrogen to do so. As much as half of the protein in many plant leaves, by weight, is rubisco—it is often said to be the world's most abundant protein. One estimate is that plants and microorganisms contain more than 11 pounds of rubisco for every person on Earth.

Evolution, one would think, should have improved rubisco. No such luck. But it did produce a work-around: C4 photosynthesis (C4 refers to a four-carbon molecule involved in the scheme). At once a biochemical kludge and a clever mechanism for turbocharging plant growth, C4 photosynthesis consists of a wholesale reorganization of leaf anatomy.

When carbon dioxide comes into a C4 leaf, it is initially grabbed not by rubisco but by a different enzyme that uses it to form a compound that is then pumped into special, rubisco filled cells deep in the leaf. These cells have almost no oxygen, so rubisco can't bumblingly grab the wrong molecule. The end result is exactly the same sugars, starches, and cellulose that ordinary photosynthesis produces, except much faster. C4 plants need less water and fertilizer than ordinary plants, because they don't waste water on rubisco's mistakes. In the sort of convergence that makes biologists snap to attention, C4 photosynthesis has arisen independently more than 60 times. Corn, tumbleweed, crabgrass, sugarcane, and Bermuda grass—all of these very different plants evolved C4 photosynthesis.

In the botanical equivalent of a moonshot, scientists from around the world are trying to convert rice into a C4 plant—one that would grow faster, require less water and fertilizer, and produce more grain. The scope and audacity of the project are hard to overstate. Rice is the world's most important foodstuff, the staple crop for more than half the global population, a food so embedded in Asian culture that the words rice and meal are variants of each other in both Chinese and Japanese. Nobody can predict with confidence how much more rice farmers will need to grow by 2050, but estimates range up to a 40 percent rise, driven by both increasing population numbers and increasing affluence, which permits formerly poor people to switch to rice from less prestigious staples such as millet and sweet potato. Meanwhile, the land available to plant rice is shrinking as cities expand into the countryside, thirsty people drain rivers, farmers switch to more-profitable crops, and climate change creates deserts from farmland. Running short of rice would be a human catastrophe with consequences that would ripple around the world.

The C4 Rice Consortium is an attempt to ensure that that never happens. Funded largely by the Bill & Melinda Gates Foundation, the consortium is the world's most ambitious genetic engineering project. But the term genetic engineering does not capture the project's scope. The genetic engineering that appears in news reports typically involves big companies sticking individual packets of genetic material, usually from a foreign species, into a crop. The paradigmatic example is Monsanto's Roundup Ready soybean, which contains a snippet of DNA from a bacterium that was found in a Louisiana waste pond. That snippet makes the plant assemble a chemical compound in its leaves and stems that blocks the effects of Roundup, Monsanto's widely used herbicide. The foreign gene lets farmers spray Roundup on their soy fields, killing weeds but leaving the crop unharmed. Except for making a single tasteless, odorless, nontoxic protein, Roundup Ready soybeans are otherwise identical to ordinary soybeans.

What the C4 Rice Consortium is trying to do with rice bears the same resemblance to typical genetically modified crops as a Boeing 787 does to a paper airplane. Rather than tinker with individual genes in order to monetize seeds, the scientists are trying to refashion photosynthesis, one of the most fundamental processes of life. Because C4 has evolved in so many different species, scientists believe that most plants must have precursor C4 genes. The hope is that rice is one of these, and that the consortium can identify and awaken its dormant C4 genes following a path evolution has taken many times before. Ideally, researchers would switch on sleeping chunks of genetic material already in rice (or use very similar genes from related species that are close cousins but easier to work with) to create, in effect, a new and more productive species. Common rice, Oryza sativa, will become something else: Oryza nova, say. No company will profit from the result; the International Rice Research Institute, where much of the research takes place, will give away seeds for the modified grain, as it did with Green Revolution rice.

When I visited IRRI, 35 miles southeast of downtown Manila, scores of people were doing what science does best: breaking a problem into individual pieces, then attacking the pieces. Some were sprouting rice in petri dishes. Others were trying to find chance variations in existing rice strains that might be helpful. Still others were studying a model organism, a C4 species of grass called Setaria viridis. Fast-growing and able to be grown in soil, not paddies, Setaria is easier to work with in the lab than rice. There were experiments to measure differences in photosynthetic chemicals, in the rates of growth of different varieties, in the transmission of biochemical markers. Half a dozen people in white coats were sorting seeds on a big table, grain by grain. More were in fields outside, tending experimental rice paddies. All of the appurtenances of contemporary biology were in evidence: flat screen monitors, humming refrigerators and freezers, tables full of beakers of recombinant goo, Dilbert and XKCD cartoons taped to whiteboards, a United Nations of graduate students a-gossip in the cafeteria, air conditioners whooshing in a row outside the windows.

Directing the C4 Rice Consortium is Jane Langdale, a molecular geneticist at Oxford's Department of Plant Sciences. Initial research, she told me, suggests that about a dozen genes play a major part in leaf structure, and perhaps another 10 genes have an equivalent role in the biochemistry. All must be activated in a way that does not affect the plant's existing, desirable qualities and that allows the genes to coordinate their actions. The next, equally arduous step would be breeding rice varieties that can channel the extra growth provided by C4 photosynthesis into additional grains, rather than roots or stalk. All the while, varieties must be disease-resistant, easy to grow, and palatable for their intended audience, in Asia, Africa, and Latin America.

"I think it can all happen, but it might not," Langdale said. She was quick to point out that even if C4 rice runs into insurmountable obstacles, it is not the only biological moonshot. Self fertilizing maize, wheat that can grow in salt water,

enhanced soil-microbial ecosystems—all are being researched. The odds that any one of these projects will succeed may be small, the idea goes, but the odds that all of them will fail are equally small. The Wizardly process begun by Borlaug is, in Langdale's view, still going strong.

## The Luddites' Moonshot

For as long as Wizards and Prophets have been arguing about feeding the world, Wizards have charged that Prophet-style agriculture simply cannot produce enough food for tomorrow. In the past 20 years, scores of research teams have appraised the relative contributions of industrial and organic agriculture. These inquiries in turn have been gathered together and assessed, a procedure that is fraught with difficulty: Researchers use different definitions of organic, compare different kinds of farms, and include different costs in their analyses. Nonetheless, every attempt to combine and compare data that I know of has shown that Prophet-style farms yield fewer calories per acre than do Wizard-style farms-sometimes by a little, sometimes by quite a lot. The implications are obvious, Wizards say. If farmers must grow twice as much food to feed the 10 billion, following the ecosystem-conserving rules of Sir Albert Howard ties their hands.

Prophets smite their brows at this logic. To their minds, evaluating farm systems wholly in terms of calories per acre is folly. It doesn't include the sort of costs identified by Vogt: fertilizer runoff, watershed degradation, soil erosion and compaction, and pesticide and antibiotic overuse. It doesn't account for the destruction of rural communities. It doesn't consider whether the food is tasty and nutritious.

Wizards respond that C4 rice will use less fertilizer and water to produce every calorie-it will be better for the environment than conventional crops. That's like trying to put out fires you started by dousing them with less gasoline! the Prophets say. Just eat less meat! To Wizards, the idea of making farms diverse in a way that mimics natural ecosystems is hooey: only hyper intensive, industrial-scale agriculture using super productive genetically modified crops can feed tomorrow's world.

Productivity? the Prophets reply. We have moon shot so fourown! And in fact, they do.

Wheat, rice, maize, oats, barley, rye, and the other common cereals are annuals, which need to be planted anew every year. By contrast, the wild grasses that used to fill the prairie are perennials: plants that come back summer after summer, for as long as a decade. Because perennial grasses build up root systems that reach deep into the ground, they hold on to soil better and are less dependent on surface rainwater and nutrients—that is, irrigation and artificial fertilizer—than annual grasses. Many of them are also more disease-resistant. Not needing to build up new roots every spring, perennials emerge from the soil earlier and faster than annuals. And because they don't die in the winter, they keep photosynthesizing in the fall, when annuals stop. Effectively, they have a longer growing season. They produce food year after year with much less plowing-caused erosion. They could be just as productive as Green Revolution-style grain, Prophets say, but without ruining land, sucking up scarce water, or requiring heavy doses of polluting, energy-intensive fertilizer.

Echoing Borlaug's program in Mexico, the Rodale Institute, the country's oldest organization that researches organic agriculture, gathered 250 samples of intermediate wheatgrass (Thinopyrum intermedium) in the late 1980s. A perennial cousin to bread wheat, wheatgrass was introduced to the Western Hemisphere from Asia in the 1930s as fodder for farm animals. Working with U.S. Department of Agriculture researchers, the Rodale Institute's Peggy Wagoner, a pioneering plant breeder and agricultural researcher, planted samples, measured their yields, and crossbred the best performers in an attempt to make a commercially viable perennial. Wagoner and the Rodale Institute passed the baton in 2002 to the Land Institute, in Salina, Kansas, a nonprofit agricultural-research center dedicated to replacing conventional agriculture with processes akin to those that occur in natural ecosystems. The Land Institute, collaborating with other researchers, has been developing wheatgrass ever since. It has even given its new variety of intermediate wheatgrass a trade name: Kernza.

Like C4 rice, wheatgrass may not fulfill its originators' hopes. Wheatgrass kernels are one-quarter the size of wheat kernels, sometimes smaller, and have a thicker layer of bran. Unlike wheat, wheatgrass grows into a dark, dense mass of foliage that covers the field; the thick layer of vegetation protects the soil and keeps out weeds, but it also reduces the amount of grain that the plant produces. To make wheatgrass useful to farmers, breeders will have to increase kernel size, alter the plant's architecture, and improve its bread-making qualities. The work has been slow. Because wheatgrass is a perennial, it must be evaluated over years, rather than a single season. The Land Institute hopes to have field-ready, bread worthy wheatgrass with kernels that are twice their current size (if still half the size of wheat's) in the 2020s, though nothing is guaranteed.

Domesticating wheatgrass is the long game. Other plant breeders have been trying for a shortcut: creating a hybrid of bread wheat and wheatgrass, hoping to marry the former's large, plentiful grain and the latter's disease resistance and perennial life cycle. The two species produce viable offspring just often enough that biologists in North America, Germany, and the Soviet Union tried unsuccessfully for decades in the mid-i900s to breed useful hybrids. Bolstered by developments in biology, the Land Institute, together with researchers in the Pacific Northwest and Australia, began anew at the turn of this century. When I visited Stephen S. Jones of Washington State University, he and his colleagues had just suggested a scientific name for the newly developed and tested hybrid: Tritipyrum aaseae (the species name honors the pioneering cereal geneticist Hannah Aase). Much work remains; Jones told me that he hoped bread from T. aaseae would be ready for my daughter's children.

African and Latin American researchers scratch their heads when they hear about these projects. Breeding perennial grains is the hard way for Prophets to raise harvests, says Edwige Botoni, a researcher at the Permanent Interstate Committee for Drought Control in the Sahel, in Burkina Faso. Botoni gave a lot of thought to the problem of feeding people from low-quality land while traveling along the edge of the Sahara. One part of the answer, she told me, would be to emulate the farms that flourish in tropical places such as Nigeria and Brazil. Whereas farmers in the temperate zones focus on cereals, tropical growers focus on tubers and trees, both of which are generally more productive than cereals.

Consider cassava, a big tuber also known as manioc, mogo, and yuca. The 11th-most-important crop in the world in terms of production, it is grown in wide swathes of Africa, Asia, and Latin America. The edible part grows underground; no matter how big the tuber, the plant will never fall over. On a per-acre basis, cassava harvests far outstrip those of wheat and other cereals. The comparison is unfair, because cassava tubers contain more water than wheat kernels. But even when this is taken into account, cassava produces many more calories per acre than wheat. (The potato is a northern equivalent. The average 2016 U.S. potato yield was 43,700 pounds per acre, more than 10 times the equivalent figure for wheat.) "I don't know why this alternative is not considered," Botoni said. Although cassava is unfamiliar to many cultures, introducing it "seems easier than breeding entirely new species."

Much the same is true for tree crops. A mature McIntosh apple tree might grow 350 to 550 pounds of apples a year. Orchard growers commonly plant 200 to 250 trees per acre. In good years this can work out to 35 to 65 tons of fruit per acre. The equivalent figure for wheat, by contrast, is about a ton and a half. As with cassava and potatoes, apples contain more water than wheat does—but the caloric yield per acre is still higher. Even papayas and bananas are more productive than wheat. So are some nuts, like chestnuts. Apples, chestnuts, and papayas cannot make crusty baguettes, crunchy tortillas, or cloud-light chiffon cakes, but most grain today is destined for highly processed substances like animal feed, breakfast cereal, sweet syrups, and ethanol—and tree and tuber crops can be readily deployed for those.

Am I arguing that farmers around the world should replace their plots of wheat, rice, and maize with fields of cassava, potato, and sweet potato and orchards of bananas, apples, and chestnuts? No. The argument is rather that Prophets have multiple ways to meet tomorrow's needs. These alternative paths are difficult, but so is the Wizards' path exemplified in C4 rice. The greatest obstacle for Prophets is something else: labor.

# The Right Way to Live

Since the end of the Second World War, most national governments have intentionally directed labor away from agriculture (Communist China was long an exception). The goal was to consolidate and mechanize farms, which would increase harvests and reduce costs, especially for labor. Farmworkers, no longer needed, would move to the cities, where they could get better paying jobs in factories. In the Borlaugian ideal, both the remaining farm owners and the factory workers would earn more, the former by growing more and better crops, the latter by obtaining better-paying jobs in industry. The nation as a whole would benefit: increased exports from industry and agriculture, cheaper food in the cities, a plentiful labor supply.

There were downsides: Cities in developing nations acquired entire slums full of displaced families. And in many areas, including most of the developed world, the countryside was emptied—exactly what Borlaugians intended, as part of the goal of freeing agriculture workers to pursue their dreams. In the United States, the proportion of the workforce employed in agriculture went from 21.5 percent in 1930 to 1.9 percent in 2000; the number of farms fell by almost two-thirds. The average size of the surviving farms increased to compensate for the smaller number. Meanwhile, states around the world established networks of tax incentives, loan plans, training programs, and direct subsidies to help big farmers acquire large-scale farm machinery, stock up on chemicals, and grow certain government-favored crops for export. Because these systems remain in effect, Vogtian farmers are swimming against the tide.

To Vogtians, the best agriculture takes care of the soil first and foremost, a goal that entails smaller patches of multiple crops—difficult to accomplish when concentrating on the mass production of a single crop. Truly extending agriculture that does this would require bringing back at least some of the people whose parents and grandparents left the countryside. Providing these workers with a decent living would drive up costs. Some labor sparing mechanization is possible, but no small farmer I have spoken with thinks that it would be possible to shrink the labor force to the level seen in big industrial operations. The whole system can grow only with a wall-to-wall rewrite of the legal system that encourages the use of labor. Such large shifts in social arrangements are not easily accomplished.

And here is the origin of the decades-long dispute between Wizards and Prophets. Although the argument is couched in terms of calories per acre and ecosystem conservation, the disagreement at bottom is about the nature of agriculture—and, with it, the best form of society. To Borlaugians, farming is a kind of useful drudgery that should be eased and reduced as much as possible to maximize individual liberty. To Vogtians, agriculture is about maintaining a set of communities, ecological and human, that have cradled life since the first agricultural revolution, 10,000-plus years ago. It can be drudgery, but it is also work that reinforces the human connection to the Earth. The two arguments are like skew lines, not on the same plane.

My daughter is 19 now, a sophomore in college. In 2050, she will be middle-aged. It will be up to her generation to set up the institutions, laws, and customs that will provide for basic human needs in the world of 10 billion. Every generation decides the future, but the choices made by my children's generation will resonate for as long as demographers can foresee. Wizard or Prophet? The choice will be less about what this generation thinks is feasible than what it thinks is good.

# Critical Thinking

1. Apocalyptic environmentalism and techno-optimism predict the future. What is the situation now?

2. What extensive changes occurred in population, environmental conditions, and resource-use technology in the last 50 years?

3. What dominant values of society affect the resource consumption behavior of individuals?

# Internet References

**New American Studies Web**
   www.georgetown.edu/crossroads/asw
**Social Science Information Gateway**
   http://sosig.esrc.bris.ac.uk
**Sociology Web Resources**
   http://www.mhhe.com/socscience/sociology/resources/index.htm
**Sociology—Study Sociology Online**
   http://edu.learnsoc.org
**Sociosite**
   http://www.topsite.com/goto/sociosite.net

CHARLES C. MANN is a contributing editor at *The Atlantic* and the author of *1491*. This article is adapted from his most recent book, *The Wizard and the Prophet*.

*Article*                              Prepared by: Kurt Finsterbusch, *University of Maryland, College Park*

# Can a Collapse of Global Civilization Be Avoided?

PAUL R. EHRLICH AND ANNE H. EHRLICH

## Learning Outcomes

*After reading this article, you will be able to:*

- Evaluate the Ehrlichs' thesis about addressing environmental problems immediately or face the possibility of the collapse of global civilization.

- Give your assessment of how to deal with the problem of Americans overusing the environment.

- Lay out the steps that should be taken to make America sustainable.

## 1. Introduction

Virtually every past civilization has eventually undergone collapse, a loss of socio-political-economic complexity usually accompanied by a dramatic decline in population size. Some, such as those of Egypt and China, have recovered from collapses at various stages; others, such as that of Easter Island or the Classic Maya, were apparently permanent. All those previous collapses were local or regional; elsewhere, other societies and civilizations persisted unaffected. Sometimes, as in the Tigris and Euphrates valleys, new civilizations rose in succession. In many, if not most, cases, overexploitation of the environment was one proximate or an ultimate cause.

But today, for the first time, humanity's global civilization—the worldwide, increasingly interconnected, highly technological society in which we all are to one degree or another, embedded—is threatened with collapse by an array of environmental problems. Humankind finds itself engaged in what Prince Charles described as 'an act of suicide on a grand scale', facing what the UK's Chief Scientific Advisor John

Beddington called a 'perfect storm' of environmental problems. The most serious of these problems show signs of rapidly escalating severity, especially climate disruption. But other elements could potentially also contribute to a collapse: an accelerating extinction of animal and plant populations and species, which could lead to a loss of ecosystem services essential for human survival; land degradation and land-use change; a pole-to-pole spread of toxic compounds; ocean acidification and eutrophication (dead zones); worsening of some aspects of the epidemiological environment (factors that make human populations susceptible to infectious diseases); depletion of increasingly scarce resources, including especially groundwater, which is being overexploited in many key agricultural areas; and resource wars. These are not separate problems; rather they interact in two gigantic complex adaptive systems: the biosphere system and the human socio-economic system. The negative manifestations of these interactions are often referred to as 'the human predicament', and determining how to prevent it from generating a global collapse is perhaps the foremost challenge confronting humanity.

The human predicament is driven by overpopulation, over-consumption of natural resources and the use of unnecessarily environmentally damaging technologies and socio-economic-political arrangements to service Homo sapiens' aggregate consumption. How far the human population size now is above the planet's long-term carrying capacity is suggested (conservatively) by ecological footprint analysis. It shows that to support today's population of seven billion sustainably (i.e. with business as usual, including current technologies and standards of living) would require roughly half an additional planet; to do so, if all citizens of Earth consumed resources at the US level would take four to five more Earths. Adding the projected 2.5 billion more people by 2050 would make the human assault on civilization's life-support systems disproportionately worse, because almost everywhere people face systems with nonlinear responses, in which environmental damage increases at a rate that becomes faster with each additional person. Of course, the claim is often made that humanity will expand Earth's carrying capacity dramatically with technological innovation, but it is widely recognized that technologies can both add and subtract from carrying capacity. The plough evidently first expanded it and now appears to be reducing it. Overall, careful analysis of the prospects does not provide much confidence that technology will save us or that gross domestic product can be disengaged from resource use.

## 2. Do Current trends Portend a Collapse?

What is the likelihood of this set of interconnected predicaments leading to a global collapse in this century? There have been many definitions and much discussion of past 'collapses', but a future global collapse does not require a careful definition. It could be triggered by anything from a 'small' nuclear war, whose ecological effects could quickly end civilization, to a more gradual breakdown because famines, epidemics and resource shortages cause a disintegration of central control within nations, in concert with disruptions of trade and conflicts over increasingly scarce necessities. In either case, regardless of survivors or replacement societies, the world familiar to anyone reading this study and the well-being of the vast majority of people would disappear.

How likely is such a collapse to occur? No civilization can avoid collapse if it fails to feed its population. The world's success so far, and the prospective ability to feed future generations at least as well, has been under relatively intensive discussion for half a century. Agriculture made civilization possible, and over the last 80 years or so, an industrial agricultural revolution has created a technology-dependent global food system. That system, humanity's single biggest industry, has generated miracles of food production. But it has also created serious long-run vulnerabilities, especially in its dependence on stable climates, crop monocultures, industrially produced fertilizers and pesticides, petroleum, antibiotic feed supplements and rapid, efficient transportation.

Despite those food production miracles, today at least two billion people are hungry or poorly nourished. The Food and Agriculture Organization estimates that increasing food production by some 70 per cent would be required to feed a 35 per cent bigger and still growing human population adequately by 2050. What are the prospects that H. sapiens can produce and distribute sufficient food? To do so, it probably will be necessary to

accomplish many or all of the following tasks: severely limit climate disruption; restrict expansion of land area for agriculture (to preserve ecosystem services); raise yields where possible; put much more effort into soil conservation; increase efficiency in the use of fertilizers, water and energy; become more vegetarian; grow more food for people (not fuel for vehicles); reduce food wastage; stop degradation of the oceans and better regulate aquaculture; significantly increase investment in sustainable agricultural and aquacultural research; and move increasing equity and feeding everyone to the very top of the policy agenda.

Most of these long-recommended tasks require changes in human behaviour thus far elusive. The problem of food wastage and the need for more and better agricultural research have been discussed for decades. So have 'technology will save us' schemes such as building 'nuclear agro-industrial complexes', where energy would be so cheap that it could support a new kind of desert agriculture in 'food factories', where crops would be grown on desalinated water and precisely machine fertilized. Unhappily, sufficiently cheap energy has never been produced by nuclear power to enable large-scale agriculture to move in that direction. Nor has agriculture moved towards feeding people protein extracted from leaves or bacteria grown on petroleum. None of these schemes has even resulted in a coordinated development effort. Meanwhile, growing numbers of newly well-off people have increased demand for meat, thereby raising global demand for feed grains.

Perhaps even more critical, climate disruption may pose insurmountable biophysical barriers to increasing crop yields. Indeed, if humanity is very unlucky with the climate, there may be reductions in yields of major crops, although near-term this may be unlikely to affect harvests globally. Nonetheless, rising temperatures already seem to be slowing previous trends of increasing yields of basic grains, and unless greenhouse gas emissions are dramatically reduced, dangerous anthropogenic climate change could ravage agriculture. Also, in addition to falling yields from many oceanic fish stocks because of widespread overfishing, warming and acidification of the oceans threaten the protein supply of some of the most nutritionally vulnerable people, especially those who cannot afford to purchase farmed fish.

Unfortunately, the agricultural system has complex connections with all the chief drivers of environmental deterioration. Agriculture itself is a major emitter of greenhouse gases and thus is an important cause of climate disruption as well as being exceptionally vulnerable to its consequences. More than a millennium of change in temperature and precipitation patterns is apparently now entrained, with the prospect of increasingly severe storms, droughts, heat waves and floods, all of which seem already evident and all of which threaten agricultural production.

Land is an essential resource for farming, and one facing multiple threats. In addition to the serious and widespread problems of soil degradation, sea-level rise (the most certain consequence of global warming) will take important areas out of production either by inundating them (a 1 m rise would flood 17.5% of Bangladesh), exposing them to more frequent storm surges, or salinizing coastal aquifers essential for irrigation water. Another important problem for the food system is the loss of prime farmland to urbanization, a trend that seems certain to accelerate as population growth steadily erodes the per capita supply of farmland.

The critical importance of substantially boosting the inadequate current action on the demographic problem can be seen in the time required to change the trajectory of population growth humanely and sensibly. We know from such things as the World War II mobilizations that many consumption patterns can be altered dramatically within a year, given appropriate incentives. If food shortages became acute, then a rapid reaction would ensue as hunger became much more widespread. Food prices would rise, and diets would temporarily change (e.g. the number of meals consumed per day or amount of meat consumed) to compensate the shortage.

Over the long term, however, expanding the global food supply and distributing it more equitably would be a slow and difficult process. Even though a major famine might well provoke investment in long-needed improvements in food production and distribution, they would take time to plan, test and implement.

Furthermore, agriculture is a leading cause of losses of biodiversity and thus of the critical ecosystem services supplied to agriculture itself (e.g. pollination, pest control, soil fertility, climate stability) and other human enterprises. Farming is also a principal source of global toxification, as has been clear since the days of Carson, exposing the human population to myriad subtle poisons. These pose further potential risks to food production.

# 3. What Needs to be done to Avoid a Collapse?

The threat from climate disruption to food production alone means that humanity's entire system for mobilizing energy needs to be rapidly transformed. Warming must be held well below a potential 58C rise in global average temperature, a level that could well bring down civilization. The best estimate today may be that, failing rapid concerted action, the world is already committed to a 2.48C increase in global average temperature. This is significantly above the 28C estimated a decade ago by climate scientists to be a 'safe' limit, but now considered by some analysts to be too dangerous, a credible assessment,

given the effects seen already before reaching a one degree rise. There is evidence, moreover, that present models underestimate future temperature increase by overestimating the extent that growth of vegetation can serve as a carbon sink and underestimating positive feedbacks.

Many complexities plague the estimation of the precise threats of anthropogenic climate disruption, ranging from heat deaths and spread of tropical diseases to sea-level rise, crop failures and violent storms. One key to avoiding a global collapse, and thus an area requiring great effort and caution is avoiding climate-related mass famines. Our agricultural system evolved in a geological period of relatively constant and benign climate and was well attuned to twentieth-century conditions. That alone is cause for substantial concern as the planet's climates rapidly shift to new, less predictable regimes. It is essential to slow that process. That means dramatically transforming much of the existing energy mobilization infrastructure and changing human behaviour to make the energy system much more efficient. This is possible; indeed, sensible plans for doing it have been put forward, and some progress has been made. The central challenge, of course, is to phase out more than half of the global use of fossil fuels by 2050 in order to forestall the worst impacts of climate disruption, a challenge the latest International Energy Agency edition of World Energy Outlook makes look more severe. This highlights another dilemma. Fossil fuels are now essential to agriculture for fertilizer and pesticide manufacture, operation of farm machinery, irrigation (often wasteful), livestock husbandry, crop drying, food storage, transportation and distribution. Thus, the phase-out will need to include at least partial substitution of non-fossil fuels in these functions, and do so without greatly increasing food prices.

Unfortunately, essential steps such as curbing global emissions to peak by 2020 and reducing them to half of present levels by 2050 are extremely problematic economically and politically. Fossil fuel companies would have to leave most of their proven reserves in the ground, thus destroying much of the industry's economic value. Because the ethics of some businesses include knowingly continuing lethal but profitable activities, it is hardly surprising that interests with large financial stakes in fossil fuel burning have launched a gigantic and largely successful disinformation campaign in the USA to confuse people about climate disruption and block attempts to deal with it.

One recurrent theme in analyses of the food problem is the need for closing 'yield gaps'. That means raising yields in less productive systems to those typical of industrial agriculture. But climatic conditions may change sufficiently that those industrial high yields can themselves no longer be sustained. Thus, reducing the chances of a collapse calls for placing much more effort into genetic and ecological research related to agriculture and adopting already known environmental-friendly techniques, even though that may require trading off immediate corporate profits for social benefits or long-term sustainability.

Rationalizing energy mobilization alone may not be enough to be enough to maintain agricultural production, let alone allow its great expansion. Human water-handling infrastructure will have to be re-engineered for flexibility to bring water to crops in an environment of constantly changing precipitation patterns. This is critical, for although today only about 15 per cent of agricultural land is irrigated, it provides some 40 per cent of the grain crop yield. It seems likely that farming areas now rain-fed may someday need to be irrigated, whereas irrigation could become superfluous elsewhere, and both could change more or less continually. For this and many other reasons, the global food system will need to quickly evolve an unprecedented flexibility, never before even contemplated.

One factor making the challenges more severe is the major participation in the global system of giant nations whose populations have not previously enjoyed the fossil energy abundance that brought Western countries and Japan to positions of affluence. Now they are poised to repeat the West's energy 'success', and on an even greater scale. India alone, which recently suffered a gigantic blackout affecting 300 million people, is planning to bring 455 new coal plants on line. Worldwide more than 1200 plants with a total installed capacity of 1.4 million megawatts are planned, much of that in China, where electricity demand is expected to skyrocket. The resultant surge in greenhouse gases will interact with the increasing diversion of grain to livestock, stimulated by the desire for more meat in the diets of Indians, Chinese and others in a growing global middle class.

# 4. Dealing with Problems Beyond Food Supply

Another possible threat to the continuation of civilization is global toxification. Adverse symptoms of exposure to synthetic chemicals are making some scientists increasingly nervous about effects on the human population. Should a global threat materialize, however, no planned mitigating responses (analogous to the ecologically and politically risky 'geoengineering' projects often proposed to ameliorate climate disruption) are waiting in the wings ready for deployment.

Much the same can be said about aspects of the epidemiological environment and the prospect of epidemics being enhanced by rapid population growth in immune-weakened societies, increased contact with animal reservoirs, high speed transport and the misuse of antibiotics. Nobel laureate Joshua Lederberg had great concern for the epidemic problem, famously stating, 'The survival of the human species is not a preordained evolutionary program'. Some precautionary steps that should be considered include forbidding the use of antibiotics as growth

stimulators for livestock, building emergency stocks of key vaccines and drugs (such as Tamiflu), improving disease surveillance, expanding mothballed emergency medical facilities, preparing institutions for imposing quarantines and, of course, moving as rapidly as possible to humanely reduce the human population size. It has become increasingly clear that security has many dimensions beyond military security and that breaches of environmental security could risk the end of global civilization.

But much uncertainty about the human ability to avoid a collapse still hinges on military security, especially whether some elements of the human predicament might trigger a nuclear war. Recent research indicates that even a regional scale nuclear conflict, as is quite possible between India and Pakistan, could lead to a global collapse through widespread climatic consequences. Triggers to conflict beyond political and religious strife easily could include cross-border epidemics, a need to gain access to food supplies and farmland, and competition over other resources, especially agricultural water and (if the world does not come to its energy senses) oil. Finding ways to eliminate nuclear weapons and other instruments of mass destruction must move even higher on civilization's agenda, because nuclear war would be the quickest and surest route to a collapse.

In thinking about the probability of collapse, one must obviously consider the social disruptions associated with elements of the predicament. Perhaps at the top of the list should be that of environmental refugees. Recent predictions are that environmental refugees could number 50 million by 2020. Severe droughts, floods, famines and epidemics could greatly swell that number. If current 'official' predictions of sea-level rise are low (as many believe they are), coastal inundations alone could generate massive human movements; a 1 m rise would directly affect some 100 million people, whereas a 6 m rise would displace more than 400 million. Developing a more comprehensive system of international governance with institutions planning to ameliorate the impacts of such catastrophes would be a major way to reduce the odds of collapse.

# 5. The Role of Science

The scientific community has repeatedly warned humanity in the past of its peril, and the earlier warnings about the risks of population expansion and the 'limits to growth' have increasingly been shown to be on the right track. The warnings continue. Yet many scientists still tend to treat population growth as an exogenous variable, when it should be considered an endogenous one—indeed, a central factor. Too many studies asking 'how can we possibly feed 9.6 billion people by 2050?' should also be asking 'how can we humanely lower birth rates far enough to reduce that number to 8.6?' To our minds, the fundamental cure, reducing the scale of the human enterprise (including the size of the population) to keep its aggregate consumption within the carrying capacity of Earth, is obvious but too much neglected or denied. There are great social and psychological barriers in growth manic cultures to even considering it. This is especially true because of the 'endarkenment'—a rapidly growing movement towards religious orthodoxies that reject enlightenment values such as freedom of thought, democracy, separation of church and state, and basing beliefs and actions on empirical evidence. They are manifest in dangerous trends such as climate denial, failure to act on the loss of biodiversity and opposition to condoms (for AIDS control) as well as other forms of contraception. If ever there was a time for evidence-based (as opposed to faith-based) risk reduction strategies, it is now.

How can scientists do more to reduce the odds of a collapse? Both natural and social scientists should put more effort into finding the best ways of accomplishing the necessary re-modelling of energy and water infrastructure. They should develop better ways of evaluating and regulating the use of synthetic chemicals, a problem that might abate somewhat as availability of their fossil fuel sources fades (even though only about 5% of oil production flows into petrochemical production). The protection of Earth's remaining biodiversity (especially the crucial diversity of populations) must take centre stage for both scientific specialists and, through appropriate education, the public. Scientists must continually call attention to the need to improve the human epidemiological environment, and for control and eventual elimination of nuclear, chemical and biological weapons. Above all, they should expand efforts to understand the mechanisms through which cooperation evolves, because avoiding collapse will require unusual levels of international cooperation.

Is it too late for the global scientific community to collect itself and start to deal with the nexus of the two complex adaptive systems and then help generate the necessary actions to move towards sustainability? There are certainly many small scale science-based efforts, often local, that can provide hope if scaled up. For example, environmental non-govenmental organizations and others are continually struggling to halt the destruction of elements of biodiversity (and thus, in some cases, of vital ecosystem services), often with success. In the face of the building extinction crisis, they may be preserving nuclei from which Earth's biota and humanity's ecosystem services, might eventually be regenerated. And some positive efforts are scaling up. China now has some 25 per cent of its land in ecosystem function conservation areas designed to protect both natural capital and human well-being. The Natural Capital Project is helping improve the management of these areas. This is good news, but in our view, many too few scientists are involved in the efforts needed, especially in re-orienting at least part of their research towards mitigating the predicament and then bringing their results to the policy front.

# 6. The Need for Rapid Social/ Political Change

Until very recently, our ancestors had no reason to respond genetically or culturally to long-term issues. If the global climate were changing rapidly for Australopithecus or even ancient Romans, then they were not causing it and could do nothing about it. The forces of genetic and cultural selection were not creating brains or institutions capable of looking generations ahead; there would have been no selection pressures in that direction. Indeed, quite the opposite, selection probably favoured mechanisms to keep perception of the environmental background steady so that rapid changes (e.g. leopard approaching) would be obvious. But now slow changes in that background are the most lethal threats. Societies have a long history of mobilizing efforts, making sacrifices and changes, to defeat an enemy at the gates, or even just to compete more successfully with a rival. But there is not much evidence of societies mobilizing and making sacrifices to meet gradually worsening conditions that threaten real disaster for future generations. Yet that is exactly the sort of mobilization that we believe is required to avoid a collapse.

Perhaps the biggest challenge in avoiding collapse is convincing people, especially politicians and economists, to break this ancient mould and alter their behaviour relative to the basic population-consumption drivers of environmental deterioration. We know that simply informing people of the scientific consensus on a serious problem does not ordinarily produce rapid changes in institutional or individual behaviour. That was amply demonstrated in the case of cigarettes, air pollution and other environmental problems and is now being demonstrated in the obesity epidemic as well as climate disruption.

Obvious parallels exist regarding reproduction and overconsumption, which are especially visible in what amounts to a cultural addiction to continued economic growth among the already well-off. One might think that the mathematics of compound interest would have convinced everyone long ago that growth of an industrialized economy at 3.5 per cent annually cannot long continue. Unfortunately, most 'educated' people are immersed in a culture that does not recognize that, in the real world, a short history (a few centuries) of exponential growth does not imply a long future of such growth.

Besides focusing their research on ways to avoid collapse, there is a need for natural scientists to collaborate with social scientists, especially those who study the dynamics of social movements. Such collaborations could develop ways to stimulate a significant increase in popular support for decisive and immediate action on the predicament. Unfortunately, awareness among scientists that humanity is in deep trouble has not been accompanied by popular awareness and pressure to counter the political and economic influences implicated in the current crisis. Without significant pressure from the public demanding action, we fear there is little chance of changing course fast enough to forestall disaster.

The needed pressure, however, might be generated by a popular movement based in academia and civil society to help guide humanity towards developing a new multiple intelligence, 'foresight intelligence' to provide the long-term analysis and planning that markets cannot supply. Foresight intelligence could not only systematically look ahead but also guide cultural changes towards desirable outcomes such as increased socio-economic resilience. Helping develop such a movement and foresight intelligence are major challenges facing scientists today, a cutting edge for research that must slice fast if the chances of averting a collapse are to be improved.

If foresight intelligence became established, many more scientists and policy planners (and society) might, for example, understand the demographic contributions to the predicament, stop treating population growth as a 'given' and consider the nutritional, health and social benefits of humanely ending growth well below nine billion and starting a slow decline. This would be a monumental task, considering the momentum of population growth. Monumental, but not impossible if the political will could be generated globally to give full rights, education and opportunities to women, and provide all sexually active human beings with modern contraception and backup abortion. The degree to which those steps would reduce fertility rates is controversial, but they are a likely win-win for societies.

Obviously, especially with the growing endarkenment, there are huge cultural and institutional barriers to establishing such policies in some parts of the world. After all, there is not a single nation where women are truly treated as equal to men. Despite that, the population driver should not be ignored simply because limiting overconsumption can, at least in theory, be achieved more rapidly. The difficulties of changing demographic trajectories mean that the problem should have been addressed sooner, rather than later. That halting population growth inevitably leads to changes in age structure is no excuse for bemoaning drops in fertility rates, as is common in European government circles. Reduction of population size in those over-consuming nations is a very positive trend, and sensible planning can deal with the problems of population aging.

While rapid policy change to head off collapse is essential, fundamental institutional change to keep things on track is necessary as well. This is especially true of educational systems, which today fail to inform most people of how the world works

and thus perpetuate a vast culture gap. The academic challenge is especially great for economists, who could help set the background for avoiding collapse by designing steady-state economic systems, and along the way destroying fables such as 'growth can continue forever if it's in service industries', or 'technological innovation will save us'. Issues such as the importance of comparative advantage under current global circumstances, the development of new models that better reflect the irrational behaviour of individuals and groups, reduction of the worship of 'free' markets that infests the discipline, and tasks such as making information more symmetrical, moving towards sustainability and enhancing equity (including redistribution) all require re-examination. In that re-examination, they would be following the lead of distinguished economists in dealing with the real world of biophysical constraints and human well-being.

At the global level, the loose network of agreements that now tie countries together, developed in a relatively recent stage of cultural evolution since modern nation states appeared, is utterly inadequate to grapple with the human predicament. Strengthening global environmental governance and addressing the related problem of avoiding failed statehood are tasks humanity has so far refused to tackle comprehensively even as cultural evolution in technology has rendered the present international system (as it has educational systems) obsolete. Serious global environmental problems can only be solved and a collapse avoided with an unprecedented level of international cooperation. Regardless of one's estimate of civilization's potential longevity, the time to start restructuring the international system is right now. If people do not do that, nature will restructure civilization for us.

Similarly, widely based cultural change is required to reduce humanely both population size and overconsumption by the rich. Both go against cultural norms, and, as long feared, the overconsumption norm has understandably been adopted by the increasingly rich subpopulations of developing nations, notably India and China. One can be thrilled by the numbers of people raised from poverty while being apprehensive about the enormous and possibly lethal environmental and social costs that may eventually result. The industrial revolution set civilization on the road to collapse, spurring population growth, which contributed slightly more than overconsumption to environmental degradation. Now population combined with affluence growth may finish the job.

Needless to say, dealing with economic and racial inequities will be critically important in getting large numbers of people from culturally diverse groups to focus their minds on solving the human predicament, something globalization should help. These tasks will be pursued, along with an emphasis on developing 'foresight intelligence', by the nascent Millennium Alliance for Humanity and the Biosphere (the MAHB; http://mahb.stanford.edu). One of its central goals is to try to accelerate change towards sustainability. Since simply giving the scientific facts to the public will not do it, among other things, this means finding frames and narratives to convince the public of the need to make changes.

We know that societies can evolve fundamentally and unexpectedly, as was dramatically demonstrated by the collapse of communist regimes in Europe in 1989. Rather than tinkering around the edges and making feeble or empty gestures towards one or another of the interdependent problems we face, we need a powerful and comprehensive approach. In addressing climate change, for instance, developing nations need to be convinced that they (along with the rest of the world) cannot afford (and do not need) to delay action while they 'catch up' in development. Indeed, development on the old model is counterproductive; they have a great opportunity to pioneer new approaches and technologies. All nations need to stop waiting for others to act and be willing to do everything they can to mitigate emissions and hasten the energy transition, regardless of what others are doing.

With climate and many other global environmental problems, polycentric solutions may be more readily found than global ones. Complex, multi-level systems may be better able to cope with complex, multi-level problems, and institutional change is required at many levels in many polities. What scientists understand about cultural evolution suggests that, while improbable, it may be possible to move cultures in such directions. Whether solutions will be global or polycentric, international negotiations will be needed, existing international agencies that deal with them will need strengthening, and new institutions will need to be formed.

# 7. Conclusions

Do we think global society can avoid a collapse in this century? The answer is yes, because modern society has shown some capacity to deal with long-term threats, at least if they are obvious or continuously brought to attention (think of the risks of nuclear conflict). Humanity has the assets to get the job done, but the odds of avoiding collapse seem small because the risks are clearly not obvious to most people and the classic signs of impending collapse, especially diminishing returns to complexity, are everywhere. One central psychological barrier to taking dramatic action is the distribution of costs and benefits through time: the costs up front, the benefits accruing largely to unknown people in the future. But whether we or more optimistic observers are correct, our own ethical values compel us to think the benefits to those future generations are worth struggling for, to increase at least slightly the chances of avoiding a dissolution of today's global civilization as we know it.

We are especially grateful to Joan Diamond, Executive Director of the MAHB, for her ideas on foresight intelligence, and to the Beijer Institute of Ecological Economics for two decades of provocative discussions on topics related to this paper. This paper has benefited from comments from Ken Arrow, Scott Barrett, Andy Beattie, Dan Blumstein, Corey Bradshaw, Greg Bratman, Paul Brest, Jim Brown, Bob Brulle, Gretchen Daily, Lisa Daniel, Timothy Daniel, Partha Dasgupta, Nadia Diamond-Smith, Tom Dietz, Anantha Duraiappah, Riley Dunlap, Walter Falcon, Marc Feldman, Rachelle Gould, Larry Goulder, John Harte, Mel Harte, Ursula Heise, Tad Homer-Dixon, Bob Horn, Danny Karp, Don Kennedy, Michael Klare, Simon Levin, Jack Liu, David Lobell, Doug McAdam, Chase Mendenhall, Hal Mooney, Fathali Moghaddam, Dennis Pirages, Graham Pyke, Gene Rosa, Lee Ross, Jose Sarukhan, Kirk Smith, Sarah Soule, Chris Turnbull and Wren Wirth. Two of the best and most thorough anonymous reviewers we have ever encountered helped us improve the manuscript. The work was supported by Peter and Helen Bing and the Mertz Gilmore Foundation.

# Critical Thinking

1. What is your assessment of the state of the planet?
2. What specifically are the most worrisome environmental problems?
3. The Ehrlichs wonder whether the collapse of global civilization can be avoided. Do they have convincing data supporting this conclusion?

# Internet References

**Sociosite**
www.topsite.com/goto/sociosite.net
**Socioweb**
www.topsite.com/goto/socioweb.com
**Sociology—Study Sociology Online**
http://edu.learnsoc.org
**Sociology Web Resources**
www.mhhe.com/socscience/sociology/resources/index.htm

**PAUL EHRLICH** is a Professor of Biology and President of the Center for Conservation Biology at Stanford University, and Adjunct Professor at the University of Technology, Sydney. His research interests are in the ecology and evolution of natural populations of butterflies, reef fishes, birds and human beings. **ANNE EHRLICH** is a Senior Research Scientist in Biology at Stanford and focuses her research on policy issues related to the environment

*Article*                    Prepared by: Kurt Finsterbusch, *University of Maryland, College Park*

# The Uninhabitable Earth

Famine, economic collapse, a sun that cooks us: what climate change could wreak—sooner than you think.

### David Wallace-Wells

## Learning Outcomes

*After reading this article, you will be able to:*

- Understand the range of possibilities for future climate change impacts on societies.

- Describe what terrors are possible from climate change in the future.

- Describe what needs to be done to prevent these terrors.

## I. 'Doomsday'
### Peering Beyond Scientific Reticence

It is, I promise, worse than you think. If your anxiety about global warming is dominated by fears of sea-level rise, you are barely scratching the surface of what terrors are possible, even within the lifetime of a teenager today. And yet the swelling seas — and the cities they will drown — have so dominated the picture of global warming, and so overwhelmed our capacity for climate panic, that they have blocked our perception of other threats, many much closer at hand. Rising oceans are bad, in fact very bad; but fleeing the coastline will not be enough.

Indeed, absent a significant adjustment to how billions of humans conduct their lives, parts of the Earth will likely become close to uninhabitable, and other parts horrifically inhospitable, as soon as the end of this century.

Even when we train our eyes on climate change, we are unable to comprehend its scope. This past winter, a string of days 60 and 70 degrees warmer than normal baked the North Pole, melting the permafrost that encased Norway's Svalbard seed vault — a global food bank nicknamed "Doomsday," designed to ensure that our agriculture survives any catastrophe, and which appeared to have been flooded by climate change less than ten years after being built.

The Doomsday vault is fine, for now: The structure has been secured and the seeds are safe. But treating the episode as a parable of impending flooding missed the more important news. Until recently, permafrost was not a major concern of climate scientists, because, as the name suggests, it was soil that stayed permanently frozen. But Arctic permafrost contains 1.8 trillion tons of carbon, more than twice as much as is currently suspended in the Earth's atmosphere. When it thaws and is released, that carbon may evaporate as methane, which is 34 times as powerful a greenhouse-gas warming blanket as carbon dioxide when judged on the timescale of a century; when judged on the timescale of two decades, it is 86 times as powerful. In other words, we have, trapped in Arctic permafrost, twice as much carbon as is currently wrecking the atmosphere of the planet, all of it scheduled to be released at a date that keeps getting moved up, partially in the form of a gas that multiplies its warming power 86 times over.

Maybe you know that already — there are alarming stories in the news every day, like those, last month, that seemed to suggest satellite data showed the globe warming since 1998 more than twice as fast as scientists had thought (in fact, the underlying story was considerably less alarming than the headlines). Or the news from Antarctica this past May, when a crack in an ice shelf grew 11 miles in six days, then kept going; the break now has just three miles to go — by the time you read this, it may already have met the open water, where it will drop into the sea one of the biggest icebergs ever, a process known poetically as "calving."

But no matter how well-informed you are, you are surely not alarmed enough. Over the past decades, our culture has gone apocalyptic with zombie movies and *Mad Max* dystopias, perhaps the collective result of displaced climate anxiety, and yet when it comes to contemplating real-world warming dangers, we suffer from an incredible failure of imagination. The reasons for that are many: the timid language of scientific probabilities, which the climatologist James Hansen once called "scientific reticence" in a paper chastising scientists for editing their own observations so conscientiously that they failed to communicate how dire the threat really was; the fact that the country is dominated by a group of technocrats who believe any problem can be solved and an opposing culture that doesn't even see warming as a problem worth addressing; the way that climate denialism has made scientists even more cautious in offering speculative warnings; the simple speed of change and, also, its slowness, such that we are only seeing effects now of warming from decades past; our uncertainty about uncertainty, which the climate writer Naomi Oreskes in particular has suggested stops us from preparing as though anything worse than a median outcome were even possible; the way we assume climate change will hit hardest elsewhere, not everywhere; the smallness (two degrees) and largeness (1.8 trillion tons) and abstractness (400 parts per million) of the numbers; the discomfort of considering a problem that is very difficult, if not impossible, to solve; the altogether incomprehensible scale of that problem, which amounts to the prospect of our own annihilation; simple fear. But aversion arising from fear is a form of denial, too.

In between scientific reticence and science fiction is science itself. This article is the result of dozens of interviews and exchanges with climatologists and researchers in related fields and reflects hundreds of scientific papers on the subject of climate change. What follows is not a series of predictions of what will happen — that will be determined in large part by the much-less-certain science of human response. Instead, it is a portrait of our best understanding of where the planet is heading absent aggressive action. It is unlikely that all of these warming scenarios will be fully realized, largely because the devastation along the way will shake our complacency. But those scenarios, and not the present climate, are the baseline. In fact, they are our schedule.

The present tense of climate change — the destruction we've already baked into our future — is horrifying enough. Most people talk as if Miami and Bangladesh still have a chance of surviving; most of the scientists I spoke with assume we'll lose them within the century, even if we stop burning fossil fuel in the next decade. Two degrees of warming used to be considered the threshold of catastrophe: tens of millions of climate refugees unleashed upon an unprepared world. Now two degrees is our goal, per the Paris climate accords, and experts give us only slim odds of hitting it. The U.N. Intergovernmental Panel on Climate Change issues serial reports, often called the "gold standard" of climate research; the most recent one projects us to hit four degrees of warming by the beginning of the next century, should we stay the present course. But that's just a median projection. The upper end of the probability curve runs as high as eight degrees — and the authors still haven't figured out how to deal with that permafrost melt. The IPCC reports also don't fully account for the albedo effect (less ice means less reflected and more absorbed sunlight, hence more warming); more cloud cover (which traps heat); or the dieback of forests and other flora (which extract carbon from the atmosphere). Each of these promises to accelerate warming, and the history of the planet shows that temperature can shift as much as five degrees Celsius within thirteen years. The last time the planet was even four degrees warmer, Peter Brannen points out in *The Ends of the World*, his new history of the planet's major extinction events, the oceans were hundreds of feet higher.

The Earth has experienced five mass extinctions before the one we are living through now, each so complete a slate-wiping of the evolutionary record it functioned as a resetting of the planetary clock, and many climate scientists will tell you they are the best analog for the ecological future we are diving headlong into. Unless you are a teenager, you probably read in your high-school textbooks that these extinctions were the result of asteroids. In fact, all but the one that killed the dinosaurs were caused by climate change produced by greenhouse gas. The most notorious was 252 million years ago; it began when carbon warmed the planet by five degrees, accelerated when that warming triggered the release of methane in the Arctic, and ended with 97 percent of all life on Earth dead. We are currently adding carbon to the atmosphere at a considerably faster rate; by most estimates, at least ten times faster. The rate is accelerating. This is what Stephen Hawking had in mind when he said, this spring, that the species needs to colonize other planets in the next century to survive, and what drove Elon Musk, last month, to unveil his plans to build a Mars habitat in 40 to 100 years. These are nonspecialists, of course, and probably as inclined to irrational panic as you or I. But the many sober-minded scientists I interviewed over the past several months — the most credentialed and tenured in the field, few of them inclined to alarmism and many advisers to the IPCC who nevertheless criticize its conservatism — have quietly reached an apocalyptic conclusion, too: No plausible program of emissions reductions alone can prevent climate disaster.

Over the past few decades, the term "Anthropocene" has climbed out of academic discourse and into the popular imagination — a name given to the geologic era we live in now, and a way to signal that it is a new era, defined on the wall chart of deep history by human intervention. One problem with the term is that it implies a conquest of nature (and even echoes the biblical "dominion"). And however sanguine you might be about the proposition that we have already ravaged the natural world, which we surely have, it is another thing entirely to consider the possibility that we have only provoked it, engineering first in ignorance and then in denial a climate system that will now go to war with us for many centuries, perhaps until it destroys us. That is what Wallace Smith Broecker, the avuncular oceanographer who coined the term "global warming," means when he calls the planet an "angry beast." You could also go with "war machine." Each day we arm it more.

## II. Heat Death
### The Bahraining of New York

Humans, like all mammals, are heat engines; surviving means having to continually cool off, like panting dogs. For that, the temperature needs to be low enough for the air to act as a kind of refrigerant, drawing heat off the skin so the engine can keep pumping. At seven degrees of warming, that would become impossible for large portions of the planet's equatorial band, and especially the tropics, where humidity adds to the problem; in the jungles of Costa Rica, for instance, where humidity routinely tops 90 percent, simply moving around outside when it's over 105 degrees Fahrenheit would be lethal. And the effect would be fast: Within a few hours, a human body would be cooked to death from both inside and out.

Climate-change skeptics point out that the planet has warmed and cooled many times before, but the climate window that has allowed for human life is very narrow, even by the standards of planetary history. At 11 or 12 degrees of warming, more than half the world's population, as distributed today, would die of direct heat. Things almost certainly won't get that hot this century, though models of unabated emissions do bring us that far eventually. This century, and especially in the tropics, the pain points will pinch much more quickly even than an increase of seven degrees. The key factor is something called wet-bulb temperature, which is a term of measurement as home-laboratory-kit as it sounds: the heat registered on a thermometer wrapped in a damp sock as it's swung around in the air (since the moisture evaporates from a sock more quickly in dry air, this single number reflects both heat and humidity). At present, most regions reach a wet-bulb maximum of 26 or 27 degrees Celsius; the true red line for habitability is 35 degrees. What is called heat stress comes much sooner.

Actually, we're about there already. Since 1980, the planet has experienced a 50-fold increase in the number of places experiencing dangerous or extreme heat; a bigger increase is to come. The five warmest summers in Europe since 1500 have all occurred since 2002, and soon, the IPCC warns, simply being outdoors that time of year will be unhealthy for much of the globe. Even if we meet the Paris goals of two degrees warming, cities like Karachi and Kolkata will become close to uninhabitable, annually encountering deadly heat waves like those that crippled them in 2015. At four degrees, the deadly European heat wave of 2003, which killed as many as 2,000 people a day, will be a normal summer. At six, according to an assessment focused only on effects within the U.S. from the National Oceanic and Atmospheric Administration, summer labor of any kind would become impossible in the lower Mississippi Valley, and everybody in the country east of the Rockies would be under more heat stress than anyone, anywhere, in the world today. As Joseph Romm has put it in his authoritative primer *Climate Change: What Everyone Needs to Know,* heat stress in New York City would exceed that of present-day Bahrain, one of the planet's hottest spots, and the temperature in Bahrain "would induce hyperthermia in even sleeping humans." The high-end IPCC estimate, remember, is two degrees warmer still. By the end of the century, the World Bank has estimated, the coolest months in tropical South America, Africa, and the Pacific are likely to be warmer than the warmest months at the end of the 20th century. Air-conditioning can help but will ultimately only add to the carbon problem; plus, the climate-controlled malls of the Arab emirates aside, it is not remotely plausible to wholesale air-condition all the hottest parts of the world, many of them also the poorest. And indeed, the crisis will be most dramatic across the Middle East and Persian Gulf, where in 2015 the heat index registered temperatures as high as 163 degrees Fahrenheit. As soon as several decades from now, the hajj will become physically impossible for the 2 million Muslims who make the pilgrimage each year.

It is not just the hajj, and it is not just Mecca; heat is already killing us. In the sugarcane region of El Salvador, as much as one-fifth of the population has chronic kidney disease, including over a quarter of the men, the presumed result of dehydration from working the fields they were able to comfortably harvest as recently as two decades ago. With dialysis, which is expensive, those with kidney failure can expect to live five years; without it, life expectancy is in the weeks. Of course, heat stress promises to pummel us in places other than our kidneys, too. As I type that sentence, in the California desert in mid-June, it is 121 degrees outside my door. It is not a record high.

## III. The End of Food
### Praying for Cornfields in the Tundra

Climates differ and plants vary, but the basic rule for staple cereal crops grown at optimal temperature is that for every degree of warming, yields decline by 10 percent. Some estimates run as high as 15 or even 17 percent. Which means that if the planet is five degrees warmer at the end of the century, we may have as many as 50 percent more people to feed and 50 percent less grain to give them. And proteins are worse: It takes 16 calories of grain to produce just a single calorie of hamburger meat, butchered from a cow that spent its life polluting the climate with methane farts.

Pollyannaish plant physiologists will point out that the cereal-crop math applies only to those regions already at peak growing temperature, and they are right — theoretically, a warmer climate will make it easier to grow corn in Greenland. But as the pathbreaking work by Rosamond Naylor and David Battisti has shown, the tropics are already too hot to efficiently grow grain, and those places where grain is produced today are already at optimal growing temperature — which means even a small warming will push them down the slope of declining productivity. And you can't easily move croplands north a few hundred miles, because yields in places like remote Canada and Russia are limited by the quality of soil there; it takes many centuries for the planet to produce optimally fertile dirt.

Drought might be an even bigger problem than heat, with some of the world's most arable land turning quickly to desert. Precipitation is notoriously hard to model, yet predictions for later this century are basically unanimous: unprecedented droughts nearly everywhere food is today produced. By 2080, without dramatic reductions in emissions, southern Europe will be in permanent extreme drought, much worse than the American dust bowl ever was. The same will be true in Iraq and Syria and much of the rest of the Middle East; some of the most densely populated parts of Australia, Africa, and South America; and the breadbasket regions of China. None of these places, which today supply much of the world's food, will be reliable sources of any. As for the original dust bowl: The droughts in the American plains and Southwest would not just be worse than in the 1930s, a 2015 NASA study predicted, but worse than any droughts in a thousand years — and that includes those that struck between 1100 and 1300, which "dried up all the rivers East of the Sierra Nevada mountains" and may have been responsible for the death of the Anasazi civilization.

Remember, we do not live in a world without hunger as it is. Far from it: Most estimates put the number of undernourished at 800 million globally. In case you haven't heard, this spring has already brought an unprecedented quadruple famine to Africa and the Middle East; the U.N. has warned that separate starvation events in Somalia, South Sudan, Nigeria, and Yemen could kill 20 million this year alone.

## IV. Climate Plagues
### What Happens When the Bubonic Ice Melts?

Rock, in the right spot, is a record of planetary history, eras as long as millions of years flattened by the forces of geological time into strata with amplitudes of just inches, or just an inch, or even less. Ice works that way, too, as a climate ledger, but it is also frozen history, some of which can be reanimated when unfrozen. There are now, trapped in Arctic ice, diseases that have not circulated in the air for millions of years — in some cases, since before humans were around to encounter them. Which means our immune systems would have no idea how to fight back when those prehistoric plagues emerge from the ice.

The Arctic also stores terrifying bugs from more recent times. In Alaska, already, researchers have discovered remnants of the 1918 flu that infected as many as 500 million and killed as many as 100 million — about 5 percent of the world's population and almost six times as many as had died in the world war for which the pandemic served as a kind of gruesome capstone. As the BBC reported in May, scientists suspect smallpox and the bubonic plague are trapped in Siberian ice, too — an abridged history of devastating human sickness, left out like egg salad in the Arctic sun.

Experts caution that many of these organisms won't actually survive the thaw and point to the fastidious lab conditions under which they have already reanimated several of them — the 32,000-year-old "extremophile" bacteria revived in 2005, an 8 million-year-old bug brought back to life in 2007, the 3.5 million-year-old one a Russian scientist self-injected just out of curiosity — to suggest that those are necessary conditions for the return of such ancient plagues. But already last year, a boy was killed and 20 others infected by anthrax released when retreating permafrost exposed the frozen carcass of a reindeer killed by the bacteria at least 75 years earlier; 2,000 present-day reindeer were infected, too, carrying and spreading the disease beyond the tundra.

What concerns epidemiologists more than ancient diseases are existing scourges relocated, rewired, or even re-evolved by warming. The first effect is geographical. Before the early-modern period, when adventuring sailboats accelerated the mixing of peoples and their bugs, human provinciality was a guard against pandemic. Today, even with globalization and the enormous intermingling of human populations, our ecosystems are mostly stable, and this functions as another limit, but global warming will scramble those ecosystems and help disease trespass those limits as surely as Cortés did. You don't worry much about dengue or malaria if you are living in Maine or France. But as the tropics creep northward and mosquitoes migrate with them, you will. You didn't much worry about Zika a couple of years ago, either.

As it happens, Zika may also be a good model of the second worrying effect — disease mutation. One reason you hadn't heard about Zika until recently is that it had been trapped in Uganda; another is that it did not, until recently, appear to cause birth defects. Scientists still don't entirely understand what happened, or what they missed. But there are things we do know for sure about how climate affects some diseases: Malaria, for instance, thrives in hotter regions not just because the mosquitoes that carry it do, too, but because for every degree increase in temperature, the parasite reproduces ten times faster. Which is one reason that the World Bank estimates that by 2050, 5.2 billion people will be reckoning with it.

# V. Unbreathable Air
## *A Rolling Death Smog That Suffocates Millions*

Our lungs need oxygen, but that is only a fraction of what we breathe. The fraction of carbon dioxide is growing: It just crossed 400 parts per million, and high-end estimates extrapolating from current trends suggest it will hit 1,000 ppm by 2100. At that concentration, compared to the air we breathe now, human cognitive ability declines by 21 percent.

Other stuff in the hotter air is even scarier, with small increases in pollution capable of shortening life spans by ten years. The warmer the planet gets, the more ozone forms, and by mid-century, Americans will likely suffer a 70 percent increase in unhealthy ozone smog, the National Center for Atmospheric Research has projected. By 2090, as many as 2 billion people globally will be breathing air above the WHO "safe" level; one paper last month showed that, among other effects, a pregnant mother's exposure to ozone raises the child's risk of autism (as much as tenfold, combined with other environmental factors). Which does make you think again about the autism epidemic in West Hollywood.

Already, more than 10,000 people die each day from the small particles emitted from fossil-fuel burning; each year, 339,000 people die from wildfire smoke, in part because climate change has extended forest-fire season (in the U.S., it's increased by 78 days since 1970). By 2050, according to the U.S. Forest Service, wildfires will be twice as destructive as they are today; in some places, the area burned could grow fivefold. What worries people even more is the effect that would have on emissions, especially when the fires ravage forests arising out of peat. Peatland fires in Indonesia in 1997, for instance, added to the global $CO_2$ release by up to 40 percent, and more burning only means

more warming only means more burning. There is also the terrifying possibility that rain forests like the Amazon, which in 2010 suffered its second "hundred-year drought" in the space of five years, could dry out enough to become vulnerable to these kinds of devastating, rolling forest fires — which would not only expel enormous amounts of carbon into the atmosphere but also shrink the size of the forest. That is especially bad because the Amazon alone provides 20 percent of our oxygen.

Then there are the more familiar forms of pollution. In 2013, melting Arctic ice remodeled Asian weather patterns, depriving industrial China of the natural ventilation systems it had come to depend on, which blanketed much of the country's north in an unbreathable smog. Literally unbreathable. A metric called the Air Quality Index categorizes the risks and tops out at the 301-to-500 range, warning of "serious aggravation of heart or lung disease and premature mortality in persons with cardiopulmonary disease and the elderly" and, for all others, "serious risk of respiratory effects"; at that level, "everyone should avoid all outdoor exertion." The Chinese "airpocalypse" of 2013 peaked at what would have been an Air Quality Index of over 800. That year, smog was responsible for a third of all deaths in the country.

# VI. Perpetual War
## *The Violence Baked into Heat*

Climatologists are very careful when talking about Syria. They want you to know that while climate change did produce a drought that contributed to civil war, it is not exactly fair to say that the conflict is the result of warming; next door, for instance, Lebanon suffered the same crop failures. But researchers like Marshall Burke and Solomon Hsiang have managed to quantify some of the non-obvious relationships between temperature and violence: For every half-degree of warming, they say, societies will see between a 10 and 20 percent increase in the likelihood of armed conflict. In climate science, nothing is simple, but the arithmetic is harrowing: A planet five degrees warmer would have at least half again as many wars as we do today. Overall, social conflict could more than double this century.

This is one reason that, as nearly every climate scientist I spoke to pointed out, the U.S. military is obsessed with climate change: The drowning of all American Navy bases by sea-level rise is trouble enough, but being the world's policeman is quite a bit harder when the crime rate doubles. Of course, it's not just Syria where climate has contributed to conflict. Some speculate that the elevated level of strife across the Middle East over the past generation reflects the pressures of global warming — a hypothesis all the more cruel considering that warming began accelerating when the industrialized world extracted and then burned the region's oil.

What accounts for the relationship between climate and conflict? Some of it comes down to agriculture and economics; a lot has to do with forced migration, already at a record high, with at least 65 million displaced people wandering the planet right now. But there is also the simple fact of individual irritability. Heat increases municipal crime rates, and swearing on social media, and the likelihood that a major-league pitcher, coming to the mound after his teammate has been hit by a pitch, will hit an opposing batter in retaliation. And the arrival of air-conditioning in the developed world, in the middle of the past century, did little to solve the problem of the summer crime wave.

# VII. Permanent Economic Collapse
## Dismal Capitalism in a Half-poorer World

The murmuring mantra of global neoliberalism, which prevailed between the end of the Cold War and the onset of the Great Recession, is that economic growth would save us from anything and everything. But in the aftermath of the 2008 crash, a growing number of historians studying what they call "fossil capitalism" have begun to suggest that the entire history of swift economic growth, which began somewhat suddenly in the 18th century, is not the result of innovation or trade or the dynamics of global capitalism but simply our discovery of fossil fuels and all their raw power — a onetime injection of new "value" into a system that had previously been characterized by global subsistence living. Before fossil fuels, nobody lived better than their parents or grandparents or ancestors from 500 years before, except in the immediate aftermath of a great plague like the Black Death, which allowed the lucky survivors to gobble up the resources liberated by mass graves. After we've burned all the fossil fuels, these scholars suggest, perhaps we will return to a "steady state" global economy. Of course, that onetime injection has a devastating long-term cost: climate change.

The most exciting research on the economics of warming has also come from Hsiang and his colleagues, who are not historians of fossil capitalism but who offer some very bleak analysis of their own: Every degree Celsius of warming costs, on average, 1.2 percent of GDP (an enormous number, considering we count growth in the low single digits as "strong"). This is the sterling work in the field, and their median projection is for a 23 percent loss in per capita earning globally by the end of this century (resulting from changes in agriculture, crime, storms, energy, mortality, and labor).Tracing the shape of the probability curve is even scarier: There is a 12 percent chance that climate change will reduce global output by more than 50 percent by 2100, they say, and a 51 percent chance that it lowers per capita

GDP by 20 percent or more by then, unless emissions decline. By comparison, the Great Recession lowered global GDP by about 6 percent, in a onetime shock; Hsiang and his colleagues estimate a one-in-eight chance of an ongoing and irreversible effect by the end of the century that is eight times worse.

The scale of that economic devastation is hard to comprehend, but you can start by imagining what the world would look like today with an economy half as big, which would produce only half as much value, generating only half as much to offer the workers of the world. It makes the grounding of flights out of heat-stricken Phoenix last month seem like pathetically small economic potatoes. And, among other things, it makes the idea of postponing government action on reducing emissions and relying solely on growth and technology to solve the problem an absurd business calculation. Every round-trip ticket on flights from New York to London, keep in mind, costs the Arctic three more square meters of ice.

# VIII. Poisoned Oceans
## Sulfide Burps off the Skeleton Coast

That the sea will become a killer is a given. Barring a radical reduction of emissions, we will see at least four feet of sea-level rise and possibly ten by the end of the century. A third of the world's major cities are on the coast, not to mention its power plants, ports, navy bases, farmlands, fisheries, river deltas, marshlands, and rice-paddy empires, and even those above ten feet will flood much more easily, and much more regularly, if the water gets that high. At least 600 million people live within ten meters of sea level today.

But the drowning of those homelands is just the start. At present, more than a third of the world's carbon is sucked up by the oceans — thank God, or else we'd have that much more warming already. But the result is what's called "ocean acidification," which, on its own, may add a half a degree to warming this century. It is also already burning through the planet's water basins — you may remember these as the place where life arose in the first place. You have probably heard of "coral bleaching" — that is, coral dying — which is very bad news, because reefs support as much as a quarter of all marine life and supply food for half a billion people. Ocean acidification will fry fish populations directly, too, though scientists aren't yet sure how to predict the effects on the stuff we haul out of the ocean to eat; they do know that in acid waters, oysters and mussels will struggle to grow their shells, and that when the pH of human blood drops as much as the oceans' pH has over the past generation, it induces seizures, comas, and sudden death.

That isn't all that ocean acidification can do. Carbon absorption can initiate a feedback loop in which underoxygenated waters breed different kinds of microbes that turn the water still more "anoxic," first in deep ocean "dead zones," then gradually up toward the surface. There, the small fish die out, unable to breathe, which means oxygen-eating bacteria thrive, and the feedback loop doubles back. This process, in which dead zones grow like cancers, choking off marine life and wiping out fisheries, is already quite advanced in parts of the Gulf of Mexico and just off Namibia, where hydrogen sulfide is bubbling out of the sea along a thousand-mile stretch of land known as the "Skeleton Coast." The name originally referred to the detritus of the whaling industry, but today it's more apt than ever. Hydrogen sulfide is so toxic that evolution has trained us to recognize the tiniest, safest traces of it, which is why our noses are so exquisitely skilled at registering flatulence. Hydrogen sulfide is also the thing that finally did us in that time 97 percent of all life on Earth died, once all the feedback loops had been triggered and the circulating jet streams of a warmed ocean ground to a halt — it's the planet's preferred gas for a natural holocaust. Gradually, the ocean's dead zones spread, killing off marine species that had dominated the oceans for hundreds of millions of years, and the gas the inert waters gave off into the atmosphere poisoned everything on land. Plants, too. It was millions of years before the oceans recovered.

# IX. The Great Filter
## *Our Present Eeriness Cannot Last*

So why can't we see it? In his recent book-length essay *The Great Derangement*, the Indian novelist Amitav Ghosh wonders why global warming and natural disaster haven't become major subjects of contemporary fiction — why we don't seem able to imagine climate catastrophe, and why we haven't yet had a spate of novels in the genre he basically imagines into half-existence and names "the environmental uncanny." "Consider, for example, the stories that congeal around questions like, 'Where were you when the Berlin Wall fell?' or 'Where were you on 9/11?'" he writes. "Will it ever be possible to ask, in the same vein, 'Where were you at 400 ppm?' or 'Where were you when the Larsen B ice shelf broke up?'" His answer: Probably not, because the dilemmas and dramas of climate change are simply incompatible with the kinds of stories we tell ourselves about ourselves, especially in novels, which tend to emphasize the journey of an individual conscience rather than the poisonous miasma of social fate.

Surely this blindness will not last — the world we are about to inhabit will not permit it. In a six-degree-warmer world, the Earth's ecosystem will boil with so many natural disasters that we will just start calling them "weather": a constant swarm of out-of-control typhoons and tornadoes and floods and droughts, the planet assaulted regularly with climate events that not so long ago destroyed whole civilizations. The strongest hurricanes will come more often, and we'll have to invent new categories with which to describe them; tornadoes will grow longer and wider and strike much more frequently, and hail rocks will quadruple in size. Humans used to watch the weather to prophesy the future; going forward, we will see in its wrath the vengeance of the past. Early naturalists talked often about "deep time" — the perception they had, contemplating the grandeur of this valley or that rock basin, of the profound slowness of nature. What lies in store for us is more like what the Victorian anthropologists identified as "dreamtime," or "everywhen": the semi-mythical experience, described by Aboriginal Australians, of encountering, in the present moment, an out-of-time past, when ancestors, heroes, and demigods crowded an epic stage. You can find it already watching footage of an iceberg collapsing into the sea — a feeling of history happening all at once.

It is. Many people perceive climate change as a sort of moral and economic debt, accumulated since the beginning of the Industrial Revolution and now come due after several centuries — a helpful perspective, in a way, since it is the carbon-burning processes that began in 18th-century England that lit the fuse of everything that followed. But more than half of the carbon humanity has exhaled into the atmosphere in its entire history has been emitted in just the past three decades; since the end of World War II, the figure is 85 percent. Which means that, in the length of a single generation, global warming has brought us to the brink of planetary catastrophe, and that the story of the industrial world's kamikaze mission is also the story of a single lifetime. My father's, for instance: born in 1938, among his first memories the news of Pearl Harbor and the mythic Air Force of the propaganda films that followed, films that doubled as advertisements for imperial-American industrial might; and among his last memories the coverage of the desperate signing of the Paris climate accords on cable news, ten weeks before he died of lung cancer last July. Or my mother's: born in 1945, to German Jews fleeing the smokestacks through which their relatives were incinerated, now enjoying her 72nd year in an American commodity paradise, a paradise supported by the supply chains of an industrialized developing world. She has been smoking for 57 of those years, unfiltered.

Or the scientists'. Some of the men who first identified a changing climate (and given the generation, those who became famous were men) are still alive; a few are even still working. Wally Broecker is 84 years old and drives to work at the Lamont-Doherty Earth Observatory across the Hudson every day from the Upper West Side. Like most of those who first raised the alarm, he believes that no amount of emissions reduction alone can meaningfully help avoid disaster. Instead, he puts his faith in carbon capture — untested technology to extract carbon dioxide from the atmosphere, which Broecker estimates will cost at least several trillion dollars — and various forms of "geoengineering," the catchall name for a variety of moon-shot technologies far-fetched enough that many climate scientists prefer to regard them as dreams, or nightmares, from science fiction. He is especially focused on what's called the aerosol approach — dispersing so much sulfur dioxide into the atmosphere that when it converts to sulfuric acid, it will cloud a fifth of the horizon and reflect back 2 percent of the sun's rays, buying the planet at least a little wiggle room, heat-wise. "Of course, that would make our sunsets very red, would bleach the sky, would make more acid rain," he says. "But you have to look at the magnitude of the problem. You got to watch that you don't say the giant problem shouldn't be solved because the solution causes some smaller problems." He won't be around to see that, he told me. "But in your lifetime . . ."

Jim Hansen is another member of this godfather generation. Born in 1941, he became a climatologist at the University of Iowa, developed the groundbreaking "Zero Model" for projecting climate change, and later became the head of climate research at NASA, only to leave under pressure when, while still a federal employee, he filed a lawsuit against the federal government charging inaction on warming (along the way he got arrested a few times for protesting, too). The lawsuit, which is brought by a collective called Our Children's Trust and is often described as "kids versus climate change," is built on an appeal to the equal-protection clause, namely, that in failing to take action on warming, the government is violating it by imposing massive costs on future generations; it is scheduled to be heard this winter in Oregon district court. Hansen has recently given up on solving the climate problem with a carbon tax alone, which had been his preferred approach, and has set about calculating the total cost of the additional measure of extracting carbon from the atmosphere.

Hansen began his career studying Venus, which was once a very Earth-like planet with plenty of life-supporting water before runaway climate change rapidly transformed it into an arid and uninhabitable sphere enveloped in an unbreathable gas; he switched to studying our planet by 30, wondering why he should be squinting across the solar system to explore rapid environmental change when he could see it all around him on the planet he was standing on. "When we wrote our first paper on this, in 1981," he told me, "I remember saying to one of my co-authors, 'This is going to be very interesting. Sometime during our careers, we're going to see these things beginning to happen.'"

Several of the scientists I spoke with proposed global warming as the solution to Fermi's famous paradox, which asks, If the universe is so big, then why haven't we encountered any other intelligent life in it? The answer, they suggested, is that the natural life span of a civilization may be only several thousand years, and the life span of an industrial civilization perhaps only several hundred. In a universe that is many billions of years old, with star systems separated as much by time as by space, civilizations might emerge and develop and burn themselves up simply too fast to ever find one another. Peter Ward, a charismatic paleontologist among those responsible for discovering that the planet's mass extinctions were caused by greenhouse gas, calls this the "Great Filter": "Civilizations rise, but there's an environmental filter that causes them to die off again and disappear fairly quickly," he told me. "If you look at planet Earth, the filtering we've had in the past has been in these mass extinctions." The mass extinction we are now living through has only just begun; so much more dying is coming.

And yet, improbably, Ward is an optimist. So are Broecker and Hansen and many of the other scientists I spoke to. We have not developed much of a religion of meaning around climate change that might comfort us, or give us purpose, in the face of possible annihilation. But climate scientists have a strange kind of faith: We will find a way to forestall radical warming, they say, because we must.

It is not easy to know how much to be reassured by that bleak certainty, and how much to wonder whether it is another form of delusion; for global warming to work as parable, of course, someone needs to survive to tell the story. The scientists know that to even meet the Paris goals, by 2050, carbon emissions from energy and industry, which are still rising, will have to fall by half each decade; emissions from land use (deforestation, cow farts, etc.) will have to zero out; and we will need to have invented technologies to extract, annually, twice as much carbon from the atmosphere as the entire planet's plants now do. Nevertheless, by and large, the scientists have an enormous confidence in the ingenuity of humans — a confidence perhaps bolstered by their appreciation for climate change, which is, after all, a human invention, too. They point to the Apollo project, the hole in the ozone we patched in the 1980s, the passing of the fear of mutually assured destruction. Now we've found a way to engineer our own doomsday, and surely we will find a way to engineer our way out of it, one way or another. The planet is not used to being provoked like this, and climate systems designed to give feedback over centuries or millennia prevent us — even those who may be watching closely — from fully imagining the damage done already to the planet. But when we do truly see the world we've made, they say, we will also find a way to make it livable. For them, the alternative is simply unimaginable.

## Critical Thinking

1. This is a one-sided article on climate change which claims that the great majority of scientific articles support it. What is your evaluation of this claim?

2. The key to low negative effects of future climate change is human behavior. How does that increase or reduce pessimism?

3. Despite facing possible horrible impacts of climate change most scientists the author talked to were positive. Why? Are you?

# Internet References

**Futures Centre | Forum for the Future**
   www.thefuturescentre.org/trends/climatechange

**New American Studies Web**
   www.georgetown.edu/crossroads/asw

**Social Science Information Gateway**
   http://sosig.esrc.bris.ac.uk

**Sociology Web Resources**
   http://www.mhhe.com/socscience/sociology/resources/index.htm

**Sociology—Study Sociology Online**
   http://edu.learnsoc.org

**Sociosite**
   http://www.topsite.com/goto/sociosite.net

David Wallace-Wells/New York Magazine.

*Article*          Prepared by: Kurt Finsterbusch, *University of Maryland, College Park*

# Climate Change 2017: What Happened and What It Means

Bruce Melton

## Learning Outcomes

*After reading this article, you will be able to:*

- Describe the many anti-climate change actions of the Trump administration.

- Describe a number unusual events which support the thesis that many of them are related to climate change.

- Explain why the scientific community is very concerned about climate change.

How many more billions of dollars in damages will it take? How many more lives? It's obvious; all the climate extremes we have been experiencing lately are indeed caused by climate change. Our climate is already far too dangerous. Scientists have been warning us for 30 years, but still they can't say for sure.

This is because scientists tell us things in terms of certainty, and this is where we get the oft-heard statement, "We can't tell if this event was caused by climate change or not." Almost nothing is certain, especially rapidly changing climate extremes, because it takes time to develop certainty about the weather.

Scientists speak in terms of certainty – probabilistic, scientific certainty. A little warming doesn't result in a little more extreme weather; it results in a lot more. Who is going to protect us from climate change?

Donald Trump and his climate-science-denying administration certainly will not. They are repealing the Clean Power Plan, which are the Environmental Protection Agency's (EPA) landmark pollution rules designed to limit carbon dioxide emissions from large sources such as power plants. They reversed the Obama administration's rejection of the Keystone XL pipeline. They shut down the EPA's climate change website in April, and when it returned in July, it was half-missing. Trump also cancelled the Climate Action Plan, dropped climate change from the list of national security threats and revoked Federal Emergency Management Agency flood risk standards accounting for sea level rise with federal infrastructure projects.

The administration has abandoned the most important climate treaty in the world, the Paris Agreement, but they still wanted to sit at the table and develop the rules at the 23rd Conference of Parties (COP23) to the United Nations Convention on Climate Change recently held in Bonn, Germany. The US delegation at COP23 asked Peabody Coal to explain how "clean coal" could slow climate change.

They have reversed Obama's ban on offshore oil exploration and are stonewalling rules for the first vehicle fuel economy standards implemented in 40 years (by Obama). Trump's EPA director Scott Pruitt sued the agency four times when he was the Oklahoma attorney general to block the Clean Power Plan, and once against methane emissions rules. Trump has scrubbed increased methane and volatile organic carbon reporting standards that began under Obama. Trump also appointed Exxon-Mobil CEO Rex Tillerson as secretary of state.

Unfortunately, new record-breaking science has made at least as much noise as Trump.

## Hurricane Harvey, a 25,000-Year Storm

Hurricane Harvey brought record setting rainfall to Texas between August 23 and 28. The most recorded rainfall was 50 inches, but more than 24 inches was recorded over more than 15,000 square miles, which is 30 times greater than the previous records.

Lawrence Berkeley National Laboratory has done some advanced modeling and found that "human induced climate change likely increased the chances of ... Hurricane Harvey in the affected areas of Houston by a factor of at least 3.5 [350 percent]." The best estimate of how much Harvey would have rained in our old climate was 36 inches, not the 50 inches recorded – a 38 percent increase because of climate change.

There are some challenges with this Berkeley work. One is that the authors compared total storm rainfall from Harvey to record events from 1950 to 2017. This means the researchers compared Harvey to the recent past, when increases in extreme rainfall have already occurred. What this means is that big storms have increased even more than if, say, the researchers had compared today to the period 1930 to 1950. It's nuanced, but it's meaningful.

Houston rainfall has increased a lot since 1950. John Nielsen-Gammon, who is Texas state climatologist, says that extreme flooding has doubled in Houston during the last 30 years. Nielsen-Gammon compares the last 30 years to the previous 30 years. But extremes really didn't start becoming so much more extreme until, at the most, 10 years ago.

Widespread reporting said that Harvey was a 1-in-1,000-year flood event (a 1,000-year storm is a storm that happens on average every 1,000 years) based on rates of rainfall. A meteorological engineering company called MetStat specializes in these types of extreme rainfall frequency analyses and analyzed the entire storm. It found that across the 15,000 square miles of southeast Texas that received greater than 24 inches of rain, making Harvey a 25,000-year storm.

## Fire! California Burns

Record drought, record rains, record fires: It's the extremes that matter in any climate. We can tell that these new California fire extremes do not belong in our old climate because of their record nature of their size and impacts. There have been almost 10,000 structures destroyed with 40 deaths in the California fires, according to Calfire.gov. This is more than twice as many structures burned and lives lost as in the previous record outbreak. Furthermore, December is the rainy season in California.

The National Oceanic and Atmospheric Administration (NOAA) says that the period of 2011 through 2015 in California was the driest four consecutive years since record-keeping began. The California Department of Water Resources said that average rainfall across California in the water year of September 2016 through August 2017, was the wettest water year in half of California and second wettest in the other half. What is causing all of this?

## The Jet Stream and Extremes

Why are all these extremes happening? One of the reasons is "Arctic amplification." As the Arctic warms, more snow melts. When snow melts, earth, plants, rock and water absorb up to 90 percent of the sun's rays and turn them into heat. Ice and snow reflect up to 90 percent of the sun's energy harmlessly back into space, so decreased ice and snow cover due to rising temperatures in the Arctic only accelerate climate change.

This Arctic amplification affects the way the jet stream behaves. It makes the jet stream loops larger and move more slowly west to east. Because the jet stream pushes (or pulls) weather systems west to east around the planet, the slower west-east movement allows weather systems to stall out, and this increases impacts. Rainfall events "train" over the same area increasing flooding; droughts are longer.

The lead scientist who developed the famous "hockey stick" temperature graph (which shows little change in temperature for thousands of years in the past, until the last 100 years) has released some new research looking at Arctic amplification that corroborates previous studies that show warming messes with the jet stream. This new work makes the science even more clear that global warming increases weather extremes.

## Western North American Wildfire

It's not just California. Wildfires have increased area burned and intensity across the Western US. Only 2015 had more area burned in the US than did 2017. The following are some forest fire statistics from 2016 that bear repeating: Sierra Nevada Research Institute's Anthony Westerling found that wildfire season in the western US has increased by over 60 percent since the 1970s, from 138 days to 222 days, because of earlier onset of spring. The average burn time of a wildfire has increased nearly 800 percent, from six days to 52 days, because of deeper drying from earlier snowmelt. Burned area increased an astonishing 1,271 percent. Human-caused ignition has played a very small role in increasing wildfire trends. Westerling also notes that, "Given projections for further drying within the region due to human-induced warming, this study underlines the potential for further increases in wildfire activity."

## Extreme Precipitation

The National Climate Assessment says extreme precipitation has increased in intensity and frequency over most of the US, with the Northeast leading the way. Importantly, clusters of extreme warm season thunderstorms are more numerous and deliver greater amounts of rainfall. Extremes and rainfall totals are expected to continue to increase.

The latest high resolution modeling on these most extreme weather events out of the National Center for Atmospheric Research says they will triple by end of century. The US will see a 15 to 40 percent increase in maximum precipitation rates in certain regions, with up to 80 percent increase in the total precipitation volume. Area covered by each individual storm increases roughly by a factor of two. These researchers also say extreme storms with a precipitation rate in excess of 3.5 inches per hour will increase in the central US by 380 percent by the end of the century. The highest increases occur in Canada and the US Northeast, where rainfall rates in excess of 3 inches per hour, as the authors state, "are almost unrepresented in the current climate and become frequent in the future."

## Very Large Negative Emissions

Extreme weather events have already increased to dangerous levels because we have delayed climate action for nearly 30 years. Further warming increases extremes nonlinearly. In other words, a little more warming creates a lot more extremes.

Scientists are now evaluating additional "negative emissions" required to prevent even greater warming. These negative emissions are in addition to the best-case scenario of the Paris Climate Accord, which calls for 80 percent emissions reductions by 2050 and net zero emissions by 2080. (Net zero is any combination of emissions reductions, energy infrastructure decarbonization and negative emissions, where the net annual emissions of carbon dioxide are zero.)

James Hansen, the 32-year director of the US government's climate modeling agency, the Goddard Institute for Space Studies, reveals the quantity of negative emissions required to meet a 350 parts per million (ppm) CO2 goal of about 1 degree Celsius warming by 2100, where the temperature rise mid-century – before it begins to fall – is less than 1.5 degrees Celsius.

To do this, Hansen says that we must use strategies to reduce already emitted carbon dioxide that remains in our sky, whether it is through plants, forests, agricultural techniques or removing CO2 directly from the air. The quantity of negative emissions required is between 7 and 32 gigatons of carbon dioxide annually through 2100, depending on whether our emissions reductions rate is zero (where emissions stay the same as today) or 6 percent per year, which is about double the Paris Accord. Today, we emit about 40 gigatons of carbon dioxide every year.

## National Climate Assessment: There Is a Significant Possibility for Unanticipated Changes

Unless we reduce already observed warming with negative emissions, we can expect these unanticipated changes that the

National Academy of Sciences note in the National Climate Assessment. What the Fourth National Climate Assessment reports is unfortunately predictable: Climate change is worse than it was supposed to be because we have delayed action and previous projections have turned out to be understated.

According to the report, the likely human contribution to warming is 92-123 percent of the observed climate warming from 1951-2010. In other words, humans have caused more warming than has been measured. This is possible because global cooling pollutants (sulfates or smog) from burning fossil fuels have masked warming that should have occurred. This masking happens because smog reflects sunlight harmlessly back into space without warming Earth.

Maybe the most important thing in the assessment, though, is excerpted below from the final chapter of the Executive Summary:

There is significant potential for humanity's effect on the planet to result in unanticipated surprises and a broad consensus that the further and faster the Earth system is pushed towards warming, the greater the risk of such surprises.

There are at least two types of potential surprises: compound events, where multiple extreme climate events occur simultaneously or sequentially (creating greater overall impact), and critical threshold or tipping point events, where some threshold is crossed in the climate system). The probability of such surprises – some of which may be abrupt and/or irreversible increases as the influence of human activities on the climate system increases.

Positive feedbacks (self-reinforcing cycles) within the climate system have the potential to accelerate human-induced climate change and even shift the Earth's climate system. . . .

**Three record setting droughts in 2005, 2010 and 2016, each more extreme than the previous, have flipped the Amazon from a carbon sink to a carbon source**

Unanticipated surprises are already underway. Three 100-year-plus droughts in the Amazon in 12 years have taken their toll. Along with continual human-created ecological compromise and climate warming, fires and forest mortality from drought have overwhelmed the capacity of the Amazon to absorb carbon dioxide.

The telling part of this research from the University of Connecticut, funded by the National Science Foundation, is that in the past, sea surface temperatures in the Pacific have been well correlated to drought, including the two 100-year-plus events in 2005 and 2010. In 2016, the drought exceeded modeling extremes and the authors believe warming, deforestation and drought mortality are to blame. These quotes from the study tell the story:

"In 2005, a severe drought in the Amazon, categorized as a 100-year event, caused record-breaking annual wild fires and carbon emissions, leading to the first ever negative annual carbon balance recorded for the rainforest."

"Five years later, a stronger and more destructive drought hit Amazonia in 2010 and the recorded rainforest carbon balance was negative for the second time."

"Here, we show that the severity of the 2015-2016 drought is unprecedented based on multiple precipitation products (since 1900)."

# Sea Level Rise Scenarios Start to Catch Up With Prehistory

The NOAA's new sea level rise report has revealed some truly meaningful realities of future impacts. With just a nine-inch rise in sea level projected by 2030, NOAA advisories for coastal flooding capable of causing "significant risks to life and property" could occur 25 times more often. This is very significant sounding on its own, but what exactly does it mean?

According to the report, flooding that we would expect to happen on average every five years (three feet) will happen every two months. This means that what would previously have been categorized as 100-year floods (13 feet) will be expected to happen every four years. And remember, this is with just nine inches of sea level rise and it is projected to happen by 2030.

Here again, Earth systems cause the increases to be exponential. In other words, a little bit of rise creates a very large amount of impact. It's not the average that is important, it is the extremes.

The Union of Concerned Scientists (UCS) goes further with NOAA's new projections. Their new report, based on NOAA's work, defines the increase of chronic flooding of 25 times greater than today, as an amount of flooding that causes "resources abandonment." This is the point that people begin to simply walk away from their homes and businesses. The UCS says this will happen to nearly 170 coastal US communities within 12 years, and under the worst-case scenario, in about 670 coastal US communities by the end of the century.

**Wind scoured blue ice in Greenland: Katabatic winds, or gravity-driven monster winds up to 150 mph sustained, can literally blow the ice away. Just off screen, a nuntak, or mountain island in the ice sheet, deflects winds in this area to create ice scour that reveals ancient blue ice**

# Ice Loss During Antarctic Cold Reversal May Spell Trouble for West Antarctic Ice Sheet Collapse

Where do these nine inches of sea level rise come from? The Intergovernmental Panel on Climate Change (IPCC) says two feet by 2100. The IPCC though, does not include abrupt sea level rise from ice sheet collapse. The latest research on ice sheet collapse from Australia shows 52 feet of sea level rise occurred in 400 years, 14,500 years ago with ocean conditions similar to today. We were coming out of the last ice age then, but then, the increasing rate of warming was far less than today.

Our climate's most meaningful and common temperature changes are classified as abrupt changes in climate science. Twenty-three of them occurred in our last 100,000-year-long ice age. They mostly happened with global temperature change of 9 to 15 degrees Fahrenheit and 25 degrees Fahrenheit or more in Greenland.

The biggest was caused by melt from the massive Laurentide ice sheet that covered the northern half of North America at the end of the last ice age, beginning about 18,000 years ago. The ice was a mile deep over what is now New York City, with an epicenter two miles high over Hudson Bay. The melt formed a giant lake over south-central Canada. About 14,600 years ago, it became so large that it broke through the lobe of ice that carved out the Great Lakes, and its outflow changed from the Mississippi River Basin to the St. Laurence, and then to the North Atlantic via New Newfoundland.

The massive influx of freshwater melt, being lighter than salt water, floated on the North Atlantic and shut down the Gulf Stream. This stopped the northward flow of warm water from the South Atlantic and plummeted our planet back into deep ice age cold. But under-ice melt continued. Some research says that parts of Greenland ice sheet and Antarctica collapsed and raised sea level 65 feet in as little as 200 years.

Today, Greenland melt has created a massive pool of buoyant fresh melt water in the North Atlantic east of Newfoundland. The pool has reduced flow in the Gulf Stream 40 percent since the mid-2000s.

Enter Chris Fogwill and a team of 21 researchers from Australia to the UK. This team has created a half mile-long "horizontal ice core" from the Ronne Ice Shelf in West Antarctica. Fogwill says gravity-driven Antarctic winds have so scoured the ice over 50 miles, that surface sampling allowed the team to look at 5,000 years of ancient ice. (The British Antarctic Survey says these gravity-driven winds can reach 200 mph.)

They found this area lost 2,000 feet in elevation during the abrupt cold reversal 18,000 years ago. Their unexpected results reveal that the return of glacial temperatures cooled surface waters, but not deeper waters, which remained warm, melting the underside of the ice.

Today, we see the same cool surface/warm deep setup. The trigger 18,000 years ago was the melting of the Laurentide ice sheet. Today, it's the West Antarctic ice sheet. Both were/are marine ice sheets, inherently unstable because their ice is grounded on the ocean floor thousands of feet below sea level.

The cool surface water in the North Atlantic today is melt from increased ice discharge in Greenland. The cooler water, just like in North Atlantic Gulf Stream shutdowns in prehistory, prevents surface water from mixing with deeper water. The researchers tell us that current projections of sea level rise "do not fully include ice-sheet-ocean dynamic feedbacks." These feedbacks "are believed to have triggered rapid continental ice-sheet retreat and driven periods of abrupt sea-level rise during the geological past."

## Summary: Resist the Trump Administration

The bottom line is that climate change, because of delayed action, is happening faster and more extremely than projected. Before Trump, the best-case scenario of emissions reductions allowed for significantly more than 2 degrees Celsius of warming. With dangerously extreme weather happening more and more frequently, and with abrupt changes plausibly already begun, now is not the time to be backpedaling climate policy.

Climate scientists warned us that our task would be more difficult the longer we delayed. The difficulty has now arrived and even further delay is real. The great risk is that a little more warming will not create a small increase in additional extremes. It is entirely plausible that a little more warming will cross thresholds and create nonlinearly more extreme events that are literally unrecoverable, if we do not reduce warming sooner rather than later.

## Critical Thinking

1. What are the present and future impacts of climate change?
2. What are some of the key findings of other major reports?
3. What do you think should be done about climate change?

## Internet References

**Energy and Environment—RAND Corporation**
https://www.rand.org/topics/energy-and-environment.html

**Futures Centre|Forum for the Future**
www.thefuturescentre.org/trends/climatechange

**Sociology Web Resources**
http://www.mhhe.com/socscience/sociology/resources/index.htm

**Sociology—Study Sociology Online**
http://edu.learnsoc.org

**Sociosite**
http://www.topsite.com/goto/sociosite.net

---

**BRUCE MELTON** is a professional engineer, environmental researcher, filmmaker, author, and CEO of the Climate Change Now Initiative in Austin, TX. The Climate Change Now Initiative is a nonprofit outreach organization reporting the latest discoveries in climate science in plain English. Information on his book, *Climate Discovery Chronicles*, can be found along with more climate change writing, climate science outreach and critical environmental issue documentary films at ClimateDiscovery.org.

*Article*　　　　Prepared by: Kurt Finsterbusch, *University of Maryland, College Park*

# The Role of Government in the Transition to a Sustainable Economy

The Need for Governmental Sustainability Policy

STEVEN COHEN

## Learning Outcomes

*After reading this article, you will be able to:*

- Discuss the need for government action on the environment and the current many problems of government actions.

- Discuss the importance of developing and deploying the technology to create and maintain a renewable resource-based economy.

- Understand why the private sector cannot produce sustainability.

I t's a great paradox that the moment the United States needs government the most, we don't seem to have one anymore. As a student of public administration, like many of my generation, I was motivated by John F. Kennedy's call to public service. I "asked not what my country could do for me" and, despite my concerns about the direction of our foreign policy in the 1960s and 1970s, I went to work for the Environmental Protection Agency in the late 1970s asking, "what can I do for my country?" Six months into Ronald Reagan's term, after he defined government as a problem rather than a calling, I was gone. I was not alone; many left and many who were needed never arrived. State and local governments continued to attract the best and brightest of our young people, but fewer and fewer seemed interested in working in our nation's capital. Most headed for private non-profits and for-profits. In Washington, public service went out of fashion, replaced by the ambition-fueled revolving door.

Today, Washington seems a place of palace intrigue, arcane policy debates, campaign cash and a political spin on everything and everyone. I suppose for me, the final breaking point was the

Obama team's failure to launch a functioning web-based sign-up system for national health care. Over a half-century of struggle to establish national healthcare culminated with a sign-up process that didn't work. We now have a federal government so incompetent that it can't manage the contractors setting up a website. President Reagan set in motion a self-fulfilling prophecy; government, at least the federal kind, has become a problem.

With this as the backdrop, we have a planet that is trapped in an economic system based on the one-time use of fossil fuels and other material resources. The population of our planet has grown from 3 billion when JFK took office to over 7 billion today. We need to develop and deploy the technology to create a renewable resource-based economy. We simply cannot continue using up materials and dumping the waste in a hole in the ground.

The private sector cannot make the transition from a waste-based economy to a renewable one by itself. This transition can only happen if we can create a public-private partnership. This is nothing new; we've been through this before. The transformation from an agrarian economy to an industrial economy could not have been done under the laissez-faire economic philosophy of the early industrial age. Teddy Roosevelt and his allies understood that and began to regulate the marketplace. Food, drugs, labor and monopolies were regulated at the start of the 20th century. FDR continued the process of increasing the role of government in our mixed economy. Government was needed to establish the rules of the game-a social safety net-along with transportation, energy and water infrastructure. Now, as we begin the transition from a fossil fuel-based economy to one based on renewable energy and other reusable resources, government has a critical role to play again.

While I am focusing here on the role of government, it is important to understand that the private sector has a much larger and even more important role to play in the transition to a sustainable economy. It is the private sector that produces the goods and services that modern life relies on. We like and want these goods and services and without capitalism's power to motivate and reduce inefficiency, there would be far fewer of these goods and services to consume. This is not an argument that government knows best. It is the argument that effective competition requires rules, referees and meaningful penalties for anti-social, criminal behavior. I am saying that in a complex economy on a crowded planet, we need a set of rules that respond to the complexity and planetary stress that our global economy has created. Just as the regulation of Wall Street builds confidence in the public marketplace for capital, we need rules to ensure that economic life does not destroy the planet that provides us with food, air and water.

The role of government in building the sustainable economy includes:

1. Funding basic science needed for renewable energy and renewable resource technology.
2. Using the tax system, government purchasing power and other financial tools to steer private capital toward investment in renewable energy and other sustainability technologies and businesses.
3. Investment in sustainability infrastructure, such as smart grids, electric vehicle charging stations, mass transit, waste management facilities, water filtration systems and sewage treatment systems.
4. Regulating land use and other private behaviors to minimize destruction of ecosystems.
5. Working with private organizations as well as state and local government to ensure that the transition is well-managed in the real world.
6. Measuring our society's progress toward sustainability by developing and maintaining a system of generally accepted sustainability metrics. This in turn should facilitate the integration of sustainability into our overall management of the economy along with the setting of national sustainable economic policy.
7. Transferring sustainability technologies to the developing world.

# 1 & 2. Funding Science and Providing Incentives for Private Investment

One of the fundamental tasks that can only be done by government is to fund the science needed to build the technological base for a sustainable economy. America's research universities remain the best in the world. They are funded by peer-reviewed, competitive government grant programs. When coupled with the creativity hard-wired into American culture, they create a unique asset that can be used to develop a leadership position in sustainability technologies. The work of our scientists and engineers could not be more important. We need to develop a way to get off of fossil fuels and more efficiently store energy. We also need more effective ways of managing and recycling our waste stream. Government must fund the basic research and enough of the applied research to demonstrate possible profitability. The tax code must then provide private firms with incentives to invest capital in these new and speculative technologies.

# 3. Funding Infrastructure

Just as government built ports, canals, dams and highways—the infrastructure of the 19th and 20th centuries—it must build the energy, communications, waste and water-management infrastructure needed for the 21st century. Constructing and operating these facilities will probably be the work of private firms, but the vision and financing will need to come from taxpayers and their government. Infrastructure requires an imaginative and aggressive government. It cannot be seen as a residual category. The neglect of investment in infrastructure is obvious to even the most casual observer of America's political economy. Our roads, railways, water systems, electric grid, broadband speed, bridges, airports and schools show signs of disinvestment and neglect. Our anti-government and anti-tax ideology has made investment difficult and will make the transition to a sustainable economy even more difficult.

# 4. Setting and Enforcing Rules to Protect the Environment and Maximize Resource Efficiency

Anti-tax and anti-government sentiment is also reflected in reflexive opposition to so-called job-killing environmental regulations. Even though the economic benefits of environmental rules are far higher than the economic costs, our delegitimized federal government has not enacted any new environmental laws in over two decades. Many sustainability-oriented local officials understand the clear connection between environmental quality and economic growth. Unfortunately, the old mindset persists: we must trade off environmental quality to achieve economic growth. While short-term benefits can be obtained by ignoring environmental conditions, our polluted land, air and water must eventually be cleaned if we are to remain healthy.

The long-term costs of clean-up are also far greater than the long-term costs of pollution prevention.

Our more complex economy and the increased use of toxics in production require rules that keep pace with economic, demographic and technological change. The food, water and air that sustain human life must be protected; only government rules and enforcement can ensure that those critical resources are maintained. Rules must prevent damage to the environment, but also must ensure that energy efficiency, recycling and water efficiency are integrated into our structures, institutions and daily routines.

## 5. Working to Ensure the Transition is Well-Managed

Making policies and setting rules is only the start of the process; these rules must be altered and adjusted to deal with the real world. Some rules prove to be impractical. Some become outdated by new technology and new social behaviors. In some cases, new rules require the use of new technology, equipment and standard operating procedures, and require a period of learning, pilot tests and experimentation. Very few new activities match the plans they are based on. Edicts from faceless bureaucrats reinforced by arrogant, "tough enforcement" attitudes almost always backfire and should be avoided. As my friend and retired EPA manager Ron Brand used to say, "Focus on the real work. There are no cash registers in headquarters." Revenues and expenditures are driven by the people on the production line delivering services and manufacturing goods. Once policies and strategies are developed and the money to implement them is allocated, the action shifts to operational management, assessment and learning. It is a mistake to ignore operations management.

## 6. Sustainability Metrics and Management

As management guru Peter Drucker famously stated, "You can't manage something if you can't measure it." Without measures, you can't tell if the actions taken by management are making things better or worse. In some respects, sustainability metrics are as primitive as accounting was before the Great Depression. While the imposition of income and corporate taxes at the start of the 20th century resulted in the growth of the accounting profession, early accounting principles were not consistently applied. According to financial writer Andrew Beattie:

*In 1917, the Federal Reserve published Uniform Accounting, a document that attempted to set industry standards for how financials should be organized both for reporting tax and for financial statements. There were no laws to back the standards so they had little effect. The stock market crash of 1929 that launched the Great Depression exposed massive accounting frauds by companies listed on the NYSE. This prompted stricter measures in 1933, including the independent audit of a company's financial statements by public accountants before being listed on the exchange.*

Sustainability metrics are still under development. Each corporation, locality and think tank seems to have their own favorite measures and methods. Some focus on physical issues such as water, waste and energy, while others include issues of equity, fairness and environmental justice. In the end, government will need to set reporting standards. Perhaps they will be integrated into standard accounting definitions and practices as the U.S. tax code evolves to encourage sustainability. Perhaps a separate set of measures will be developed. I have proposed that the U.S. government establish a National Commission on Sustainability Metrics to bring academics, government officials, industry, labor and environmentalists together to develop a set of generally accepted sustainability metrics. I have also begun a major research project to inventory and assess the current state of sustainability metrics now in use throughout the world.

## 7. Transferring Technology to the Developing World

As the developed world makes the transition to a more sustainable, renewable resource-based economy, it is important that newly developing nations are provided with incentives to use the new technologies instead of older ones that might get cheaper as they are discarded by the developed world. Coal and coal-fired power plants could get very inexpensive as they are replaced by cleaner sources of energy, and if the U.S. lowers its greenhouse gas emissions while developing nations increase theirs, the climate will continue to be degraded. I believe that the mitigation of climate change will require new energy technology, but without effective technology transfer, the climate problem will remain. Fortunately, a variety of financial tools could be used to lower the cost of new technology for export to the developing world.

## Government Needs a Sophisticated, Agile Sustainability Policy

The issues identified here cannot be addressed by the private sector and the free market alone; they require government action. Unfortunately, it requires a degree of management savvy we have not seen in the United States' federal government in decades. The people that rolled out Obamacare, bailed out the financial system at the expense of the middle class, and invaded Iraq to destroy non-existent weapons of mass destruction will not be able to handle the management challenges of this transition. Nevertheless, there is no choice. The U.S. government will need to assume global leadership of the transition to a sustainable economy. The probability of this happening today is low. I see far more evidence of this capacity in local government than I do at the federal level.

The future well-being of this country and of the planet as a whole depends on the U.S. government playing a more strategic and future-oriented role to bring about the transition to a renewable resource-based economy. This country seems to do its best work when confronted with a crisis. While this crisis has arrived, many people do not believe it is here. We need a national leader willing to communicate the need for change and a strategy for getting from here to there. While no one immediately comes to mind, perhaps someone will emerge.

# Critical Thinking

1. How will the needed technology be produced and funded?
2. Explain the need for new policies regulating economic actions. What is the opposition to such regulations?
3. How can the developing world be made more sustainable?

# Internet References

**Energy and Environment—RAND Corporation**
https://www.rand.org/topics/energy-and-environment.html

**New American Studies Web**
www.georgetown.edu/crossroads/asw

**Social Science Information Gateway**
http://sosig.esrc.bris.ac.uk

**Sociology Web Resources**
http://www.mhhe.com/socscience/sociology/resources/index.htm

**Sociology—Study Sociology Online**
http://edu.learnsoc.org

**Sociosite**
http://www.topsite.com/goto/sociosite.net

# Article

Prepared by: Kurt Finsterbusch, *University of Maryland, College Park*

# Is a Digitally Connected World a Better Place?

The plusses and minuses of this "Brave New World" represent the greatest change to the way people live and interact on this planet humankind has ever seen. We'll see more change in the next five years than we've seen in the last five. If we take some basic precautions, I believe the utility of the mobile Internet far outweighs the risks.

## Dan Hesse

## Learning Outcomes

*After reading this article, you will be able to:*

- Explain the economic benefits of the Internet and digital connections.

- Explain the explosion of available knowledge and its impacts that are produced by the digital revolution.

- Discuss the issue of cyber attacks.

W e are living at a time when technology is changing the world at a pace never before experienced in human history. Of all technological advances, in my view, the one that is changing the life we share on this planet the most, whether one lives in a G8 country or in the developing world, is the mobile Internet.

These dramatic changes bring with them many plusses, but also some negatives and risks. F. Scott Fitzgerald's quote, "The test of a first-rate intelligence is the ability to hold two opposed ideas in mind at the same time and still retain the ability to function" is perhaps a good theme for this talk.

I'm not claiming to have a first rate mind, but I have learned a bit about telecommunications during a 37-year career in the industry. Will Rogers said it well, "Everybody is ignorant, only in different subjects," and perhaps this could apply here as this is one of the few subjects I don't feel ignorant about.

I feel fortunate to have been in this rapidly-changing industry. I had the opportunity to launch AT&T's Internet division

in the mid-90's when I was jokingly referred to as "Rubber Ducky" in the Halls of headquarters, a reference to the popular song about a trucker with a Citizens Band radio, as some thought that the Internet would be a passing fad like the CB. The BMW ad on TV with Katie Couric and Bryant Gumble brings back memories of the 90's.

After launching AT&T's Internet service provider business, Worldnet, I was sent to Seattle to run a recent acquisition, McCaw Cellular, which became AT&T Wireless.

Both the Internet and wireless were growth businesses, but it took the merging of the two for each to explode. When Internet browsers were put into cell phones (the early "smartphones" like the first IPhone in 2007), it was like peanut butter meeting chocolate. Wireless had been useful in connecting people with people, but when wireless connected people with the information and utility of the Internet, growth of both wireless and the Internet accelerated rapidly.

Wireless went from zero to 6 billion users in 25 years, the most rapidly-adopted technology in history. There are roughly ten cell phones produced daily for every baby born in the world.

Wireless's next big growth period will not be driven by cell phones. Wireless chips are, or will be, put into almost every object imaginable: motor vehicles, health monitors, home appliances, wearables like fitness bracelets and watches, even into our bodies. Connecting not people, but things to the Internet, what has been referred to as "machine to machine" or the "Internet of things" will usher in the next big growth phase. Cisco estimates there will be 25 billion things connected to the Internet this year and 50 billion things connected by 2020.

Some would argue that this much change to the way we live our lives and communicate with one another is a scourge. Others see a blessing. I don't know the answer. Bertrand Russell said, "The trouble with the world is that the stupid are cocksure and the intelligent are full of doubt," so I guess it's OK not to be sure. In the time I have tonight, I'll try to give you both sides of the argument.

First, let's consider the impact on the global economy. One study indicates that for each 10 percentage points of cell phone penetration (the percentage of the population with a cell phone), a nation's GDP increases from a half to one-and-a-half points. Recon Analytics projects that wireless will contribute $1.5 trillion to US GDP over the next ten years. And, with the rare exception of countries like North Korea, there is not a large difference in penetration rates between developed and developing countries. Peter Diamandis, in his book *Abundance,* gives the example of the Masai warrior in Africa with a smartphone and Google having better access to information than the US President had 15 years ago. From a telecom infrastructure perspective, wireless has allowed the developing world to "leapfrog" the expensive landline access networks deployed by more developed countries.

Some gaps still exist, between countries, and within countries, what is referred to as the "Digital Divide".North America has less than 10% of the world's wireless subscribers, but 45% of the 4G LTE connections.

The greatest economic benefits may still be ahead of us with the productivity that will be driven by the "Internet of things." The information gathered by billions of "always on" devices, utilizing cloud and quantum computing, sophisticated analytics and algorithms, machine learning and artificial intelligence could have great economic potential. For example, UPS uses these technologies to track packages and vehicles, and each mile saved per day per driver adds $50 million per year to the bottom line. On the other hand, if a company is going to invest in embedding 3G wireless chips in thousands of vehicles with long productive lives, they may require their wireless carrier to maintain an outdated technology like 3G longer instead of investing in 5G.

I've been watching the History Channel program "The Men Who Built America", about how this country and our way of life was radically transformed in the late 19th and early 20th centuries by Vanderbilt's rail-roads, Rockefeller's oil, Carnegie's steel, JP Morgan's electricity, and Ford's automobiles, and the important interrelationship of these industries. We're seeing this same kind of new industry creation and interrelationship now in the digital domain.

The business model of every industry could be transformed in a world where every device and every person is connected all the time. This is an enormous opportunity for those who understand this power and harness it. On the other hand, seismic disruption like this could usher in great risk to incumbents.

There are two areas of expertise every board of directors and every "C-suite" should be steeped in: the mobile Internet and cybersecurity. For good reason, cybersecurity is rising to the top of the business risk list. There are two kinds of companies: those that know and those that don't know they've been hacked. Attacks can be harmful to current and to future operations. Examples include loss of trade secrets, customer and financial information, online advertising "pay by the click" scamming, and outright extortion threats to the company's website or systems if a ransom isn't paid. Perhaps the greatest risk is to a company's valuable brand. Sony, Target and Home Depot are examples.

Just as systems that use the Internet increase productivity, protecting these systems reduce productivity by requiring added investment. It's estimated cybersecurity costs the typical firm of 1000+ employees $9 million/year. US labor productivity has been stagnant in recent years, perhaps partly due to the unproductive investments required for cybersecurity and for Sarbanes-Oxley compliance. The cybersecurity industry is a new industry, which will create some jobs, but like any new growth industry, it will come with its share of marketing hype.

There are opportunities and new challenges in education as well. Advanced Placement and specialized courses have historically only been available at large or elite high schools, but the connected Internet is democratizing education in the US and around the world through resources like online high school equivalent and college degrees, and the excellent Kahn Academy (which also has helped this father brush up on high school algebra in order to be a more effective tutor). But all students still do not have access to tablets or smartphones, or to high speed Internet access at school or at home in the evening when home-work needs to be done.

These tools create new challenges. 35% of teens admit to using cell phones to cheat, and 65% say others cheat using cell phones. Some worry about the effect this technology will have on the quality of spoken and written language. One study found 13% of people pretend to be talking on their phone to avoid interacting with those around them. You've likely seen students texting each other across the lunchroom table instead of conversing. If we call our sons, it goes to voicemail. We need to text them to get an answer. Few would claim texting is the epitome of the "King's English." 64% of teens were found to use improper grammar while texting, something many of us are regularly guilty of.

School administrators and parents have another new worry—cyberbullying. One study found one in ten students were victims of, and one in five participated in, cyberbullying. "Sexting" is a new word in the vernacular. 20% of teens admit to posting nude photos online.

An Elon University study found that students with this digitally enhanced education possess something called "fast-twitch wiring". "Always on" students are nimble, quick-acting multi-taskers, but with a thirst for instant gratification, quick fixes, and with little patience and deep-thinking.

But, social networking can be a constructive form of human interaction. I've used social media to connect with many old friends I would have lost touch with. Smartphones also allow us to be productive by staying in touch with the office at home or on vacation, which is certainly a quality-of-life double-edged sword. Some argue that the information and entertainment of the Internet improves the quality of life by reducing boredom.

The news is a form of education. Does the Internet improve the quality of news we get? From personal experience, and admitted to by reporters, the 24 hour online news cycle and the need to break a story first means verifying the accuracy of information or getting a second source often goes by the wayside. Reporters don't have the time that the next morning's paper edition gave them.

It also seems that "real" news curated by professionals is being replaced with the trivial from new news sources like Facebook, Twitter and Buzzfeed, with national or world events replaced by the exploits of Kim Kardashian, videos of water-skiing squirrels, or debates about the color of a dress.

On the other hand, the amount and depth of news available has never been greater. If you grew up in a "one paper town", far less news was available to you from around the globe vs. what you can access now at a reasonable cost.

Maybe talking to computers will replace some human interaction. I watched my son's fingers fly as he typed feverishly on his PC, and looking over his shoulder, I saw indecipherable characters—computer code. He was creating a new video game, for fun. On the one hand, this is encouraging to see, but on the other hand, will this essential new language create another wave of untrained "have-nots?" For example, appliance or engine repair is moving away from screwdrivers to software programming and analysis. And the new machines: self-driving cars, trucks, trains, robots, and self-diagnosing and self-repairing machines, may replace many jobs. 3D printer programming skills will replace craftsmanship in some industries. The same son owns two 3D printers he is very skilled with. If manufacturing done via 3D printer largely eliminates the need for assembly, what will happen to the economies of countries which depend on low-cost labor as their primary export? But, manufacturing and product design intellectual property is now much easier to steal or compromise.

To increase our safety, cell phones allow us to call 911, locate our children, provide alerts and information helpful with natural disasters and aid first-responders. Cell phone fund-raising campaigns have raised millions for relief efforts.

But digital connectivity can reduce safety by distracting drivers. Texting while driving has led to fatalities, which is why you've seen wireless carriers join together with distracted driving campaigns.

Vehicles come connected with wireless digital monitoring capabilities for engines or tires and with GPS tracking and "On-Star"-like emergency buttons. These add to safety, but the reverse could be true if the connected vehicle is hacked.

In terms of environmental impact, computers use an enormous amount of energy to run and cool them. In addition, the US produces 2.5 million tons of e-waste annually, enough to fill a line of dump trucks from Washington DC to Disney World.

On the other hand, GPS saves fuel and miles driven as does teleconferencing and telecommuting, all enabled by mobile technology. Cell phones built to the new UL-E standard are more energy efficient, are designed for reuse and recycling, and contain fewer harmful chemicals. The mobile industry is also driving "dematerialization." The smartphone, akin to a Swiss Army Knife, can replace a PC, watch, alarm clock, camera, hand-held GPS, flashlight, transistor radio, portable music player, TV, even plastic credit cards, keeping a lot of material out of landfills.

Because early cell phones had small storage and processing capabilities, and networks were slow, even though these devices made music more portable, the cell phone industry contributed to what many consider the "Dark Age" of music fidelity.

Recorded music was "sampled" to create MP3 files and compressed streaming services, played through small tinny speakers or "throw away" low-fi earbuds included in the phone's box. But, new smartphones, like HTC's Harman/Kardon edition, not only come with high-quality earphones, but can play high-resolution audio files from sources like HDTracks, with approximately 60 times the musical information of an MP3 or streaming service, providing better fidelity than a compact disc. So, after helping to create the "Dark Age" of fidelity, the mobile Internet is helping to usher in a new "Golden Age" of sound.

Perhaps no industry will be transformed more by the mobile Internet than healthcare. Imagine taking a pill with a small wireless chip inside that sends a voltage to a patch you wear on your skin, which in turn communicates with your smartphone to tell your doctor how your medicine is interacting with your body's chemistry. No need to wait for blood work to return from the lab. This is in use today.

In much of the developing world, knowing whether water is safe to drink is a big issue. Photospectrometers to test the water for viruses, bacteria and toxins traditionally cost about $50,000. A capability has been developed to use a smartphone's camera and processor, plus about $200 in parts, to provide similar functionality.

Telemedicine has the potential to save billions and keep sick people at home, where they want to be and should be, to keep them from infecting others. Wearables like fitness bracelets, chips in pacemakers, and digital medical records are improvements, but also add risk if this information could be compromised or hacked. To take advantage of medical innovations, we may need to rethink our approval processes as well. When I ask entrepreneurs with health care innovations what their biggest challenge is, they don't say funding, they say the FDA.

If we live longer, couldn't the aging population become even more out-of-touch with current technology given the greater number of years out of the workforce? The elderly represent America's largest "minority" group. My personal view is that this group will benefit the most from the mobile Internet. Smartphone speech-to-text and text-to-speech capabilities can improve the quality of life for the hearing or visually impaired. Mobile health monitoring will help people live in their own homes longer, as will connected smart appliances, self-driving cars and connected robotic personal assistants.

Social media will help the elderly stay connected with family, friends and with those who share common interests. Crowdsourcing techniques will provide a way to tap into the collective expertise and wisdom of a graying society while stimulating this generation with renewed purpose.

So far, I've been discussing the tradeoffs this digital, connected world brings to education, the news, the environment, economies, health care, music, safety, and aging, but perhaps the greatest challenge will be balancing the tradeoff between the tremendous utility potential of the wireless Internet with threats to our privacy and security.

In terms of national security, despotic regimes are legitimately concerned with the access to information and communication capabilities of mobile devices and social networking. We likely would not have seen the "Arab Spring" regime changes in Egypt or Tunisia if citizens did not have the mobilizing power of cell phones. These countries had mobile penetration of roughly 90%. North Korea, on the other hand, keeps penetration low, at roughly 5%. And, we've read of countries censoring the Internet as a way of mitigating internal threats to their security.

Social networking, plus access to Google, Google maps, and emerging digital currencies can be a threat to democracies too in the hands of even small groups of terrorists, and we've read of how easy it is to learn how to make a bomb, or print an undetectable plastic gun using a 3D printer on the Internet.

The Internet was created based on trust to facilitate sharing information. 90% of the Internet is privately owned, not under government control. The Internet is basically an architecture and protocol that links multiple private networks, where the word "inter-net"came from. The challenge is balancing sharing with protecting information. Just as personal privacy and security is inversely related to utility, network security is also inversely related to utility. Network utility increases with network size, but larger networks have more points of vulnerability.

Woody Allen said, "There are two kinds of people in this world, good and bad. The good sleep better, but the bad seem to enjoy the waking hours more." One can't pick up the newspaper without reading about a computer attack, whether it be attributed to a state-sponsored or criminal APT (Advanced Persistent Threat), attempting to steal information from government, business, or individuals.

It seems like a Cold War is re-emerging, filled with suspicion. The good news is that the alleged cyber-attacks between nations haven't been as lethal as conventional war, but in conventional war, who the enemy is can be more apparent, as cyberattacks can take place from machines distributed across the globe. I've read that 25% of the machines used in the famous cyberattack against Estonia were US-based. And governments can support, yet hide behind, "patriotic hackers" to carry out attacks, giving a government plausible deniability. This complicates diplomacy. Responses are more complex when the effects are asymmetrical, when one side has much and the other very little to lose from a digital attack, like the US vs North Korea.

I can speak from personal experience that this new arena is difficult for Internet companies to navigate. Which CEO is more patriotic, the one who provides all of the information the government requests to help catch a criminal or prevent a terrorist attack, or the CEO whose company creates tools that make it difficult for law enforcement or the government to acquire a customer's information, believing protecting civil liberties is a higher calling. I don't have an answer, but there is perhaps no more important area for public/private dialogue and cooperation than this.

The most effective cyberattacks on companies have internal complicity, either by a mole or through an untrained employee. Well-trained employees don't plug in USB drives they don't know the origin of, don't click on links they're not sure about, don't connect to free Wi-Fi networks they don't know, recognize when social engineering or "phishing" attempts are being made, password protect all devices, and don't put company logos on themselves or their computers when traveling.

In conclusion, we all share a responsibility to protect the Internet. Please pattern or password protect your devices. A study showed that if your phone is lost or stolen, there is a 90% chance your data will be breached, and a 50% chance you'll never see your phone again. You can buy security apps like Lookout from your carrier to protect against malware and also remotely lock or wipe information from your phone.

There are a lot of free aps out there. Be careful. If it seems like they're asking for more personal information than the utility of the app requires, like access to your contacts and to your location, they probably are. It's free because you're paying by providing personal information. Be selective.

Laws may need to change to make the Internet safer. The U.S. President has made it easier for competitors in the same industries to share information to protect against attacks, what would have been an antitrust concern not long ago.

It can be argued that the meteoric growth in the Internet is because it has been unregulated. America's Internet looks like it may be regulated soon like a utility of centuries past. On a global level, Russia and China have urged the ITU (International Telecommunications Union) to govern the Internet, citing cybersecurity issues, a move resisted by the US and Europe who are concerned this will be a tool to limit freedom. Once again, there are two sides to this coin.

The plusses and minuses of this "Brave New World" represent the greatest change to the way people live and interact on this planet humankind has ever seen. We'll see more change in the next five years than we've seen in the last five. There are no absolutes, only shades of gray and two sides to practically every argument. If we take some basic precautions, I believe the utility of the mobile Internet far outweighs the risks.

I feel privileged to be able to hear what Admiral Rogers will have to say tonight. Continued dialogue and cooperation will be needed between governments, businesses and the citizens of the world to achieve a "Gold-ilocks" solution, a.k.a. getting it "just right."

Thank you.

## Critical Thinking

1. Is a digitally connected world a better place?
2. What are the risks of the world wide Internet?
3. What are the changes that the Internet is likely to cause in the near future?

## Internet References

**New American Studies Web**
   https://blogs.commons.georgetown.edu/vkp/
**Social Science Information Gateway**
   http://www.ariadne.ac.uk/issue2/sosig
**Sociology–Study Sociology Online**
   http://edu.learnsoc.org/
**Sociology Web Resources**
   http://www.mhhe.com/socscience/sociology/resources/index.htm
**Sociosite**
   http://www.topsite.com/goto/sociosite.net
**Socioweb**
   http://www.topsite.com/goto/socioweb.com

*Article*                    Prepared by: Kurt Finsterbusch, *University of Maryland, College Park*

# How Innovation Could Save the Planet

Ideas may be our greatest natural resource, says a computer scientist and futurist. He argues that the world's most critical challenges—including population growth, peak oil, climate change, and limits to growth—could be met by encouraging innovation.

RAMEZ NAAM

## Learning Outcomes

*After reading this article, you will be able to:*

- Understand both the benefits and the costs of long-term economic progress.

- Evaluate Ramez Naam's thesis that "Innovation could save the planet."

- Notice the many specific ideas and innovations that could address the major problems.

## The Best of Times: Unprecedented Prosperity

There are many ways in which we are living in the most wonderful age ever. We can imagine we are heading toward a sort of science-fiction Utopia, where we are incredibly rich and incredibly prosperous, and the planet is healthy. But there are other reasons to fear that we're headed toward a dystopia of sorts.

On the positive side, life expectancy has been rising for the last 150 years, and faster since the early part of the twentieth century in the developing world than it has in the rich world. Along with that has come a massive reduction in poverty. The most fundamental empowerer of humans—education—has also soared, not just in the rich world, but throughout the world.

Another great empowerer of humanity is connectivity: Access to information and access to communication both have soared. The number of mobile phones on the planet was effectively zero in the early 1990s, and now it's in excess of 4 billion. More than three-quarters of humanity, in the span of one generation, have gotten access to connectivity that, as my

friend Peter Diamand is likes to say, is greater than any president before 1995 had. A reasonably well-off person in India or in Nigeria has better access to information than Ronald Reagan did during most of his career.

With increased connectivity has come an increase in democracy. As people have gotten richer, more educated, more able to access information, and more able to communicate, they have demanded more control over the places where they live. The fraction of nations that are functional democracies is at an all-time high in this world—more than double what it was in the 1970s, with the collapse of the Soviet Union.

Economically, the world is a more equal place than it has been in decades. In the West, and especially in the United States, we hear a lot about growing inequality, but on a global scale, the opposite is true. As billions are rising out of poverty around the world, the global middle classes are catching up with the global rich.

In many ways, this is the age of the greatest human prosperity, freedom, and potential that has ever been on the face of this planet. But in other ways, we are facing some of the largest risks ever.

## The Worst of Times: The Greatest Risks

At its peak, the ancient Mayan city of Tikal was a metropolis, a city of 200,000 people inside of a civilization of about 20 million people. Now, if you walk around any Mayan city, you see mounds of dirt. That's because these structures were all abandoned by about the mid-900s A.D. We know now what happened: The Mayan civilization grew too large. It overpopulated.

To feed themselves, they had to convert forest into farmland. They chopped down all of the forest. That, in turn, led to soil erosion. It also worsened drought, because trees, among other things, trap moisture, and create a precipitation cycle.

When that happened, and was met by some normal (not human caused) climate change, the Mayans found they didn't have enough food. They exhausted their primary energy supply, which is food. That in turn led to more violence in their society and ultimately to a complete collapse.

The greatest energy source for human civilization today is fossil fuels. Among those, none is more important than oil. In 1956, M. King Hubbert looked at production in individual oil fields and predicted that the United States would see the peak of its oil production in 1970 or so, and then drop. His prediction largely came true: Oil production went up but did peak in the 1970s, then plummeted.

Oil production has recently gone up in the United States a little bit, but it's still just barely more than half of what it was in its peak in the 1970s.

Hubbert also predicted that the global oil market would peak in about 2000, and for a long time he looked very foolish. But it now has basically plateaued. Since 2004, oil production has increased by about 4 percent, whereas in the 1950s it rose by about 4 percent every three months.

We haven't hit a peak; oil production around the world is still rising a little bit. It's certainly not declining, but we do appear to be near a plateau; supply is definitely rising more slowly than demand. Though there's plenty of oil in the ground, the oil that remains is in smaller fields, further from shore, under lower pressure, and harder to pump out.

Water is another resource that is incredibly precious to us. The predominant way in which we use water is through the food that we eat: 70 percent of the freshwater that humanity uses goes into agriculture.

The Ogallala Aquifer, the giant body of freshwater under the surface of the Earth in the Great Plains of the United States, is fossil water left from the melting and the retreat of glaciers in the end of the last Ice Age, 12,000–14,000 years ago. Its refill time is somewhere between 5,000 and 10,000 years from normal rainfall. Since 1960, we've drained between a third and a half of the water in this body, depending on what estimate you look at. In some areas, the water table is dropping about three feet per year.

If this was a surface lake in the United States or Canada, and people saw that happening, they'd stop it. But because it's out of sight, it's just considered a resource that we can tap. And indeed, in the north Texas area, wells are starting to fail already, and farms are being abandoned in some cases, because they can't get to the water that they once did.

Perhaps the largest risk of all is climate change. We've increased the temperature of the planet by about 2°F in the last 130 years, and that rate is accelerating. This is primarily because of the carbon dioxide we've put into the atmosphere, along with methane and nitrous oxide. $CO_2$ levels, now at over 390 parts per million, are the highest they've been in about 15 million years. Ice cores go back at least a million years, and we know that they're the highest they've been in that time. Historically, when $CO_2$ levels are high, temperature is also high. But also, historically, in the lifetime of our species, we've actually never existed as human beings while $CO_2$ levels have been this high.

For example, glaciers such as the Bear and Pedersen in Alaska have disappeared just since 1920. As these glaciers melt, they produce water that goes into the seas and helps to raise sea levels. Over the next century, the seas are expected to rise about 3 to 6 feet. Most of that actually will not be melting glaciers; it's thermal expansion: As the ocean gets warmer, it gets a little bit bigger.

But 3 to 6 feet over a century doesn't sound like that big a deal to us, so we think of that as a distant problem. The reality is that there's a more severe problem with climate change: its impact on the weather and on agriculture.

In 2003, Europe went through its worst heat wave since 1540. Ukraine lost 75 percent of its wheat crop. In 2009, China had a once-in-a-century level drought; in 2010 they had another once-in-a-century level drought. That's twice. Wells that had given water continuously since the fifteenth century ran dry. When those rains returned, when the water that was soaked up by the atmosphere came back down, it came down on Pakistan, and half of Pakistan was under water in the floods of 2010. An area larger than Germany was under water.

Warmer air carries more water. Every degree Celsius that you increase the temperature value of air, it carries 7 percent more water. But it doesn't carry that water uniformly. It can suck water away from one place and then deliver it in a deluge in another place. So both the droughts are up and flooding is up simultaneously, as precipitation becomes more lumpy and more concentrated.

In Russia's 2010 heat wave, 55,000 people died, 11,000 of them in Moscow alone. In 2011, the United States had the driest 10-month period ever in the American South, and Texas saw its worst wildfires ever. And 2012 was the worst drought in the United States since the Dust Bowl—the corn crop shrank by 20 percent.

So that's the big risk the world faces: that radical weather will change how we grow food, which is still our most important energy source—even more important than fossil fuels.

A number of people in the environmentalist movement are saying that we have to just stop growing. For instance, in his book *Peak Everything: Waking Up to the Century of Declines*, Richard Heinberg of the Post-Carbon Institute says that the Earth is full. Get used to it, and get ready for a world where you live with less wealth, and where your children live with less wealth, than any before.

I don't think this idea of stopping growth is realistic, because there are a top billion people who live pretty well and there are another 6 billion who don't and are hungry for it. We see demand rising for everything—water, food, energy—and that demand is rising not in the United States or Europe or Canada or Australia. It's rising in the developing world. This is the area that will create all of the increased demand for physical resources.

Even if we could, by some chance, say That's enough, sorry, we're not going to let you use these resources, which is doubtful, it wouldn't be just, because the West got rich by using those natural resources. So we need to find a different way.

## Ideas as a Resource Expander, Resource Preserver, and Waste Reducer

The best-selling environmental book of all time, *Limits to Growth,* was based on computer modeling. It was a simple model with only about eight variables of what would happen in the world. It showed that economic growth, more wealth, would inevitably lead to more pollution and more consumption of finite resources, which would in turn take us beyond the limits and lead ultimately to collapse.

While it's been widely reported recently that its predictions are coming true, that's actually not the case. If you look at the vast majority of the numbers that the researchers predict in this model, they're not coming true.

Why did they get these things wrong? The most important thing that the forecasters did was underestimate the power of new ideas to expand resources, or to expand wealth while using fewer resources. Ideas have done tremendous things for us. Let's start with food.

In *The Population Bomb* (1968), Paul Ehrlich predicted that food supply could not support the population, just as Malthus did. But what's happened is that we've doubled population since 1960, and we've nearly tripled the food supply in total. We've increased by 30–40 percent the food supply per person since the 1960s.

Let's look at this on a very long time scale. How many people can you feed with an acre of land? Before the advent of agriculture, an acre of land could feed less than a thousandth of a person. Today it's about three people, on average, who can be fed by one acre of land. Preagriculture, it took 3,000 acres for one person to stay alive through hunting and gathering. With agriculture, that footprint has shrunk from 3,000 acres to one-third of one acre. That's not because there's any more sunlight,

which is ultimately what food is; it's because we've changed the productivity of the resource by innovation in farming—and then thousands of innovations on top of that to increase it even more.

In fact, the reason we have the forests that we have on the planet is because we were able to handle a doubling of the population since 1960 without increasing farmland by more than about 10 percent. If we had to have doubled our farmland, we would have chopped down all the remaining forests on the planet.

Ideas can reduce resource use. I can give you many other examples. In the United States, the amount of energy used on farms per calorie grown has actually dropped by about half since the 1970s. That's in part because we now only use about a tenth of the energy to create synthetic nitrogen fertilizer, which is an important input.

The amount of food that you can grow per drop of water has roughly doubled since the 1980s. In wheat, it's actually more than tripled since 1960. The amount of water that we use in the United States per person has dropped by about a third since the 1970s, after rising for decades. As agriculture has gotten more efficient, we're using less water per person. So, again, ideas can reduce resource use.

Ideas can also find substitutes for scarce resources. We're at risk of running out of many things, right? Well, let's think about some things that have happened in the past.

The sperm whale was almost hunted into extinction. Sperm whales were, in the mid-1800s, the best source of illumination. Sperm whale oil—spermaceti—was the premier source of lighting. It burned without smoke, giving a clear, steady light, and the demand for it led to huge hunting of the sperm whales. In a period of about 30 years, we killed off about a third of the sperm whales on the planet.

That led to a phenomenon of "peak sperm-whale oil": The number of sperm whales that the fleet could bring in dropped over time as the sperm whales became more scarce and more afraid of human hunters. Demand rose as supply dropped, and the prices skyrocketed. So it looked a little bit like the situation with oil now.

That was solved not by the discovery of more sperm whales, nor by giving up on this thing of lighting. Rather, Abraham Gesner, a Canadian, discovered this thing called kerosene. He found that, if he took coal, heated it up, captured the fumes, and distilled them, he could create this fluid that burned very clear. And he could create it in quantities thousands of times greater than the sperm whales ever could have given up.

We have no information suggesting that Gesner was an environmentalist or that he cared about sperm whales at all. He was motivated by scientific curiosity and by the huge business opportunity of going after this lighting market. What he did was dramatically lower the cost of lighting while saving the sperm whales from extinction.

One more thing that ideas can do is transform waste into value. In places like Germany and Japan, people are mining landfills. Japan estimates that its landfills alone contain 10-year supplies of gold and rare-earth minerals for the world market. Alcoa estimates that the world's landfills contain a 15-year supply of aluminum. So there's tremendous value.

When we throw things away, they're not destroyed. If we "consume" things like aluminum, we're not really consuming it, we're rearranging it. We're changing where it's located. And in some cases, the concentration of these resources in our landfills is actually higher than it was in our mines. What it takes is energy and technology to get that resource back out and put it back into circulation.

## Ideas for Stretching the Limits

So ideas can reduce resource use, can find substitutes for scarce resources, and can transform waste into value. In that context, what are the limits to growth?

Is there a population limit? Yes, there certainly is, but it doesn't look like we're going to hit that. Projections right now are that, by the middle of this century, world population will peak between 9 billion and 10 billion, and then start to decline. In fact, we'll be talking much more about the graying of civilization, and perhaps underpopulation—too-low birthrates on a current trend.

What about physical resources? Are there limits to physical resource use on this planet? Absolutely. It really is a finite planet. But where are those limits?

To illustrate, let's start with energy. This is the most important resource that we use, in many ways. But when we consider all the fossil fuels that humanity uses today—all the oil, coal, natural gas, and so on—it pales in comparison to a much larger resource, all around us, which is the amount of energy coming in from our Sun every day.

The amount of energy from sunlight that strikes the top of the atmosphere is about 10,000 times as much as the energy that we use from fossil fuels on a daily basis. Ten seconds of sunlight hitting the Earth is as much energy as humanity uses in an entire day; one hour of sunlight hitting the Earth provides as much energy to the planet as a whole as humanity uses from all sources combined in one year.

This is an incredibly abundant resource. It manifests in many ways. It heats the atmosphere differentially, creating winds that we can capture for wind power. It evaporates water, which leads to precipitation elsewhere, which turns into things like rivers and waterfalls, which we can capture as hydropower.

But by far the largest fraction of it—more than half—is photons hitting the surface of the Earth. Those are so abundant that, with one-third of 1 percent of the Earth's land area, using current technology of about 14 percent-efficient solar cells, we could capture enough electricity to power all of current human needs.

The problem is not the abundance of the energy; the problem is cost. Our technology is primitive. Our technology for building solar cells is similar to our technology for manufacturing computer chips. They're built on silicon wafers in clean rooms at high temperatures, and so they're very, very expensive.

But innovation has been dropping that cost tremendously. Over the last 30 years, we've gone from a watt of solar power costing $20 to about $1. That's a factor of 20. We roughly drop the cost of solar by one-half every decade, more or less. That means that, in the sunniest parts of the world today, solar is now basically at parity in cost, without subsidies, with coal and natural gas. Over the next 12–15 years, that will spread to most of the planet. That's incredibly good news for us.

Of course, we don't just use energy while the Sun is shining. We use energy at night to power our cities; we use energy in things like vehicles that have to move and that have high energy densities. Both of these need storage, and today's storage is actually a bigger challenge than capturing energy. But there's reason to believe that we can tackle the storage problem, as well.

For example, consider lithium ion batteries—the batteries that are in your laptop, your cell phone, and so on. The demand to have longer-lasting devices drove tremendous innovations in these batteries in the 1990s and the early part of the 2000s. Between 1991 and 2005, the cost of storage in lithium ion batteries dropped by about a factor of nine, and the density of storage—how much energy you can store in an ounce of battery—increased by a little over double in that time. If we do that again, we would be at the point where grid-scale storage is affordable and we can store that energy overnight. Our electric vehicles have ranges similar to the range you can get in a gasoline-powered vehicle.

This is a tall order. This represents perhaps tens of billions of dollars in R&D, but it is something that is possible and for which there is precedent.

Another approach being taken is turning energy into fuel. When you use a fuel such as gasoline, it's not really an energy source. It's an energy carrier, an energy storage system, if you will. You can store a lot of energy in a very small amount.

Today, two pioneers in genome sequencing—Craig Venter and George Church—both have founded companies to create next-generation biofuels. What they're both leveraging is that gene-sequencing cost is the fastest quantitative area of progress on the planet.

What they're trying to do is engineer microorganisms that consume $CO_2$, sunlight, and sugar and actually excrete fuel as a byproduct. If we could do this, maybe just 1 percent of the Earth's surface—or a 30th of what we use for agriculture—could provide all the liquid fuels that we need. We would conveniently grow algae on saltwater and waste water, so biofuel production wouldn't compete for freshwater. And the possible yields are vast if we can get there.

If we can crack energy, we can crack everything else:

\* Water. Water is life. We live in a water world, but only about a tenth of a percent of the water in the world is freshwater that's accessible to us in some way. Ninety-seven percent of the world's water is in the oceans and is salty. It used to be that desalination meant boiling water and then catching the steam and letting it condense.

Between the times of the ancient Greeks and 1960, desalination technology didn't really change. But then, it did. People started to create membranes modeled on what cells do, which is allow some things through but not others. They used plastics to force water through and get only the fresh and not the salty. As a result, the amount of energy it takes to desalinate a liter of water has dropped by about a factor of nine in that time. Now, in the world's largest desalination plants, the price of desalinated water is about a tenth of a cent per gallon. The technology has gotten to the point where it is starting to become a realistic option as an alternative to using up scarce freshwater resources.

\* Food. Can we grow enough food? Between now and 2050, we have to increase food yield by about 70 percent. Is that possible? I think it is. In industrialized nations, food yields are already twice what they are in the world as a whole. That's because we have irrigation, tractors, better pesticides, and so on. Given such energy and wealth, we already know that we can grow enough food to feed the planet.

Another option that's probably cheaper would be to leverage some things that nature's already produced. What most people don't know is that the yield of corn per acre and in calories is about 70 percent higher than the yield of wheat. Corn is a C 4 photosynthesis crop: It uses a different way of turning sunlight and $CO_2$ into sugars that evolved only 30 million years ago. Now, scientists around the world are working on taking these C 4 genes from crops like corn and transplanting them into wheat and rice, which could right away increase the yield of those staple grains by more than 50 percent.

Physical limits do exist, but they are extremely distant. We cannot grow exponentially in our physical resource use forever, but that point is still at least centuries in the future. It's something we have to address eventually, but it's not a problem that's pressing right now.

\* Wealth. One thing that people don't appreciate very much is that wealth has been decoupling from physical resource use on this planet. Energy use per capita is going up, $CO_2$ emissions per capita have been going up a little bit, but they are both widely outstripped by the amount of wealth that we're creating.

That's because we can be more efficient in everything—using less energy per unit of food grown, and so on.

This again might sound extremely counterintuitive, but let me give you one concrete example of how that happens. Compare the ENIAC—which in the 1940s was the first digital computer ever created—to an iPhone. An iPhone is billions of times smaller, uses billions of times less energy, and has billions of times more computing power than ENIAC. If you tried to create an iPhone using ENIAC technology, it would be a cube a mile on the side, and it would use more electricity than the state of California. And it wouldn't have access to the Internet, because you'd have to invent that, as well.

This is what I mean when I say ideas are the ultimate resource. The difference between an ENIAC and an iPhone is that the iPhone is embodied knowledge that allows you to do more with less resources. That phenomenon is not limited to high tech. It's everywhere around us.

So ideas are the ultimate resource. They're the only resource that accumulates over time. Our store of knowledge is actually larger than in the past, as opposed to all physical resources.

## Challenges Ahead for Innovation

Today we are seeing a race between our rate of consumption and our rate of innovation, and there are multiple challenges. One challenge is the Darwinian process, survival of the fittest. In areas like green tech, there will be hundreds and even thousands of companies founded, and 99 percent of them will go under. That is how innovation happens.

The other problem is scale. Just as an example, one of the world's largest solar arrays is at Nellis Air Force Base in California, and we would need about 10 million of these in order to meet the world's electricity needs. We have the land, we have the solar energy coming in, but there's a lot of industrial production that has to happen before we get to that point.

Innovation is incredibly powerful, but the pace of innovation compared to the pace of consumption is very important. One thing we can do to increase the pace of innovation is to address the biggest challenge, which is market failure.

In 1967, you could stick your hand into the Cuyahoga River, in Ohio, and come up covered in muck and oil. At that time, the river was lined with businesses and factories, and for them the river was a free resource. It was cheaper to pump their waste into the river than it was to pay for disposal at some other sort of facility. The river was a commons that anybody could use or abuse, and the waste they were producing was an externality. To that business or factory, there was no cost to pumping waste into this river. But to the people who depended upon the river, there was a high cost overall.

That's what I mean by a market externality and a market failure, because this was an important resource to all of us. But no one owned it, no one bought or sold it, and so it was treated badly in a way that things with a price are not.

That ultimately culminated when, in June 1969, a railway car passing on a bridge threw a spark; the spark hit a slick of oil a mile long on the river, and the river burst into flames. The story made the cover of *Time* magazine. In many ways, the environmental movement was born of this event as much as it was of Rachel Carson's *Silent Spring*. In the following three years, the United States created the Environmental Protection Agency and passed the Clean Water and Clean Air acts.

Almost every environmental problem on the planet is an issue of the commons, whether it's chopping down forests that no one owns, draining lakes that no one owns, using up fish in the ocean that no one owns, or polluting the atmosphere because no one owns it, or heating up the planet. They're all issues of the commons. They're all issues where there is no cost to an individual entity to deplete something and no cost to over-consume something, but there is a greater cost that's externalized and pushed on everybody else who shares this.

Now let's come back again to what Limits to Growth said, which was that economic growth always led to more pollution and more consumption, put us beyond limits, and ends with collapse. So if that's the case, all those things we just talked about should be getting worse. But as the condition of the Cuyahoga River today illustrates, that is not the case.

GDP in the United States is three times what it was when the Cuyahoga River caught on fire, so shouldn't it be more polluted? It's not. Instead, it's the cleanest it's been in decades. That's not because we stopped growth. It's because we made intelligent choices about managing that commons.

Another example: In the 1970s, we discovered that the ozone layer was thinning to such an extent that it literally could drive the extinction of all land species on Earth. But it's actually getting better. It's turned a corner, it's improving ahead of schedule, and it's on track to being the healthiest it's been in a century. That's because we've reduced the emissions of CFCs, which destroy ozone; we've dropped the amount of them that we emit into the atmosphere basically to zero. And yet industry has not ground to a halt because of this, either. Economic growth has not faltered.

And one last example: Acid rain—which is primarily produced by sulfur dioxide emitted by coal-burning power plants—is mostly gone as an issue. Emissions of sulfur dioxide are down by about a factor of two. That's in part because we created a strategy called cap and trade: It capped the amount of $SO_2$ that you could emit, then allowed you to swap and buy emission credits from others to find the optimal way to do that.

The cost, interestingly enough, has always been lower than projected. In each of these cases, industry has said, This will

end things. Ronald Reagan's chief of staff said the economy would grind to a halt, and the EPA would come in with lower cost estimates. But the EPA has always been wrong: The EPA cost estimate has always been too high.

Analysis of all of these efforts in the past shows that reducing emissions is always cheaper than you expect, but cleaning up the mess afterwards is always more expensive than you'd guess.

Today, the biggest commons issue is that of climate change, with the $CO_2$ and other greenhouse gases that we're pumping into the atmosphere. A logical thing to do would be to put a price on these. If you pollute, if you're pumping $CO_2$ into the atmosphere and it's warming the planet, so you're causing harm to other people in a very diffuse way. Therefore, you should be paying in proportion to that harm you're doing to offset it.

But if we do that, won't that have a massive impact on the economy? This all relates to energy, which drives a huge fraction of the economy. Manufacturing depends on it. Transport depends on it. So wouldn't it be a huge problem if we were to actually put a price on these carbon emissions?

Well, there has been innovative thinking about that, as well. One thing that economists have always told us is that, if you're going to tax, tax the bad, not the good. Whatever it is that you tax, you will get less of it. So tax the bad, not the good.

The model that would be the ideal for putting a price on pollution is what we call a revenue-neutral model. Revenue-neutral carbon tax, revenue-neutral cap and trade. Let's model it as a tax: Today, a country makes a certain amount of revenue for its government in income tax, let's say. If you want to tax pollution, the way to do this without impacting the economy is to increase your pollution tax in the same manner that you decrease the income tax. The government then is capturing the same amount of money from the economy as a whole, so there's no economic slowdown as a result of this.

This has a positive effect on the environment because it tips the scales of price. Now, if you're shopping for energy, and you're looking at solar versus coal or natural gas, the carbon price has increased the price of coal and natural gas to you, but not the cost of solar. It shifts customer behavior from one to the other while having no net impact on the economy, and probably a net benefit on the economy in the long run as more investment in green energy drives the price down.

## Toward a Wealthier, Cleaner Future

The number-one thing I want you to take away is that pollution and overconsumption are not inevitable outcomes of growth. While tripling the wealth of North America, for instance, we've gone from an ozone layer that was rapidly deteriorating to one that is bouncing back.

The fundamental issue is not one of limits to growth; it's one of the policy we choose, and it's one of how we structure our economy to value all the things we depend upon and not just those things that are owned privately.

What can we do, each of us? Four things:

First is to communicate. These issues are divisive, but we know that beliefs and attitudes on issues like this spread word of mouth. They spread person to person, from person you trust to person you trust. So talk about it. Many of us have friends or colleagues or family on the other side of these issues, but talk about it. You're better able to persuade them than anyone else is.

Second is to participate. By that I mean politically. Local governments, state and province governments, and national governments are responsive when they hear from their constituents about these issues. It changes their attitudes. Because so few constituents actually make a call to the office of their legislator, or write a letter, a few can make a very large impact.

Third is to innovate. These problems aren't solved yet. We don't have the technologies for these problems today. The trend lines look very good, but the next 10 years of those trend lines demand lots of bright people, lots of bright ideas, and lots of R&D. So if you're thinking about a career change, or if you know any young people trying to figure out what their career is now, these are careers that (A) will be very important to us in the future and (B) will probably be quite lucrative for them.

Last is to keep hope, because we have faced problems like this before and we have conquered them every time. The future isn't written in stone—it could go good or bad—but I'm very optimistic. I know we have the ability to do it, and I think we will. Ultimately, ideas are our most important natural resource.

## Critical Thinking

1. Do the facts seem to support an optimistic future or a pessimistic future?

2. What is the potential of new ideas and new technologies?

3. Technologies have brought great benefits and considerable problems. Can technologies and new ideas now solve those problems?

## Internet References

**National Center for Policy Analysis**
www.ncpa.org

**Social Science Information Gateway**
http://sosig.esrc.bris.ac.uk

**SocioSite**
www.pscw.uva.nl/sociosite/TOPICS/Women.html

**Sociology—Study Sociology Online**
http://edu.learnsoc.org

**Sociology Web Resources**
http://www.mhhe.com/socscience/sociology/resources/index.htm

**Sociosite**
http://www.topsite.com/goto/sociosite.net

**Socioweb**
http://www.topsite.com/goto/socioweb.com

**WWW Virtual Library: Demography & Population Studies**
http://demography.anu.edu.au/VirtualLibrary

**RAMEZ NAAM** is a computer scientist and author. He is a former Microsoft executive and current fellow of the Institute for Ethics and Emerging Technologies. He lives in Seattle, Washington.

*Article*                    Prepared by: Kurt Finsterbusch, *University of Maryland, College Park*

# Globalization Is Good for You!

New research demonstrates the amazing power of open markets and open borders.

RONALD BAILEY

## Learning Outcomes

*After reading this article, you will be able to:*

- Describe Bailey's view of globalization.

- Critically analyze the considerable evidence that Bailey provides that globalization has increased the equality of women, improved job opportunities, and expanded other benefits.

- Analyze the opposing ideas that theoretically freer trade should make most people better off but some countries could lose jobs with globalization.

How important is the open exchange of goods to the spreading of prosperity? This important: Since 1950, world trade in goods has expanded from $600 billion (in 2015 dollars) to $18.9 trillion in 2013. That's a more than 30-fold increase, during a period in which global population grew less than three-fold.

This massive increase in trade was kicked off in 1948 by the General Agreement on Tariffs and Trade, which began the liberalization process of lowering tariff and non-tariff barriers. As a result, autarkic national economies became more integrated and intertwined with one another. The World Bank reports that openness to trade—the ratio of a country's trade (exports plus imports) to its gross domestic product (GDP)—has more than doubled on average since 1950.

Immigration has also contributed significantly to economic growth and higher wages. Today some 200 million people, about 3 percent of the world's population, live outside their countries of birth. According to the Partnership for a New American Economy, 28 percent of all U.S. companies started in 2011 had immigrant founders—despite immigrants comprising

roughly 13 percent of the population. In addition, some 40 percent of Fortune 500 firms were founded by immigrants or their children.

All of this open movement of people and stuff across borders pays off in many measurable ways, some obvious, some more surprising.

## Longer, Healthier Lives

A 2010 study in World Development, titled "Good For Living? On the Relationship between Globalization and Life Expectancy," looked at data from 92 countries and found that economic globalization significantly boosts life expectancy, especially in developing countries. The two Swedish economists behind the study, Andreas Bergh and Therese Nilsson, noted that as Uganda's economic globalization index rose from 22 to 46 points (almost two standard deviations) over the 1970–2005 period, average life expectancy increased by two to three years.

Similarly, a 2014 conference paper titled "The long-run relationship between trade and population health: evidence from five decades," by Helmut Schmidt University economist Dierk Herzer, concluded, after examining the relationship between economic openness and population health for 74 countries between 1960 and 2010, that "international trade in general has a robust positive long-run effect on health, as measured by life expectancy and infant mortality."

## Women's Liberation

A 2012 working paper by University of Konstantz economist Heinrich Ursprung and University of Munich economist Niklas Potrafke analyzed how women fare by comparing globalization trends with changes in the Social Institutions and Gender Index (SIGI), which was developed by the

Organisation for Economic Co-operation and Development (OECD). SIGI takes several aspects of gender relations into account, including family law codes, civil liberties, physical integrity, son preference, and ownership rights. It's an index of deprivation that captures causes of gender inequality rather than measuring outcomes.

"Observing the progress of globalization for almost one hundred developing countries at ten year intervals starting in 1970," Ursprung and Potrafke concluded, "we find that economic and social globalization exert a decidedly positive influence on the social institutions that reduce female subjugation and promote gender equality." They further noted that since globalization tends to liberate women from traditional social and political orders, "social globalization is demonized, by the established local ruling class, and by western apologists who, for reasons of ideological objections to markets, join in opposing globalization."

## Less Child Labor

A 2005 World Development study, "Trade Openness, Foreign Direct Investment and Child Labor," by Eric Neumayer of the London School of Economics and Indra de Soysa of the Norwegian University of Science and Technology, looked at the effects of trade openness and globalization on child labor in poor countries. Their analysis refuted the claims made by anti-globalization proponents that free trade induces a "race to the bottom," encouraging the exploitation of children as cheap laborers. Instead the researchers found that the more open a country is to international trade and foreign investment, the lower the incidence of exploitation. "Globalization is associated with less, not more, child labor," they concluded.

## Faster Economic Growth

A 2008 World Bank study, "Trade Liberalization and Growth: New Evidence," by the Stanford University economists Romain Wacziarg and Karen Horn Welch, found that trade openness and liberalization significantly boost a country's rate of economic growth.

The authors noted that in 1960, just 22 percent of countries representing 21 percent of the global population had open trade policies. This rose to 73 percent of countries representing 46 percent of world population by the year 2000. The study compared growth rates of countries before and after trade liberalization, finding that "over the 1950–1998 period, countries that liberalized their trade regimes experienced average annual growth rates that were about 1.5 percentage points higher than before liberalization" and that "investment rates rose by 1.5–2.0 percentage points."

## Higher Incomes

Trade openness boosts economic growth, but how does it affect per-capita incomes? A 2009 Rutgers University-Newark working paper, "Trade Openness and Income—a Re-examination," by economists Vlad Manóle and Mariana Spatareanu, calculated the trade restrictiveness indices for 131 developed and developing countries between 1990 and 2004. Its conclusion: A "lower level of trade protection is associated with higher per-capita income."

## Less Poverty

A 2011 Research Institute of Industrial Economics working paper—"Globalization and Absolute Poverty—A Panel Data Study," by the Swedish economists Bergh and Nilsson—analyzed the effects of globalization and trade openness on levels of absolute poverty (defined as incomes of less than $1 per day) in 100 developing countries. The authors found "a robust negative correlation between globalization and poverty."

Interestingly, most of the reduction in absolute poverty results from better information flows—for example, access to cellphones—that improve the functioning of markets and lead to the liberalization of trade. For example, the globalization index score for Bangladesh increased from 8 points in 1980 to 30 points in 2000, which yielded a reduction in absolute poverty of 12 percentage points.

## More Trees

A number of studies have found that trade openness tends to improve environmental quality in rich countries while increasing pollution and deforestation in poor countries. For example, a 2009 *Journal of Environmental Economics and Management* study by three Japanese researchers, titled "Does Trade Openness Improve Environmental Quality?," found that air and water pollution decline among rich-country members of the OECD, whereas it increases in poor countries as they liberalize and embark on the process of economic development.

But as poor countries become rich, they flip from getting dirtier to becoming cleaner. A 2012 *Canadian Journal of Agricultural Economics* study, "Deforestation and the Environmental Kuznets Curve in Developing Countries: A Panel Smooth Transition Regression Approach," explored the relationship between deforestation and real income for 52 developing countries during the 1972–2003 period. The study found that deforestation reverses when average incomes reach a bit more than $3,000 per year.

These studies basically confirm the Environmental Kuznets Curve hypothesis, in which various indicators of environmental degradation tend to get worse during the early stages of economic growth, but when average income reaches a certain point, subsequent economic growth leads to environmental improvement. Since trade openness and globalization boost economic growth and incomes, this suggests that opposing them slows down eventual environmental improvement in poor countries.

## Peace

In 1943, Otto T. Mallery wrote, "If soldiers are not to cross international boundaries, goods must do so. Unless the shackles can be dropped from trade, bombs will be dropped from the sky." This insight was bolstered by a 2011 working paper, "Does Trade Integration Contribute to Peace?," by the University of California, Davis researcher Ju Hyun Pyun and the Korea University researcher Jong-Wha Lee. The two evaluated the effects of bilateral trade and global openness on the probability of conflict between countries from 1950 to 2000, and concluded that "an increase in bilateral trade interdependence significantly promotes peace." They added, "More importantly, we find that not only bilateral trade but global trade openness also significantly promotes peace."

## More Productive Workers

The economic gains from unfettered immigration are vastly more enormous than those that would result from the elimination of remaining trade restrictions. Total factor productivity (TFP) is the portion of output not explained by the amount of inputs used in production. Its level is determined by how efficiently and intensely the inputs are utilized in production. In other words, it is all those factors-technology, honest government, a stable currency, etc.—that enable people to work "smarter" and not just harder.

A 2012 working paper titled "Open Borders," by the University of Wisconsin economist John Kennan, found that if all workers moved immediately to places with higher total factor productivity, it would produce the equivalent of doubling the world's supply of laborers. Using U.S. TFP as a benchmark, the world's workers right now are the equivalent of 750 million Americans, but allowing migration to high TFP regions would boost that to the equivalent of 1.5 billion American workers.

Think of it this way: A worker in Somalia can produce only one-tenth the economic value of a worker in the United States. But as soon as she trades the hellhole of Mogadishu for the comparative paradise of Minneapolis, she can immediately take advantage of the higher American TFP to produce vastly more.

Multiply that by the hundreds of millions still stuck in low-productivity countries.

Assuming everybody moved immediately, Kennan calculated that it would temporarily depress the average wages of the host countries' natives by 20 percent. If emigration were more gradual, there would be essentially no effects on native-born wages.

In a 2011 working paper for the Center for Global Development, "Economics and Emigration: Trillion Dollar Bills on the Sidewalk?," Michael Clemens reviewed the literature on the relationship between economic growth and migration. He concluded that removing mobility barriers could plausibly produce overall gains of 20–60 percent of global GDP. Since world GDP is about $78 trillion now, that suggests that opening borders alone could boost global GDP to between $94 and $125 trillion.

## Better Job Prospects

A 2013 University of Munich working paper on immigration and economic growth by the University of Auvergne economist Ekrame Boubtane and her colleagues analyzed data from 22 OECD countries between 1987 and 2009. It found that "migration inflows contribute to host country economic prosperity (positive impact on GDP per capita and total unemployment rate)." The authors concluded that "immigration flows do not harm the employment prospects of residents, native- or foreign-born. Hence, OECD countries may adjust immigration policies to labour market needs, and can receive more migrants, without worrying about a potential negative impact on growth and employment."

In a 2009 National Bureau of Economic Research study, "The Effect of Immigration on Productivity: Evidence from U.S. States," the University of California, Davis economist Giovanni Peri looked at the effects of differential rates of immigration to various American states in the 1990s and 2000s. Peri found that "an increase in employment in a U.S. state of 1% due to immigrants produced an increase in income per worker of 0.5% in that state." In other words, more immigrants meant higher average wages for all workers.

## Critical Thinking

1. What are some of the wonderful benefits that Bailey thinks will result from globalization?

2. What evidence does Bailey provide to show that globalization makes for longer and healthier lives?

3. With all the benefits of globalization why do so many people oppose it?

# Internet References

**New American Studies Web**
https://blogs.commons.georgetown.edu/vkp/

**Social Science Information Gateway**
http://www.ariadne.ac.uk/issue2/sosig

**Sociology—Study Sociology Online**
http://edu.learnsoc.org/

**Sociology Web Resources**
http://www.mhhe.com/socscience/sociology/resources/index.htm

**Sociosite**
http://www.topsite.com/goto/sociosite.net

**Socioweb**
http://www.topsite.com/goto/socioweb.com

Science Correspondent **Ronald Bailey** is the author of the forthcoming *The End of Doom: Environmental Renewal in the 21st Century* (St. Martin's).